SATHER CLASSICAL LECTURES
VOLUME TWENTY-FOUR
1951

THE DEVELOPMENT OF
ATTIC BLACK-FIGURE

THE DEVELOPMENT of ATTIC BLACK-FIGURE

By J. D. BEAZLEY

UNIVERSITY OF CALIFORNIA PRESS
BERKELEY AND LOS ANGELES 1951
CAMBRIDGE UNIVERSITY PRESS LONDON

UNIVERSITY OF CALIFORNIA PRESS
BERKELEY AND LOS ANGELES
CALIFORNIA

◇

CAMBRIDGE UNIVERSITY PRESS
LONDON, ENGLAND

TO H. R. W. SMITH

σοὶ τόδε δῶρον ἑταῖρε θοαῖς πέτεται πτερύγεσσι
Κιμμερίων ἀπὸ γῆς χῶρον ἐς Ἑσπερίδων

PREFACE

THESE LECTURES are printed almost exactly as they were delivered, except for the addition of notes. Since the subject is "the development of Attic black-figure," I have tried to present main lines, omitting much that seemed of secondary importance. In general I have not added to my already published lists of works by the several painters, unless for a special reason; complete lists will be given in my *Attic Black-figure Vase-painters*, which is well advanced.

The plates give only a selection of the original illustrations, as I have preferred fair-sized pictures of some to minute pictures of all; but the choice has been made as representative as possible, and many of the vases not figured may be found in easily accessible publications. For kind permission to reproduce unpublished pieces I am much indebted to the Marchesa Isabella Guglielmi di Vulci, Mrs. Semni Karouzou, the Earl of Elgin, Mr. Bernard Ashmole, Dr. Herbert Cahn, Professor George H. Chase, Professor Einar Gjerstad, Dr. Wilfred Hall, and Dr. Antonio Minto; for sending me better photographs of pieces published already, to Miss Christine Alexander, Professor Hansjörg Bloesch, Mr. Pierre Devambez, Dr. Hans Diepolder. Mr. Ashmole has kindly allowed me to reproduce his fine detail-photographs of vases in Athens and London. Mr. Humfrey Wakefield has saved me from some errors of description. Others who have earned my deep gratitude for all sorts of services are my wife, Dr. Dietrich von Bothmer, Professor H. R. W. Smith, and my other colleagues, friends, generous and graceful hosts, at the University of California and in the cities of the Bay.

J.D.B.

[PUBLISHERS' NOTE: The author had returned to England before this book was completed and hence did not see the plates through the press.]

CONTENTS

LIST OF PLATES

I

THE ROAD TO BLACK-FIGURE

BLACK-FIGURE is the name of a technique. By black-figure one means not simple silhouette, but silhouette elaborated and enlivened in two ways: first, by plenty of details engraved with a sharp point, incised, as it is called; secondly, by plentiful addition of dark red paint, and of white paint, one of the chief uses of white being for female flesh. This gives a sober scheme of four colours: the orange of the ground, which is the native colour of the clay vase; the lustrous black of the glaze paint; the white; the deep cherry or crimson, sometimes purplish, red. The black-figure technique may seem very unrealistic, and so it is; but so is outline drawing, only we are more accustomed to it. If the Greek vase-painter had painted in outline on his orange surface, the effect would have been meagre, and the strong colour of the background would have eaten up the thin line. The black-figure technique gave contrast and a proper balance of light and dark.

Black-figure is a *vase*-technique. It was not used by painters on wooden panel or on wall. It was used, however, for clay tablets or plaques, some of them complete in themselves and suitable for votive offerings, others decorating the outer walls of tombs. The material is the same as in vases, the black-figure technique is the same, the artists the same; and if we are studying vases we should not neglect the plaque.

Although black-figure in its prime was a four-colour technique, the name cannot be refused to vases in which either the red or the white, or both, are omitted: silhouette with incised details—that is enough to justify the term.

Black-figure seems to have been invented not in Athens but in Corinth, where the technique of silhouette with incised details appears soon after the beginning of the seventh century before Christ.[1] Red details were soon added at Corinth. White does not become common there for a long time; Corinthian clay was itself whitish, and white details would not have shown up plainly against a whitish background. At Athens, incision first appears not much later than at Corinth, but it is not plentiful until the middle of the seventh century. By that time white is popular. Red comes in in the third quarter of the seventh century. After a period of what might be called semi-black-figure—the term will be clear later,—black-figure attains its full development in the last decades of the seventh century. Its sway is undisputed

---

[1] **For** numbered notes to chapter i see pages 105–106 below.

I

until the invention of the red-figure technique nearly a hundred years later. In the new technique, red-figure, the figures, instead of being painted in lustrous black on the light background, are reserved, as it is called, that is, left in the natural colour of the clay, while the background is filled in with black. The two techniques competed, but the older, black-figure, was soon forced to give ground. After a single generation, by 500, it was reduced to a humble place. Yet it never died out, and by a curious fate even survived red-figure. By 300, no more red-figured vases were being painted, but there was still black-figure of a sort.

The quality of black-figured vases varies greatly, from the masterpiece to the paltry mass-product. The style also. Greek vases are important to us, not only because they are often beautiful, and because they shed all manner of light on the beliefs and customs of the Greeks in the springtime and summer of their civilisation, but also because, in an incomparable series, they enable us to trace the steps whereby a simple and even primitive kind of drawing gradually became freer, bolder, and more subtle—the rise, one might say, of Western drawing. Only the earlier phases of this process are revealed by black-figure, and red-figure is airier and more splendid; most of us, I think, prefer it at first. We may continue to do so, and yet recognise the excellence of much black-figure, and enjoy it.

At first sight black-figure vases may seem much alike in style—the technique is a little overpowering,—but presently, when one's eyes, as it were, get accustomed to the dark, one begins to notice differences of style and to distinguish the individualities of the several artists. The stylistic study of Attic black-figure has not advanced so far as that of Attic red-figure, and some tracts have been only imperfectly mapped. There are many reasons for this: the objects, as a whole, *are* less attractive to most of us; the conventional element is stronger; and for important periods, especially in the earlier reaches, the material, in spite of valuable accessions from recent excavation, is still very fragmentary.

In this opening chapter we shall give a brief account of the story of Attic vase-painting down to the appearance of the full black-figure style in the last decades of the seventh century.

❖   ❖   ❖

Good vases were made in Athens long before what is called the Protogeometric period, but it was then that Athenian potters first showed themselves superior to their contemporaries in other Greek lands. The shape of a "stamnoid amphora" in the Ceramicus Museum at Athens[2] is well considered, the technique skilful, and the decoration of concentric semicircles in lustrous black on the warm light-brown background is not ineffective in its simple way. The date may be the tenth century B.C. There is a long con-

flict in earlier Greek art between the curve and the straight line, and in the
Geometric period that follows the Protogeometric the straight line and sharp
corner, both in shape and decoration, tend to prevail. The feeling for form is
strong, and Geometric vases, especially in Athens, often have a kind of un-
pretending beauty that appeals to us more than it did to our forefathers.
A group of small vases in Berlin[3]—bowls and boxes of various shapes, one
like a hazel-nut, the other with a leg for handle,—ornamented with simple
rectilinear patterns, belong to the beginning of the Geometric period, probably
in the latter half of the ninth century. Later Geometric vases, however large
and elaborate, do not, as works of art, surpass these. There were one or two
animals in Protogeometric, though no human beings; but many Geometric
vases have figures on them, animal or human, and we can speak of a Geometric figure-style. No better example can be given than the picture, familiar
though it is, on the best-known of the huge amphorae that stood as monuments
on Attic graves in the ninth and eighth centuries.[4] The foot of the vase is modern, but restored after similar pieces. Ovoid body and long neck are covered
evenly with many bands of pattern, a broad between narrower, all rectilinear
and abstract, except the very formal leaves, as they must be, near the base. On
the shoulder, and at two points on the neck, small figures take the place of the
pattern-bands. On the neck, a long row of deer, grazing, and a long row of goats,
resting but looking round. The shoulder-picture is firmly anchored between the
handles by upright bands of pattern. The subject is the prothesis: the dead man
lying in state, with the mourners about him, beating their heads. It is a real
composition, and viewed as a rendering of life it is a solemn scene reduced to
its barest terms, terms telling from their very bareness. Here is an artist
who has not attempted more than he could exactly perform; an art not child-
ish, but planned and austere. As to the technique, the figures, all small, are
in pure silhouette; but the seats, the cover of the couch, and the awning over
it are in outline, filled in with hatching, parallel zigzags, or chequers. Geometric drawing avoids sharp contrasts, and so that the figures may not be
too staring the background between is toned down with filling-patterns. The
same strong, collected style appears in other subjects, above all in the naval
battles on fragments in the Louvre and Athens,[5] with the galleys, the rowers,
the captains, the dead on the deck and in the water. These, like the Athens
prothesis vase, are exceptional pieces, but a huge krater in Sydney,[6] though
not equal to the vase in Athens, is close to it in style; and gives, besides the
prothesis, an example of another subject, one which always remains a special favourite in vase-painting as elsewhere, the chariot or line of chariots.
This will serve for comparison with chariots on later vases. Three horses
are given; the helmeted driver and his fully armed passenger are shown, for
clearness, as if they were standing on the car and not in it. For the same
reason, most of the chariots show both wheels; in one only, the hither wheel

alone is rendered. In this vase the glaze has somewhat suffered, producing a restless effect which was not intended by the artist.

These are specimens of the Geometric figure-style at its height. The exact dating of such early vases is disputed, but no one would place the Athens prothesis and its companions later than the middle of the eighth century. In the last quarter of the eighth century a new spirit enters the Geometric style; new motives, too, make their appearance; soon there is a rush of them, and before long the Geometric style has given place to another, very different, what is called, although the name is rather misleading, the Proto-Attic.[7] In scores of vases one can watch the Geometric figures gradually rounding out, until the match-like look has disappeared. This is part of the transformation that came over Greek art, to some extent under the influence of Oriental models, at the end of the eighth century and in the first half of the seventh. Wild animals come in, especially lion, panther, and sphinx; plants, growing, or in pattern-bands. The human figures grow larger and more substantial, their stances firmer, movements bolder, proportions more just; and presently myth—the legends of gods and heroes—becomes, for choice pieces, one of the artist's favourite themes. The style is enterprising, unconstrained, and, especially perhaps in Attica, has a child-like gaiety and vigour. Sometimes one even seems to sense the wondering delight of the naïve artist who has *never drawn a man before*.

A fragmentary cauldron, with stand, in Athens,[8] still belongs to the Geometric period, but is on the threshold of the new age. The ornament includes a curvilinear element, the spiral or tendril; and, more important, the whole character of the drawing has changed. The classic control of the prothesis vase in Athens has given way to a furious energy, seen in the eager march of the women in the chief picture, in their electric hair, in the straining necks of the chariot team, and in the bold figure of a horse jumping or rearing on one of the tall, narrow divisions of the fenestrated stand. Somewhat later, perhaps, than the Athens cauldron are a pair of Late Geometric neck-amphorae, by one painter, in Oxford and London. In the Oxford vase (pl. 1, 2)[9] the principal picture represents a procession of chariots; below this, hounds pursue a fox; on the shoulder, hounds pursue a hare; on the neck, another chariot. There is more contrast than in earlier Geometric; the chief scene is larger in proportion to the vase; there is less filling-ornament, indeed one feels that what is left might soon blow away; there is more breathing-space in the pictures. The charioteer, in his long robe, now stands *in* the car, not on it. Not only has he an eye (a reserved circle, with dot), as already in some earlier Geometric, but he has a distinct face. Two horses are shown, but in one chariot one horse only—the off horse being thought of as completely concealed by the near one; it is a simplification that might not seem urgent if one looked at the Sydney vase only, but which many Geometric teams cry out for when the horses are a desperate tangle of legs and manes. The horses, with their large eyes and heavy hooves, have a strange, self-centred, spectral appearance. On the London vase by the same artist (pl. 1, 1),[10] their pair is reduced to a single horse. The figures have a dramatic, almost histrionic air. The grazing deer on the shoulder are loosely built, and their lumbering, unlovely gait is very different from the quiet movement of those on the prothesis vase in Athens. Lastly, on each side of the neck, a large lion lays its paw triumphantly on a cowering deer. There are one or two Greek lions earlier than this, but the picture gives early examples of two subjects that soon become extremely popular in Greek art: first, the lion; second, the group of one animal attacking another.

The birds (vultures? or crows?) are loosely put together, like the beasts except the lion.

In both vases the subordinate decoration, the pattern-work, is neglected; the artist is interested in the pictures only. There are none of the new curvilinear elements, one of which was seen on the Athens cauldron. These Late Geometric vases stress now one of the new elements, now another. A few years later all the novelties may appear on a single vase, and the Proto-Attic period proper has begun.

The style of the Athens cauldron is continued by another vase in Athens, the hydria (water-pot) found at Analatos in Attica.[11] The figures are now quite large. In the chief picture on the body two lions face one another with a plant between, one of those symmetrical, antithetic, one is inclined to say heraldic, designs which by this time have had a long history in the Orient but which appear only seldom in Geometric Greece. Below this, a narrow band of small, huddling water-birds; then, grazing fawns just like those of the Athens cauldron; then, two bands of careless pattern. More care has been bestowed on the new, floral pattern above the chief picture, the garland of leaves pointing downward which will henceforth be the regular decoration on the shoulder of a vase. On the neck, a dance of men and maidens, holding branches, each party hand in hand, the men headed by a lyre-player. On the back of the chief zone, a bold design of plants. Under each handle a long-necked water-bird pecks at one of the plants. The bird, and the small flower behind it—crocus one might think,—are drawn with free brush-strokes. The date is about 700 B.C.

An ovoid krater in the collection of Lord Elgin at Broomhall in Fife (pl. 2) gives us our first view of a figure which barely appears in the Geometric period but which is very popular in the Proto-Attic, and remains so, woven into legend, throughout antiquity—the centaur.[12] Here he returns gaily from the chase, a branch, his usual weapon, in one hand, a deer in the other. Long thin barrel; bristly back, tail, and hind-legs; large head and eye; open mouth; long sharp nose and chin; wavy hair. The face is drawn in outline, with more detail than in any of the vases we have looked at so far. A plant is seen beside him, another between his legs; birds perch and float. It is tempting to guess that the other ingredients of the picture are not mere filling-ornament but represent real objects: rocks, stones, serpents or worms:

> ceu duo nubigenae cum vertice montis ab alto
> descendunt Centauri Homolen Othrymque nivalem
> linquentes cursu rapido; dat euntibus ingens
> silva locum, et magno cedunt virgulta fragore.[13]

Below, an old subject, horses grazing, but with a grand new swing from ear to rump. The vase is fragmentary; the missing parts of the body, and the lid, can be restored after a complete vase of the same shape and of very much the same style, but far inferior, in Cambridge.[14] The Cambridge horse looks like a broken-down version of the Broomhall.

A neck-amphora in the Louvre takes us back to the Analatos vase, and is probably a later work by the Analatos Painter, as he is called, himself.[15] Chariots on the body; on the neck a dance, and sphinxes. Many curvilinear and floral motives. There is much use of outline, not only for the faces, but for the garments—chitons—of the girls, and the sphinxes' wings. In the horses, the first step is taken towards the black-figure technique: the hither horse is outlined by means of incision, and so are the long wavy locks of the manes.

This is the earliest extant picture of a dance in which men alternate with maids. The next picture is much later, on the François vase: and it has been thought that the subject might be the same here as there, the famous dance of the fourteen young Athenians to celebrate their deliverance from the Minotaur by Theseus. This is very unlikely; for one thing, the music here is the flute, whereas an essential feature of the famous dance was that it was led by Theseus playing the lyre. The scene on the Louvre vase is doubtless taken from contemporary life.

A mythological scene, however—the story of Herakles, the centaur Nessos, and Deianeira,—is certainly represented on a fragmentary stand in Athens, found in the Argive Heraion,[16] Attic work from the second quarter of the seventh century, poor in quality but important to us. Nessos looks round, giving tongue, towards Herakles, who has wounded him with an arrow and is about to despatch him with the sword; Deianeira raises her arm towards her deliverer. Other pictures on the stand represent a battle, a war-chariot ready to depart, and groups of wild animals, one of them a fairly compact composition of two lions attacking a bull, which heralds the great interlocked animal-groups that play an important role in the art of the late seventh century, and the sixth. The drawing is muddled, but the artist uses all the technical devices of his time: much of the figure-work is in outline; there is a good deal of white; incision appears in the lions; and the human part of Nessos is painted a brown flesh-colour, rare in Attica though not uncommon elsewhere. It has been said of the Nessos scene that it is "the earliest definitely recognisable mythological scene on an Attic, almost the earliest in any archaic Greek, work of art."[17] There are, however, a few mythological scenes earlier than this, in the Geometric period itself, and the relief on a bronze tripod-leg recently found at Olympia, which represents Herakles and Apollo struggling for the tripod, cannot be later than 700 B.C.[18]

Another and better picture of Herakles in conflict with a centaur appears on a large neck-amphora in New York.[19] Not much of the Geometric tradition persisted in the vase from the Argive Heraion; on the New York vase, which may be somewhat later, one has to look hard to find any trace at all. The figures, both men and animals, are large, thickset, and fully rounded. Rich curves prevail everywhere, and the effect is exuberant and excited. The centaur has dropped his branch and stumbles forward, hands open; Herakles, sword in hand, seizes the centaur by the forelock. His chariot waits, facing outward, and the driver, holding reins and goad, looks round. Below, concealing part of Herakles' leg, is what seems to be a long chiton. A piece of the vase is missing here, and there is a difficulty; I cannot see that the chiton can belong to the person holding the reins, and wonder if there may not be two figures, but cannot restore them. The horses, with their short legs and thick barrel, are very un-Geometric; the long dank manes and rocking-horse heads are common all over Greece in seventh-century art. An owl flies near the centaur, a bird of good omen, for Herakles: the target-like head is meant for a side-view. On the right of the picture a small man runs up as if he were in danger of not getting into the picture. This small man has the appearance of an afterthought; at least he seems to have been drawn without meditation, on the spur of the moment. Horses with long silky manes graze on the shoulder of the vase. On the neck a lion, with round frontal face, attacks a deer from behind. In all three pictures plants grow and hang, large rosettes are prominent among the filling-ornaments, and tiny shivering water-birds seek their food in the nooks and crannies of the design. A great part of the drawing is in outline; there is much white, in particular for the flesh of Herakles and his sword; much incision too, for the animals, including the centaur, except the heads; here one might really speak of semi-black-figure. The reverse of the vase is given up to curvilinear motives, mostly floral, treated broadly and with gusto.

Another mythological scene is depicted on a stand in Berlin.[20] The figures are still larger than before, about thirteen inches high. Five men in long chiton and himation, holding spears. The foremost of them is inscribed, *Menelas*, and the subject must be Menelaos leading the Achaean princes, who had sworn to join him in taking vengeance if he should be deprived of

Helen, to his brother Agamemnon, their overlord. Without the name we should not have been able to divine the subject. This is our first inscription. There are a few others, fragmentary, on Attic vases of about the same period: one gives the name of the owner;[21] in another the verb is missing, and *Antenor* might be either the dedicator, or the owner, or the potter.[22] The earliest certain signature of an artist on an Attic vase is much later, *Sophilos*, about 575 B.C.* Outside of Attica, the potter Aristonothos signs on a krater of uncertain fabric,[23] a hundred years before Sophilos; Kallikleas signs on a vase from Ithaca of about the same period as Aristonothos;[24] and another seventh-century potter on a Melian vase found at Selinus.[25] It may be by chance that no signature of an early Attic potter has been preserved. All these inscriptions, painted on the vase before firing, must of course be distinguished from incised inscriptions, added after the completion of the vase: these include the oldest of all Greek inscriptions, that which begins ὃς νῦν ὀρχηστῶν, on an Attic Geometric oinochoë (wine-pitcher) in Athens which cannot have been made later than the end of the third quarter of the eighth century.[26]

The smaller pictures above the Menelaos are, first, a cavalcade; above that, a row of sphinxes; and on the flaring top of the stand, two animal groups, each of two lions attacking a deer (the upper half missing). The men and the sphinxes are in outline, but the wings of the sphinxes, the faces, arms, chitons of the men are filled in with white, and there are white spots on the himatia. There is no incision in the main picture, but much in the horses and lions.

The Menelaos stand has been attributed to one of the principal Proto-Attic artists, the Painter of the Ram Jug;[27] and it is at least close to his work. The Aegisthus vase in Berlin (pl. 3)[28] is certainly by the Painter of the Ram Jug, but earlier than the name-piece, to which we shall come presently. It is an ovoid krater, the same shape as the Centaur vase in Broomhall. There are four pictures in the main zone, and below it a file of grazing horses. The Death of Aegisthus is the earliest representation in art, by a century, of one of the chief episodes in the tale of Pelops' line.[29] Orestes, sword in hand, marches Aegisthus forward, holding him by the long hair; Clytaemestra precedes Aegisthus, beating her head. Of the fourth figure, behind Orestes, only the fingers remain: it may have been his sister, Elektra or Laodike, urging him on. The names are not inscribed, but there can be no doubt of the interpretation: this is certainly not, as has been suggested, the Death of Agamemnon; it is the death of a coward. There is a singular fascination in this picture, so rude and yet so forcible and so felt. As to the technique, Orestes is black, with the face in outline; incision for fingers, wrists, toes, the patterns of his chitoniskos, and for the ornaments—painting, perhaps,

---

* See below, pp. 17–19.

rather than tattooing—on his thighs.[30] The other figures are white, with much detail in brown or black lines. Male figures, and not only female, are often white in early archaic art; the Herakles of the New York centaur vase was white. Often, too, there is no reason why one male in a picture should be white or black rather than another; it is for variety, or to mark one figure well off from the next. Here it is plain that the artist has wished to distinguish Orestes as the chief actor from the women and the effeminate man.

The scene on the other side of the vase is unfortunately fragmentary. The right-hand figure is Artemis,[31] the left probably Apollo; a fragment with part of a cithara may belong. Who the two persons in the middle were one cannot tell. In the space under each handle there is a black-figure picture. Under one hande it is a hairy creature, throwing stones. He looks round, retreating—or is it simply the follow-through of the swing as he throws? To make it quite clear that this is a picture by itself, and has nothing to do with the tragic scene to left of it, the artist drew a thick vertical line from the handle downward. Then it occurred to him to enliven the line by planting two grasshoppers on it. Under the other handle two men are fighting, with stones. The empty hand claws the rump with a gesture often used by dancers in later pictures. Who are these handle-figures? The couple are human, and may be simply a slice of low life; one remembers also that mischievous pair of brothers, the Kerkopes. The stone-thrower under the other handle, though hairy, has the same ornament on the rump and cable-pattern on the thigh as the couple and the heroes, and is human apart from the mouth. He is not an ape, but perhaps a wild man of the woods, a Pilosus, a kind of proto-satyr or proto-Silenos, solitary, uncompanionable, repelling intruders with stones; but one cannot be sure. Early Greek art is full of surprises, and Proto-Attic above all: this vase really takes one's breath away.

The Ram Jug itself, after which "the Painter of the Ram Jug" is named, has long been known.[32] The fragmentary picture decorates the almost flat shoulder of a low-bodied jug, and is on a smaller scale than those we have just left. The subject is taken from the Odyssey: the Escape from the Cave of Polyphemos. Two rams are seen advancing, each with a naked youth clinging under it and holding on to the horns; part of a third ram is preserved, the leader, doubtless with a similar burden. The animals are in outline, except legs and tail, which are black. The youths are filled in with white. There is no incision. The heads of the youths have suffered, and the drawing looks less firm now than it did once. The episode in the Odyssey has been simplified: in Homer, Odysseus fastens the rams three abreast, and ties a man under the middle ram only of each three. Even much later artists avoid the difficulty of rendering this complicated arrangement, and no wonder. Our painter does not even indicate the attachment, for the rings round the waists of the youths are belts, and those round wrist and ankle, as in the Aegisthus

vase, either bracelets and anklets, or more probably only the divisions between hand and arm, and foot and leg.

The masterpiece of Proto-Attic art is also by the Painter of the Ram Jug:
the Berlin neck-amphora with Peleus bringing Achilles to Chiron (pl. 4).[33]
It is fragmentary, but no essential part of the design is missing. On the neck
of the vase a handsome plant. The subject on the body is divided between
the two sides of the amphora: on one side, Peleus; on the other, Chiron—an
early example of a type of decoration used in many masterpieces of later
vase-painting, one large figure on each side of the vase. Here we seem to
breathe mountain air. This is far the earliest representation of a subject
which was popular with Attic painters, both black-figure and red, in the
later archaic period. Ancient commentators on Homer observed that according to him Achilles was brought up by his mother Thetis, not by Chiron
as what they call "more modern writers" (οἱ νεώτεροι) said. The story that
the wise centaur Chiron was Achilles' foster-father, for which Pindar is the
earliest authority in extant literature, had already been traced back to the
middle of the sixth century, for it is depicted, as will be seen, on black-
figured cups by the Heidelberg Painter;* the publication of the Berlin vase
showed that the story is at least as old as the middle of the seventh. Peleus
holds the infant Achilles out in his hands. Not much of the large figure is
preserved, but the head is almost intact; a good head with large low eye,
roomy aquiline nose, shapely lips and chin. The long hair is bound with a
fillet which has a floral ornament, a palmette, in front. One would expect
that Peleus, a father, would be given a beard, as in most of the early pictures, but fortunately he is beardless here; it is perhaps an example of the
preference for smooth cheeks which is characteristic of the "Daedalic" style
in contemporary sculpture. The infant Achilles wears a spotted chiton with
plain short sleeves. His neck is in outline, like the neck and face of Peleus;
his arm is in black, and the arm of Peleus is also in black. There is hardly
any white on the vase, only a few lines at the wrist of Peleus and to mark
the horizontal grooves on the back-hair of Peleus and Achilles. On the other
side of the vase, Chiron: body black, with plenty of incised detail, face
reserved. He extends his right hand to receive the child, and with his left
hand holds over his shoulder the long branch which is the usual staff and
weapon of centaurs. In most of the other pictures, Chiron, as a hunter,
carries his quarry slung from the branch: a hare and a fox, a hare, or a brace
of hares. On the Berlin vase the animals are not the ordinary fox or hare,
but three small young creatures, the first of which is a lion, the second a
boar, and the third, I believe, a wolf.[34] Now the mythographer known as
Apollodorus, about the first century after Christ, tells us that Chiron fed
the infant Achilles on the inwards of lions and the marrow of wild boars and

---

* See pp. 50–52 below, and pl. 20.

bears;[35] and in the *Achilleis* of Statius, "My food," says Achilles, "is said to have been the compact inwards of lions, and the marrow of the half-living she-wolf":

dicor

> non ullos ex more cibos hausisse, nec almis
> uberibus satiasse famem, sed spissa leonum
> viscera, semianimisque lupae traxisse medullas.[36]

These descriptions of the young Achilles' diet had been supposed to be a late addition to the legend: the Proto-Attic vase now shows that they are at least as old as the middle of the seventh century B.C., and a characteristic part of an ancient epic story, probably related in the *Cypria*.

Quoting the lines of Statius some time ago, I had surmised that the gruesome touch "half-living"—"the marrow of the half-living she-wolf"—might be due to the Roman poet. Recently Donald Robertson has restudied the question in an article entitled "The Food of Achilles."[37] He quotes evidence, from many times and places, for the belief that by eating the flesh and drinking the blood of strong and fearless animals—lion, wolf, dragon—a man becomes more fearless and stronger; and he adds that the fresher the food or drink, the more potent; best of all, perhaps, to take them from a living body. *Semianimis*, then, is probably an original stroke. Robertson also shows that a word in Pindar's revised account of the education of Achilles may be owing to the same trait in the traditional version;[38] in Pindar the infant Achilles is said to have killed lions and boars and dragged their bodies while they were still panting, ἀσθμαίνοντα, to Chiron's cave. Pindar, here as often, substitutes a story of his own for the epic legend which offends his moral notions, but retains a detail, while carefully excluding its original significance: "in the epic the beasts were still breathing because the small Achilles wished to suck the living marrow in the cave."

The epilogue to this section shall be from three poets. First, Shakespeare:

> Now could I drink hot blood . . .

Again, seeing what a bloodthirsty writer Nonnus is, it is not surprising that he speaks of drinking the hot blood fresh from the veins of a lioness as a suitable preparation for battle.[39] But there is another poet from whom one might not at first expect a reference to diet, or to the lapping of the blood of lions and bears; Racine, in his *Iphigénie*,[40] borrows from Apollodorus, and makes Eriphyle describe Achilles as:

> Ce héros si terrible au reste des humains,
> Qui ne connoist de pleurs que ceux qu'il fait répandre,
> Qui s'endurcit contr' eux dés l'âge le plus tendre;
> Et qui, si l'on nous fait un fidelle discours,
> Suça mesme le sang des lions et des ours.

The phase of Proto-Attic that immediately follows the work of the Painter of the Ram Jug is less attractive: at least the principal piece, the very fragmentary neck-amphora, from Kynosarges, in Athens,[41] is not of the same quality. We look at the restoration first, and then at details from photographs. On the body, a man and a young driver stand in a chariot drawn by winged horses. Both turn the head, and the man his whole body, towards a person of whom not much is preserved. The subject is unexplained. Horses graze on the shoulder of the vase, and the neck has a well-planned group of two wrestlers. There was a third figure to left of the pair, but part of the hand is all that remains. These are less probably ordinary athletes—although athletic scenes are found occasionally even on Geometric vases—than persons from heroic legend, and very possibly Argonauts. The technique is in one respect novel: besides much incision (in the animals, in the chariot-car, and for some details of the human figures) and much white (for flesh, garments, and so forth), there is also much red. This colour, not used hitherto on Attic pottery, now becomes a regular component of the decorative scheme. As to the figure-drawing, it is less lively than in the New York centaur vase or the works of the Ram Jug Painter, but somewhat more compact and controlled. The filling-ornament, on the other hand, is more obtrusive. The wrestlers are good; in physique and complexion they are quite like wrestlers. It is worth noting that the men at last have proper foreheads, and that the eye is better set in the face than it was before; the pupil, too, is indicated, by a red dot, and the artist has even suggested the eye-socket by leaving it in the colour of the clay instead of painting it white with the rest of the face.

Up to now there have been quarter-black-figure vases, and even semi-black-figure. We now reach, in the last decades of the seventh century, full Attic black-figure in its earliest stage. This phase of Attic vase-painting has been called "Late Proto-Attic," and there is something to be said for the term; but it is better called "Early (or "Earliest") Black-figure."[42] It is the period of the Piraeus vase, and the Nessos vase, both in Athens;* a classic period in one sense, the first since the high Geometric style of the prothesis vase. Imagination no longer tends to outrun skill of hand and grasp of form. In our next chapter we shall find the vase-painter in possession of a settled technique and a settled style. Henceforward we shall sometimes miss the freshness and spontaneity of the very early work we have just been considering, but shall often be compensated by other qualities.

* See pp. 13–14.

II

EARLY BLACK-FIGURE, AND THE C PAINTER

THE LAST decades of the seventh century find the Attic vase-painter in possession of a settled technique and in a fuller sense than before of a settled style. The neck-amphora from Piraeus, in Athens, is a black-figured vase.[1] The whole design is in black, with much incision, much red, and some white. The chief picture is once more a chariot-scene: two pair-horse chariots, one driven by a man, the other by a youth. The horses are of the same breed as in the New York centaur vase. They still have huge hooves, long dank manes, and rocking-horse heads; the barrel is even thinner than before. The drivers stand bolt upright, and have a solemn air, as if on parade. More significant, perhaps, than the chariot-scene is the animal under one handle. With its massive neck, thick legs, large paws, firm curves, it is a good exam-ple of those ponderous and powerful lions which take a front place in the repertory of the early black-figure artist. On the Piraeus vase it is a lion sejant; the heraldic term comes naturally to one's mind. There will be many such lions, and we may speak of a *type*. The typical and traditional element, indeed, now becomes very strong, and remains so throughout the history of black-figure. It is strong in Greek art as a whole. This has its drawbacks, but also great advantages: the blend of tradition and individuality, of past and present, makes for health and power. Before the end of the seventh century, the elusive multiplicity of the visible world has been condensed into a few well-pondered, crystalline forms, which are adequate to express the main activities and attitudes of man and beast—standing, walking, running, sitting, reclining, riding, thrusting, throwing. This small world of forms is a nucleus capable of expansion and transformation; it is the foundation on which Greek art of the fifth century was based, and through it all Western art. In the creation of *types*, or say of *standard forms*, Athens did not take the lead; a greater part was played by seventh-century Corinth. Lions like those on the Piraeus vase are descended from Protocorinthian lions; the neat filling-ornaments, too, and the thoroughly ornamentalised plants, are derived from Corinthian originals. In this period, and for a long time to come, we shall continually be referring to Corinth.

It is possible that we have another work by the painter of the Piraeus vase;[2] but the first black-figure artist whose personality is fairly clear to us

---

[1] For numbered notes to chapter ii see pages 106–108 below.

13

is the Nessos Painter.[3] He has his name from one of the inscriptions on a large neck-amphora in Athens[4] which served, like the prothesis vase long before, as a monument on a grave. The picture on the body is taken from the legend of Perseus. Medusa, beheaded, collapses; her sisters rush off in pursuit of Perseus. Perseus is not shown, but the situation is clear. There is much movement. Medusa, wings folded, is falling, not yet prostrate; she has clutched her knee in a last effort as her legs failed her. Her sisters fly, or rather plunge off through the air; the forward leg has not yet left the ground. The space above Medusa is filled by a flying bird, emphasizing the motion forward. The Gorgons, as Hesiod tells, dwelt on the farther shore of Ocean, and the chase is over the sea, which is indicated by the border of leaping dolphins under the picture.[5] This is the earliest Attic representation of the legend; in Corinthian art it appears earlier. Corinth also seems to have created the type of the Gorgoneion, the gorgon-head alone;[6] Corinthian artists, that is, stylized and made shapely a primitive and artless thing, the hideous face that must long have been used in Greece as a counter-charm to the evil eye. The Gorgoneion is found in Corinthian art before the middle of the seventh century, but the earliest Attic example is again by the Nessos Painter; the interior decoration of one of his slighter pieces, a lekane (basin-shaped bowl) in Athens, is a gorgoneion.[7] The face is not black with dark red patches as on the Nessos vase, but reserved—pallid—as in most gorgoneia, and the tusks are lacking; the lines, however, are the same, and so are several unusual particulars, the pointed tongue, the long hair parted in the middle, the thick tufts of the beard which makes the female face more horrid. Few Attic Gorgons can match those on the Nessos vase (pl. 5, 1). The size of head and wings contributes to the effect; this is not so much a body culminating in a head, as a monstrous head that has grown a body.

   The thick band of intricate floral pattern above the picture is derived from Corinthian models, and so is the discreet filling-ornament, which is much as in the Piraeus vase. On the unpierced handles, owls and swans; on the mouth, a file of sturdy geese; on the neck, a compact and vivid version of a subject already old, Herakles and a centaur. Both names are inscribed; the centaur is Nessos, Nettos in Attic; as usual in early inscriptions, a single letter is written for the double. Herakles, sword in hand, overtakes Nessos, sets a foot on his back, catches him by the hair; Nessos staggers and implores. The two figures are contrasted, even in beard and moustache, in the shape of the nose, in tight lips and open mouth. Nearly all the figures overlap their borders, which increases the impression of bulk—gorgons, dolphins, Herakles, swans. Besides the dark-red parts, there was some white, which has faded; the aspect of the vase was originally a little less sombre than it is now. And since we are speaking of technique, let us notice that the Nessos vase gives us our first instance of the scratched "sketch" which is used sporadically in black-figure, and regularly in red-figure, to fix the main lines of the composition before the painting begins.[8]

The story of Perseus is told in two other works by the Nessos Painter. One, in Leipsic,[9] is a fragment only, but of special interest because it was found at Caere in Etruria—the earliest Attic vase found in Italy, the forerunner of an immense trade. The other Perseus vase is a fragmentary bowl, with upright handles and a spout, in Berlin (pl. 5, 2).[10] The foot is lost, but the tips of the "rays" or leaves at the base remain. Above them is the same floral band as on the Nessos vase; above this, animals in pairs—sphinxes, lions, panthers, bulls; and horses (ponies) grazing. Then, on the upper part, two scenes from myth. One of the scenes was divided into two panels by the spout: the right-hand panel is preserved (pl. 5, 2): the Harpies—Αρεπυια— make off, running, not yet air-borne, pursued by the winged sons of Boreas, Zetes and Kalais, who must have been figured in the left-hand panel, now missing. The story is taken from the adventures of the Argonauts: King Phineus, blinded for a misdeed, was pestered by the Harpies, who as soon as food was laid before him flew up, snatched some of it, and fouled the rest; at last the sons of Boreas chased them away. This is the earliest representation of the legend. The Harpies, apart from their wings, are human, as always in earlier art. The vase cannot have had more than one spout, so that the other picture must have run from handle to handle. Perseus is pursued by the Gorgons; and by a happy coincidence those portions which in the Nessos vase were left to the imagination are here preserved, while the three Gorgons are lost. Perseus (Perrheus in Attic, here with a single *rho* for the double) rushes through the air, borne by his winged shoes. He wears the cap of darkness, secured by a chin-strap, has his sword braced tight to his body so as not to dangle, and carries Medusa's head (which is not, however, visible) in a bag. Behind him stands Athena his protectress, and before the fragment ends one sees the boot of Hermes. Then the sisters of Medusa must have come, pursuing, and Medusa, falling or fallen. The flesh of Athena is left in outline. This, as it happens, is the earliest figure of the goddess in extant Attic art, and without the inscription or the context one would scarcely have recognised her. Armed Athenas occur before this, but are extremely rare until the second quarter of the sixth century.[11]

A vase by the Nessos Painter, found in the American excavations of the Athenian Agora,[12] is an early example of what will be one of the leading vase-shapes in Attica for over a hundred years, the one-piece amphora, or "amphora," unqualified, for short. The decoration consists of a single huge and solemn figure on each side of the vase, a sphinx in the same attitude as those on the vase in Berlin. A fragment in Hamburg,[13] also by the Nessos Painter, from a kind of krater (mixing-vessel), has one of the earliest Attic figures of another monster, the woman-headed bird, the siren.[14] There must have been a pair of them, confronted; and another pair of animals, or several pairs. Below, a row of swans.

The Nessos Painter is one of several allied painters not always easily distinguished from each other, especially in fragments. Another is the Chimaera Painter,[15] as he may be called from a very large amphora, fragmentary, in Aegina, with two chimaeras on the body and a pair of sphinxes on the neck.[16] An amphora in London,[17] with a lion on each side and on the neck two birds feeding, seems to be by the same hand; probably also fragments of a krater in the Ceramicus Museum at Athens, with Chimaera (pl. 6, 3)[18] and Pegasos, and under the belly of Pegasos a hound.

These monsters, and those on the three vases by the Nessos Painter, were either alone, or in pairs confronted. On other vases of the group they are locked in combat; lion and pantheress, for example, attack a young bull on a krater in Athens which may be by the Chimaera Painter.[19] Such strong and fierce animals, to the Nessos Painter and his contemporaries, must have had deep significance as symbols or manifestations of terror and power; and their likenesses may have enhanced in the beholder the feeling of strength and confidence to a degree not easily apprehended by an age so glutted with visual aids as our own.

Of equal force are the prowling lions on a lid in Athens which belongs to the same stylistic group and is not far from the Chimaera Painter. (Pl. 6, 1.)

In front of these monsters, as of the mountainous beast-groups that filled the pediments of the early stone temples on the Acropolis of Athens, one begins to think of Leviathan and Behemoth in the Book of Job, or of Blake's Tiger

burning bright
In the forest of the night.

Before leaving the earliest period of Attic black-figure, let us glance at a scene from ordinary life which is not inferior to any of the great animal or mythological pieces: the cavalcade on fragments of a krater in Athens (pl. 6, 2).[20] The vase has been attributed to the succeeding period,[21] but resembles the works of the Nessos Painter, and cannot be far from them in date. There is much overlapping, and an off horse's head is even thrust on this side of a hither rider. This is the acme of the seventh-century horse, and one almost hears the clatter of hooves and the jingle of harness.

❖   ❖   ❖

The tradition of the Nessos Group was continued, in the early decades of the sixth century, by the Gorgon Painter,[22] so called from the subject of his "dinos" in the Louvre.[23] The dinos is a sort of krater: the simple, handsome shape was borrowed from metal cauldrons; once adopted, it was retained throughout the history of vase-painting, but it is especially important in the first half of the sixth century. As it has no handles, the decoration can run unimpeded round the vase. In the Louvre dinos, the principal zone, on the shoulder, has two subjects; the next broadest band, below this, is floral; then come four rows of animals, and on the bottom of the vase a cable-pattern and a whirligig design.[24] Dinoi will barely keep upright without a support: the support of the Louvre dinos is decorated with three rows of floral ornament and five of animals. The floral designs on stand and bowl are of the same nature as in the Nessos Painter, but much drier and more conventional. The same may be said of the animals. The *arrangement* of the animals, which has Corinthian antecedents,[25] is that which prevails in vase-painting from this time onwards. Pairs are still found, but the animals are often grouped in threes, fours, or fives. A siren, or a pair of sirens, facing each other between a pair of lions; a siren between sphinxes between two lions; and so on, the outer animals facing towards the middle. In the upper-most zone we notice first of all that the field has been swept clear of filling-ornaments. One of the two subjects is again Perseus pursued by the Gorgons, a six-figure composition such as we restored on the Nessos Painter's vase in Berlin: Medusa collapsing, her sisters pursuing Perseus, Athena standing, Hermes moving up. If this were the only picture of the subject it might be quite interesting, but after the Nessos Painter it seems rather tame. The other subject is a symmetrical arrangement of two warriors fighting, with their charioteers, one on each side, holding the chariots ready for their masters. Without practice in such clear, simple, symmetrical compositions the masterpieces of later painters, Kleitias and his successors, would not have been possible. There is a certain amount of repainting on the dinos, but not enough to account for the limpness of the human figures. The Gorgon Painter could do better, but he never reaches the height of the preceding age.

The Louvre dinos, with its stand, is typical of a very numerous class of early sixth-century vases, large and small, in which the decoration consists, wholly or in great part, of zones of animals. The tradition of the Gorgon Painter is carried on by the first Attic vase-painter whose name is known, Sophilos.[26] None of his many all-animal vases are signed: his name appears on three vases with scenes from *myth*, all belonging to his later period. On a large dinos by Sophilos, found on the Acropolis of Athens,[27] the mythological scene ran right round the vase, a many-figured composition far more elaborate than any we have seen hitherto. Only fragments remain, and were it not that the same subject was treated by Kleitias, somewhat later, on the François vase, we should not be able to interpret them all with certainty. Above, a floral band; below, a zone of animals—a wing, and parts of two boars are preserved. The theme of the picture is the Wedding of Peleus and Thetis, the gods coming to visit the newly wedded pair: more will be said about it when we speak of Kleitias. We see on the extreme right of the scene the house of Peleus. It is the first representation of a building we have found on a vase. There is an *indication* of a building on an earlier vase, from the Group of the Nessos Painter, in Athens, where a procession of women moves towards a temple, as it must be, indicated by two columns.[28] Sophilos is not content with an indication; he *represents* the house. There are many such buildings on black-figured vases, Corinthian and Attic, from the second quarter of the sixth century onwards, and they furnish valuable information about early architecture.[29] We see the front view of a building *in antis*. Parts of both antae remain; one of the two Doric columns between the antae, and half the door, with the keyhole. The artist signs between door and column, *Sophilos egrapsen*, "painted by Sophilos." Peleus stands in front of his house; one foot, booted, and the edge of his long white chiton are preserved. Now comes a gap, which can be supplied with the help of the François vase, although the missing figures need not all have been the same. The second fragment (*d*) gives the head of the procession, or nearly the head. Iris, wearing a short chiton, belt, winged boots, walks in front, holding a caduceus. In the François vase she is accompanied by the centaur Chiron, and she may have been so here. Two pairs follow: the goddesses Hestia and Demeter; the goddess Leto, with the wife of Chiron, Chariklo. All four wear peploi, sandals, and himatia placed shawl-wise and held out with one hand. The peploi are richly ornamented with floral bands and zones of animals—sphinxes, lions, panthers.* Then came the gods in their chariots: Zeus with Hera; Poseidon and Amphitrite; and others, of whom little remains. The position of the Nysai, as the painter calls them, is uncertain: the heads of three women remain, two side by side, the third full-face and playing the flute: they would seem to correspond to the Muses who accompany the chariots on the François vase and who sang at the wedding; but the name Nysai, which in the plural occurs here only, points to these being attendants of Dionysos. The rear is brought up, as in Kleitias, by the sea-god, merman, Triton, and by Hephaistos riding a donkey: part of Triton's tail remains, and part of the donkey's tail.[30]

A second signature of Sophilos is on fragments of another dinos, found at Pharsalos in Thessaly and now in Athens.[31] There were three rows of animals; a fourth, on the top side of the mouth, is rather less debased in style; but it is plain that Sophilos is by now sick of animals and interested only in the mythological subject. It is probable that here also the picture ran right round the vase, although if so it must have been made up of several distinct groups. Only one fragment of it has survived, but it tells us a good deal. The artist signs *Sophilos: megrapsen*, "Sophilos painted me," and on the left of the fragment there is the beginning of a second inscription,

---

* See p. 27.

Soph[*ilos*] again, which was very likely followed by the predicate *mepoiesen*, "Sophilos made me." On the right of the fragment is the name of one of the figures, *Achiles* (for *Achilleus*); the figure itself is lost. Lastly, beside the painter-signature there is a fourth inscription of a kind familiar in modern times, but rare in antiquity: it gives the *subject* of the picture ΓΑΤΡΟΟΛVϟ: ΔΤΙΔ (both words misspelt), "the Games in honour of Patroklos." The subject is therefore taken from the Iliad. Part of the chariot-race is preserved, the leading team, at full gallop; and a stand packed with spectators—two of them stretch out their arms, another waves his stick, a young man rises from his seat. This is another sort of building, not very often shown in Greek art. To get the stand in, the artist has had to make the spectators very small, mere minikins. One cannot help thinking of them as being small because they are in the distance, but that was not the painter's intention; it was a very long time before distant figures came to be diminished. The seating arrangements are not clear, and Sophilos' rendering of the stand should not perhaps be taken too literally. Achilles, who is in charge of the games, must have been full-size, facing the oncoming chariots. The stand is not really between him and the horses.

The same subject, the Games in honour of Patroklos, appears on the François vase.[32] There only one event is depicted, the chariot-race. In Sophilos it is quite likely that other events were figured. There are several comprehensive pictures of famous sports meetings from this period and even a little earlier.[33]

One technical detail calls for remark; the white colour of the hither horse, and of the female figures on the Acropolis dinos, is laid directly on the clay ground of the vase, as often in earlier black-figure, but the contour and inner lines are in matt red, which is very rare: on vases, it is found only in works by Sophilos and in one or two fragments that are close to him.[34] It occurs, however, on the sixth-century wooden panels, of Corinthian style, found at Pitsa between Sicyon and Corinth and not yet published; they are later than Sophilos, but it is possible that he borrowed the device from earlier painters on wood.

Sophilos is not a good draughtsman; but he evidently had enterprise, and his many-figured mythological representations, if they are really earlier than those of Kleitias, as they seem to be, may have pointed the way to the greater artist. Sophilos' figures are comparatively small, but he had not the fineness of hand or mind to achieve a true miniature style which yet has a real seriousness and even grandeur; that was reserved for Kleitias.

A better artist than Sophilos, although the two have much in common, is the KX Painter, whose name requires explanation. He is the chief painter in the Komast Group,[35] so called from one of the favourite subjects in it, komasts—revellers—of a rather special conformation, sometimes naked, sometimes clad in short chitons, dancing vigorously. They are the earliest of the countless revellers in Attic vase-painting; and they are borrowed from Corinth. "KX" is short for "Komast Painter X"; there is also "Komast Painter Y," and other companions can be distinguished. The revellers appear on several kinds of vase, but above all on drinking-vessels of fine make and no great size: skyphoi, and kylikes or cups. A skyphos in Athens is by the KX Painter (pl. 7, 3); a cup in New York belongs to the Komast Group and is close to him (pl. 7, 4).[36] Both shapes—kylix, skyphos—are borrowed from Corinth, the skyphos with little change, the kylix with considerable modification. These are the earliest Attic kylikes to which the term can be properly applied, and the adoption of the shape from Corinth is a landmark in the history of ancient pottery; the cups of the Komast Group stand at the head of a long and magnificent series which includes a great proportion of the masterpieces of Attic vase-painting.

The kylix of the Komast Group might be thought to have a sort of fore-runner in an Attic geometric shape, the shallow cup with offset lip but without a stem:[37] this, however, seems to have died out long before, and there does not appear to be any link between the two classes. There can be no doubt that the new shape was borrowed from Corinth.[38] The general form, with short offset lip and short conical foot, is the same as in the Corinthian cup, but the Attic potter has remodelled the shape, lightened it, and improved it. The subjects, too, are different; the dancing komasts are Corinthian, but although they appear on Corinthian skyphoi, they do not actually appear on Corinthian cups. The scheme of decoration is different; the floral ornament at the handles has no Corinthian antecedent, and while the Corinthian cup often has a gorgoneion inside, the interior of the Komast cup is always plain black: it is not until the next phase of the Attic cup that there is decoration inside as well as out.

Fragments, found in Samos, come from an unusually large and fine cup by the KX Painter,[39] but it was not of Komast type either in shape or in decoration. The offset lip has an intricate floral design instead of the usual net-pattern or rosettes, and there are two rows of pictures. Below, sphinxes face each other with a plant between. Above, a symposion. The subject appears in Corinth earlier than in Attica, and the early Attic symposia are strongly influenced by the Corinthian.[40] Women share the couches of the men, women play the flute and serve the wine. Couches and tables are richly adorned; dogs, dark and white, gnaw their bones under the couches. The drinking-vessels represented are skyphoi, mastoi, kantharoi; there is no kylix among them, as if the kylix were not yet regarded as indispensable to a feast. The white of the female flesh is laid directly on the clay; the details added in brown on top of the white have flaked off.

It is not on cups, however, that the KX Painter is seen at his best, but in small scenes from legend on other kinds of vase; for instance, in the Herakles struggling with Nereus on a hydria-fragment in Samos (pl. 7, 1), or in the Judgement of Paris—the earliest Attic representation of the subject extant—on a fragment, probably of a column-krater, in Berlin (pl. 7, 2).[41]

Cups formed only a small part of the KX Painter's output, but the next generation saw one artist at least who was primarily a painter of cups. The dominant type of kylix in the second quarter of the sixth century is given the conventional name of "Siana cup,"[42] because two well-known examples of it happen to have been found at Siana in Rhodes. It is a continuation of the Komast cup with its offset lip and conoid foot, but the proportions are different; foot and lip are both larger; and there are other changes. One of the chief is that the cup is regularly decorated inside as well as out. Now begins the great line of tondi, circular pictures inside cups, which lasts for nearly two hundred years.[43] These are not quite the earliest tondi in Attica: the lekanai of the KX Painter, and, earlier, that of the Nessos Painter with its gorgoneion,* had round pictures inside; some of the Corinthian cups had gorgoneia; and a rudiment may be traced in the Attic stemless cups, already mentioned, of the Geometric period;† but it is during the second quarter of the sixth century that the series sets in strongly. The subject is usually, within a thick border, a single human figure in swift movement, running or flying; or a horseman; or an animal, lion, sphinx, siren, cock; but two-figure pictures soon appear. The design often approximates to a cross or whirligig within the circle, a simple but effective scheme. Outside the cup, there are two chief systems of decoration. The more natural course is to accept the division caused by the offset lip, and to place one design on the narrow handle-zone and another, usually floral, on the lip—two-row decoration, "double-decker"; but often the picture is carried over both lip and handle-zone—"overlap decoration." This enables the painter to make his figures larger, but although one gets accustomed to it, it remains an error of taste. Many artists painted Siana cups, but two are prominent. The elder of them was the C Painter;[44] the letter C stands for "Corinthianizing": there is a good deal of Corinthian influence in his work. The younger will be treated in a later chapter.‡

The cups of the C Painter are well made and well proportioned, and they have a cheerful look owing to the fine orange clay and the plentiful use of white and red. The drawing of the short, thickset figures is often quaint, but always lively and clear. The Troilos cup in New York is a good example of the C Painter's work at its ordinary level (pl. 8, 2).[45] Inside, a gorgon at high speed fills the circle well, and shows a happy balance of the four colours; the lotus-buds too are not so dry as they often are. Outside, the subject of one half is a favourite in the sixth century, and more will be said about it

* See above, p. 14.   † See above, p. 20.   ‡ See below, pp. 50–52.

when we come to the François vase: Achilles pursuing Troilos. The young Troilos rode to the fountain outside the city of Troy to water his horses, accompanied by his sister Polyxena who came to fetch water; Achilles sprang out from behind the fountain where he was lurking and gave chase. The C Painter confines his picture to the main elements: the fountain, Achilles, Troilos, Polyxena. Achilles, his heavy shield on his arm and the spear in his right hand, hurtles forward with large and lumbering strides; Troilos rides one horse and leads another; Polyxena flees at a tripping run, no doubt looking back (the upper half is missing); she drops her hydria, which is here seen, shedding its contents, between the legs of Achilles. These figures are repeated, with variations, in most pictures of the subject; they form a scheme. In archaic representations of riders there is often an animal—hound or hare—under the horse's belly; it fills the void, and underlines the notion of speed.* Here the hare is in place; the fountain is outside the city wall, in a lonely spot. The Corinthian-looking cavalcade of youths, holding spears, on the other half of the exterior, has no connexion with the Troilos scene. It will be noticed that although on the one hand the artist ignores the corner between lip and handle-zone by drawing right through it, on the other hand he stresses it by means of a thick black line; so strong is the Greek tendency to emphasize articulations, to mark one member of an object distinctly off from the rest.

The same riders appear on one half of an overlap cup in Heidelberg.[46] Inside, a winged goddess, probably Nike, rushes with legs and arms outspread. The other half of the exterior represents the conquering hero. Carrying on his head the bronze tripod won as a prize at the games, he is met by the worthies of his family and village, who hold phialai and drinking-horns for the rejoicings to come. The posse is headed by a flute-player, and one can even guess what he is playing—the ancient triumph-song of Archilochus:

$$\tau\acute{\eta}\nu\epsilon\lambda\lambda\alpha \; \kappa\alpha\lambda\lambda\acute{\iota}\nu\iota\kappa\epsilon,$$
$$\chi\alpha\hat{\iota}\rho' \; \acute{\alpha}\nu\alpha\xi \; {}^{\backprime}H\rho\acute{\alpha}\kappa\lambda\epsilon\epsilon\varsigma.$$

There are other pictures of the subject, but this is the earliest and most vivid.[47] An increasing interest in athletic contests is among the characteristics of Attic vase-painting in the second quarter of the sixth century. Here one remembers the cup by the C Painter in Berkeley;[48] inside, it has a winged goddess, Nike, in the same attitude as on the Heidelberg cup, but looking round, and wearing a long garment; outside, a long procession of twenty persons, youths and men; the youths all raise their hands in greeting, as if to a victor, although as a matter of fact no victor is to be seen.

A third cup with the same riders on one half of the exterior is in Athens.[49] The other half has a battle-piece, consisting of three groups of two warriors

---

* See also below, p. 34.

each. These formal pairs, like the cavalcade, are very close to those on Corinthian vases, and, although one might think that such simple motives could be invented anywhere, were probably borrowed from Corinth all the same.[50] The warriors recur on another cup in Athens, but restricted to the handle-zone.[51] The same warriors, in the same style, form the decoration of a cup in Würzburg.[52] There, as often in our painter, the shield-devices were incised instead of being painted in white, and so stood a better chance of being perfectly preserved: horse's head, ram's head, chinless lion, head of a hoplite, flying eagle, head of a bull. These well-planned devices occur again and again in the C Painter and add a relish to his stock groups. The *shape* of the Würzburg cup is new. Such cups are found, side by side with the far more popular Siana cup, in the second quarter of the sixth century; we call them "merrythought cups," from the form of the handles, which recall a merry-thought or wishbone.[53] More important than the handles is the shape of bowl and foot. First, the bowl has no offset lip: this form of bowl is slow in asserting itself, but in the later part of the sixth century it prevails over the bowl with offset lip; although cups with offset lips continued to be made, they took the second place in late black-figure and in red-figure. Secondly, the foot: it is much taller and slenderer than in the Siana cup, and more like the foot of the Little-Master cup, the new type which, as will be seen, re-places the Siana cup in the middle of the century.

Although most of the C Painter's vases are cups, some of his best work was done on other shapes. A tripod-pyxis in the Louvre (pl. 8, 1; pl. 9)[54] has four pictures, one on each rectangular leg, and one on the upper side of the bowl. The bowl-subject is a battle, in which we recognise the warriors of the C Painter's cups, shields and all, but instead of fighting reduced to a row of repetitive single combats, there is a more varied picture, recalling not the monotonous groups on later Corinthian vases, but the fine miniature battle-pieces of seventh-century Protocorinthian. One warrior falls but tries to defend himself, or begs for mercy, from the opponent who follows up the blow; a friend steps forward to help the man in straits; one warrior turns tail, and is pursued, caught, cut down. Many attitudes, much force. In the heraldry, the chinless lion predominates, but there are also a female head and the head of a satyr. The three pictures on the upright legs of the tripod (pl. 9) are on a larger scale, and at first glance look earlier, and more formal, but the hand is the same. The chief of the three is the earliest picture of a very Attic subject, the Birth of Athena.[55] Zeus sits on his throne, his feet on a stool, gripping his thunderbolt in one hand and in the other a rather curious sceptre or stick.[56] Athena rushes out of his head, helmeted, brandishing a spear, her shield-device a gorgoneion, the first armed Athena we have seen.* The throne, doubtless thought of as the work of Hephaistos, has no back,

* See p. 15.

but between the stout ornamented legs it has handsome supports in the form of naked youths sitting on the ground. The Eileithyiai stand on each side of the father, one hand making an upward pass, the other laid soothingly on the poor head. To left of this trio, Hephaistos, who has split the skull, moves away, looking back, the axe in one hand, the other raised in a gesture of wonder; to right of the trio, Poseidon with his trident also moves away, looking round, surprised. A goddess at each end completes the symmetrical composition. The second picture is a chariot-scene: a woman stands in the car, one hand grasping the rail, the other holding her himation, which veils the back of her head and is drawn aside from the face with a gesture, much used by brides and matrons, which first appears in the seventh century and persists throughout antiquity.[57] A god, or hero, mounts, holding reins and goad. Three women approach, proffering wreaths, all three—and this is unusual—on the hither side of the horses and almost concealing them. The persons can hardly be named with certainty; one thinks of Zeus, Hera, and the Horai. On the third leg of the tripod, Hermes conducts three goddesses; a fourth female precedes him, holding a pair of wreaths; and in front of her a man hurries off, looking round. It is an episode in the Judgement of Paris; Hermes, conducting the three goddesses towards Paris, who, alarmed, tries to escape, is a favourite scene in black-figure, and we shall meet it again.* The fourth female, who leads the procession, may be Iris, who accompanies Paris in the same scene on a later vase.[58] This is an early picture of the Judgement; still earlier, the fragment by the KX Painter in Berlin: but once more Corinth has the priority with the Judgement of Paris on the Protocorinthian Chigi vase in the seventh century.[59]

The white of the female flesh, as usual in the C Painter, is laid not direct on the clay ground, but on a black or brown undercoat: the details, except the cornea of the eye, are incised. This technique, which is more durable than the other (white laid direct on the clay, details in brown), occurs as early as the period of the Gorgon Painter,[60] and is the rule in middle and later black-figure.

The finest work of the C Painter is on a lekane-lid in Naples (pl. 10),[61] with the earliest representation of a subject which becomes frequent later, the death of Astyanax at the sack of Troy. Priam is usually shown sitting on the altar of Zeus Herkeios, to which he has fled for refuge, in the court-yard of his palace, while Neoptolemos, who has seized the young son of Hector, Astyanax, by the ankle, brings the child down on top of him. Here Priam stands at the altar instead of sitting, his arms extended in entreaty; his wife Hecuba stands behind him, also raising her arms.[62] Meanwhile the Greeks, horse and foot, have poured through the city gates. First, two horse-men, side by side, ready to hurl their javelins. "Congruent" figures—figures

---

* See below, p. 44.

set abreast and overlapping—become common in this period, but the C
Painter takes special delight in them, and likes so nearly to superpose the
nearer on the farther that at first one sees a single only. Then seven warriors
run side by side. Then a warrior running beside a man riding one horse and
leading another; then, twice repeated, the alternation of seven warriors with
a single warrior and rider. The heraldry is particularly rich: Neoptolemos
bears a gorgoneion, the other warriors satyr-head, ship's prow, stag's head,
plane-leaf, insect, panther's head, ram's head twice, sphinx, cock, twice a
man's head, boar's head, hare, flying eagle, horse's head, goat's head, youth's
head, helmet, satyr's head, bull's head, lion's head, and two other charges.

Fragments of a lekane in the Acropolis collection at Athens[63] seem to be
somewhat later than the lid in Naples. There were two subjects, perhaps
three. The best-preserved is the Departure of Amphiaraos, the earliest Attic
picture of it and the nearest in treatment to the famous Corinthian krater in
Berlin.[64] Amphiaraos takes hold of the rail and mounts his chariot, but looks
round at his small son Alkmeon, who embraces him. Baton his driver holds
the reins; he wears the long robe of the charioteer, and has his shield slung
over his back by a broad band, as he needs both hands. Both warriors wear
a corslet of leather, adorned with a gorgoneion—one of the earliest occur-
rences of the leather corslet. On the ground, a hedgehog, as in the Corinthian
picture. Eriphyle draws her rich mantle aside from her face, and holds the
magic necklace for which she betrayed her husband and sent him to his
death. Behind her stands one of her daughters, or the nurse. The Entry of
Herakles into Olympus is one of the earliest representations of the subject;[65]
parts of Herakles, Athena, Artemis, and another goddess remain. A second
fragment makes one think of the Birth of Athena: Hephaistos, Eileithyia,
the throne of Zeus supported by a small naked figure sitting frontal on a
stool. The remaining fragments might belong either to the second scene or
to the third.

A cup-fragment recently found on the Acropolis joins a fragment already
known and gives part of a battle-scene by the C Painter, together with a
signature, [Ch]eiron epoiesen, "made by Cheiron."[66] Cheiron may have
painted the vase as well as fashioned it, but this cannot be assumed, and the
old designation "C Painter" had better be retained.

The gift of vivid narrative, such as we have found in the work of the C
Painter, is widespread in sixth-century Greece. Our next chapter will be
devoted to a younger contemporary of the C Painter, Kleitias, who may
fairly be termed a master of narrative art.

III

THE FRANÇOIS VASE

A HUNDRED and six years have passed since the François vase,[1] now in the Archaeological Museum at Florence, was discovered just outside the Etruscan city of Chiusi by the devoted Italian excavator whose name it not unjustly bears. The tomb in which it had been placed had been robbed in antiquity; the robbers had taken the objects in precious metal, but had contented themselves with shattering the clay vase and scattering many of the pieces far and wide outside the tomb. In his search for these, it was estimated at the time that Alessandro François had dug an area equal to that of the Colosseum at Rome. Long after, one of the fragments still missing was turned up by a ploughman; and it is not impossible that others may still come to light.

The vase was made about 570 B.C. It bears the signatures of two artists, the potter Ergotimos and the painter Kleitias. It is strange to think how little we should know of either if this one vase had not been found. The same pair of signatures occurs on two small vases, and on figureless fragments of two small cups. We have also fragments of a few vases, without signature, which we see to be by Kleitias; but without the François vase we should not have been able to name the artist.

The shape—Ergotimos' work—is what is known as a volute-krater, a krater with volute-handles (pl. 11, 1). This is the earliest Attic volute-krater, and one of the earliest Greek. It is a finer and more elaborate version of the column-krater, which originally may have been a Corinthian type of vase, but if so had long been acclimatised in Attica.[2] Later potters enlarged the volutes of the volute-krater, added a lip above the mouth, altered the form of the foot, and made the whole vase taller, but Ergotimos' model remains unsurpassed. The volute-handles may have been invented by workers in metal, but the bronze volute-kraters that have reached us have no special connexion with the François vase, the design of which is thoroughly ceramic.

The vase, nearly twenty-seven inches high, is decorated all over with many rows of small figures, precise, angular, and keen, nearly all identified by inscriptions. The surface has suffered, and the white parts of the painting especially; many of the brown lines added on top of the white have disappeared, so that the female figures have a somewhat spectral appearance which

---

[1] For numbered notes to chapter iii see pages 108–109 below.

is not original. Fragments of another vase by Kleitias, in Athens, are almost perfectly preserved (pl. 12, 1–2), and give a notion of what the female figures on the François vase looked like when they were fresh.

There are a few photographs of the entire vase, but we use, for the most part, the drawings made by Reichhold in 1900; they are not perfect, but as nearly so as one could hope for; they are a wonder of patience and skill.[3]

Before examining the several pictures, let us consider the subject-matter as a whole. It is not uniform; there are several themes. First: the subjects of the chief picture, running right round the vase, and of the three other figure-zones on the obverse, are taken from the lives of the hero *Peleus* and his son *Achilles*; while the lower picture on each handle figures, as will be seen, in narrow space, the last episode in that story, the dead body of Achilles borne from the field. Second: *Theseus* is the hero of the upper neck-picture on the *reverse* of the vase, and he also takes part in the centauromachy below it. Third: the remaining figure-scene, the *Return of Hephaistos*, is not taken from heroic legend, but from life in Olympus, viewed Homerically from its comic side. It is ingeniously linked, or hooked, to the chief picture by the special role which two gods, Dionysos and Hephaistos, play in both. Fourth: the lowermost of the figure zones is devoted to the *wild animals* which, as we saw, meant much to the Greeks of the earlier archaic period: sphinxes, and griffins, stationary; lions and panthers attacking bull, deer, and boar. The sphinxes are repeated, smaller, in the upper corners of the mouth of the vase on one side. The chief picture on each handle is taken from the same realm, for it represents the goddess *Artemis* conceived as *Queen of Wild Animals*. Fifth: there is *plant-life* as well as animal, though highly stylized—plant-complexes between the sphinxes and between the griffins, in the animal-zone; floral bands on the edges of the handles; and the subordinate decoration, the so-called tongue-pattern and ray-pattern, is also floral. Sixth: a last far-off glimpse of the heroic world is given by the *Gorgons* on the inner sides of the handles, for they evoke a great hero of an elder generation, *Perseus*. Seventh and last: the narrow zone on the foot of the vase is filled by a serio-comic conflict, the Battle between the *Pygmies and the Cranes*.

The chief picture, which runs right round the shoulder and middle of the vase, is the Wedding of Peleus, or, to be precise, the gods visiting the newly-wedded pair. The story was told in epic poems now lost. The sea-goddess Thetis, eldest of the fifty daughters of the sea-god Nereus, was wooed by both Zeus and Poseidon, but when they learned that she was destined to bear a son stronger than his father they desisted, agreed that she should wed not a god but a mortal, and chose the hero Peleus. The wedding was one of the most famous in antiquity, and was attended by all the gods. It was at the wedding-feast that the dispute arose among the three goddesses which led to the Judgement of Paris and so to the fault of Helen, the Trojan War,

the death of Achilles, and the ruin of Troy. On the right is the house of
Peleus, and Thetis sitting in it, drawing her mantle aside from her face, and
looking through the half-open door at what approaches; Peleus stands at
the altar in front of the house to welcome the gods. Really, of course, the
house would be seen in profile, and Thetis would not be seen at all; but
Kleitias has boldly turned the house towards us, while leaving Thetis in
profile. The house is one of three buildings represented on the vase, and these
are important for the history of Greek architecture, especially of early con-
structions part in timber, part in stone. It is a gabled building, with a porch
formed by the projection of the side walls, and with two columns between
the decorated wall-ends. Almost everything is given, even to the cat-hole,
as it must be, the hole for a pet animal to pass out and in. The long procession is headed by Chiron and Iris. Most of the centaurs were wild, but a few
were not, and the chief of these was Chiron, δικαιότατος Κενταύρων, as Homer
calls him, justest or most civilised of centaurs. The more civil centaurs are
often represented as wearing clothes, and as having a complete human
body, to which the barrel and hindquarters of a horse are attached; and so
Chiron. He was the great educator of heroes, of Peleus, of Achilles, of Jason,
and of many others: he taught them not only their accomplishments, shoot-
ing, riding, hunting, first-aid, and the rest, but their principles of conduct
as well. He clasps Peleus by the hand, and as a great hunter he shoulders a
fir-branch, with two hares tied to it, and another animal. Iris is here as
herald of the gods, wearing a short tunic, so as to be able to run, with a
dappled fawnskin round the waist. Then come three females side by side,
sharing, as often in earlier archaic art, a single large mantle. In the middle
is Chariklo, wife of Chiron; beside her, Hestia and Demeter, sisters of Zeus
and eldest daughters of Kronos. They are followed by a strange figure. It is
Dionysos, but nowhere else is he represented like this. He hastens, almost
stumbles forward, holding an amphora full of wine on his shoulder, wine
for the feast. The head is turned towards us, frontal. One or two faces on the
vase are frontal instead of in profile. Frontal human faces occur as early as
the seventh century (there are no three-quarter faces in Greek painting till
after the beginning of the fifth). In archaic painting the frontal face is not
used haphazard.[4] The god here, feeling the weight and the effort, turns
towards the spectator, almost as if for sympathy, a contrast to the easy,
unconscious bearing of the other deities. Then come, sharing a mantle as
before, the three Horai, daughters of Zeus—Seasons, not our four, but
goddesses of all seasonable increase, and so in place at a wedding. The peplos
of the farthest Hora is one of those magnificent garments, adorned with
rows of chariots, horsemen, animals, and flowers, of which there are seven
on our vase. The earliest reference to such garments in poetry is in the
Iliad,[5] where Helen is found weaving a large red web with scenes from the

Trojan War, which reminds one of the Bayeux Tapestry. No such garments have survived from the Greek archaic period, but they begin to be represented in the middle of the seventh century. Now the chariots begin. First, Zeus and Hera. The horses, instead of planting all four hooves flat on the ground, as horses walking do in all earlier Greek art,[6] lift the off fore-hoof so that it touches the ground with the tip only; it is a small change, but it gives a lighter effect, and was a novelty in the time of Kleitias. The pole-horses all wear topknots, and hold their heads up, while the trace-horses bend theirs.[7] This chariot and the two succeeding ones are accompanied by the nine Muses, daughters also of Zeus, headed (as in Hesiod) by Kalliope, who plays not the flute, which is the instrument of the Muses when we first hear of them in poetry, but the syrinx or Pan-pipes. Her head is frontal. The Muses sang at the wedding-feast. Then comes Poseidon with his wife Amphitrite, and Ares with Aphrodite, who are often coupled as if husband and wife.[8] The artist asks you to think that the picture was complete, and that the handle was then set on top of it; but of course that is only a fiction. Then comes Apollo, and perhaps his mother Leto, accompanied, probably, by the Charites or Graces, also daughters of Zeus. Then Athena, driving a goddess who is hard to name—the inscription is lost—but might be Artemis. Athena, the goddess of Athens, is specially honoured, for she is welcomed by the bride's father and mother—old Nereus, pointing the way, and Doris his wife. Then Hermes in his chariot, with his mother Maia, escorted by the Moirai, the Fates, who have much to do with marriage and birth; and last, as dwelling farthest away, Okeanos, the ocean-stream believed to encompass the whole earth, with Tethys his spouse. Hardly anything of these last two figures remains, but enough to show that Okeanos was represented with a human body but the head and neck of a bull.[9] River-gods were thought of by the early Greeks as bull-like, and Okeanos was the greatest of rivers. Euripides, long after, calls him bull-headed, ταυρόκρανος.[10] Okeanos and his wife are attended by a trio of females, probably Nereids, sisters of Thetis, and by a sea-god ending in the tail of a fish, or rather of a sea-serpent, a pristis, Triton. This is the last chariot, but not the end of the procession. As in the earlier picture of the subject by Sophilos,[11] the lame god Hephaistos brings up the rear. Hephaistos, when cast out of Heaven by his mother Hera, found refuge with Eurynome and Thetis, daughter and grand-daughter of Okeanos, and spent nine years working for them in a cave of Ocean; perhaps he is thought of as still their guest. As Dionysos came in front of the chariots, on foot, hurrying, burdened, face turned aside, so Hephaistos comes behind the chariots, not driving, but riding side-saddle on a donkey, he also in part turned towards the spectator. These two gods, who in this scene take a lowly place, will be compensated later, by their triumph in another scene, the Return of Hephaistos.

The subject occupying the front half of the zone below the Wedding is taken from the lost epic, the *Cypria*; it is one of the earliest episodes in the Trojan War. According to an oracle, Troy could not be taken if Troilos, youngest son of Priam, reached his twentieth year. Achilles lay in wait at the fountain outside the city, and when Troilos came to water his horses, sprang out. Troilos mounted, and made off towards the altar of Apollo, hoping for sanctuary; but the fleet Achilles, though in heavy armour, pursued him, overtook him, and slew him on the altar itself. Troilos in this scene is regularly accompanied by his sister Polyxena, who has come to the fountain to fill her hydria, which she drops as she runs away. Athena encourages Achilles; Hermes says something to Thetis, Achilles' mother, who is apprehensive. On the left is the fountain, turned towards us as the house of Peleus was; a youth and a girl are still drawing water. At the extreme left Apollo comes up incensed; he has seen Troilos heading for sanctuary, and suspects that Achilles will not hesitate to trespass. Achilles, in fact, incurred the anger of the god, who did not forget, and long after helped Paris to slay Achilles. On the right of the picture is another building, the city wall of Troy. In front of it sits the aged Priam, who has been taking the air with his friend Antenor. Antenor has seen with alarm what is taking place in the distance (the interval between Antenor and Polyxena is not actual: the archaic artist does not leave a great gap between one figure and another, but spaces them all out evenly). Antenor hastens back to Priam, who, startled, instinctively rises from his seat. Priam is an unusual and expressive figure. Bald, with clipped beard, and wrinkles on forehead and neck, he has a patient, meagre face, and the brittle look of old age. Moreover, one of his feet is drawn right back and rests on the ground with toes and ball only. In early Greek art, seated figures keep their legs close together, and their feet flat on the ground. This, and another figure on the François vase (Ares in the next scene), are the earliest seated figures which draw one of the legs back—earliest in Greek art at least; in Egyptian and Mesopotamian there are much earlier examples.[12] The alarm has been given and a rescue party, headed by Troilos' brothers, Hector and Polites, issues from the heavy city gates. On the battlements, in the embrasures, there are heaps of stones to throw at attackers. Stone-throwing was a substantial part of ancient defence-tactics, and even in the fourth century the military expert Aeneas Tacticus describes a method of retrieving the stones under cover of night.[13] Taking a last glance at this picture, we see that the composition is far from primitive. In the middle, six figures; to left and right three figures and a building (the two brothers tell as a single figure), the left side-group linked with the middle one by the girl Rhodia looking round and raising her arms in dismay, the right side-group linked with the middle one by the figure of Antenor, also looking round—enough remains to make this certain—and extending his arms.

The scene on the other half of this zone is the Return of Hephaistos. This is one of those gay and irreverent stories about the gods of which there are good examples in Homer, above all the lay of Demodokos in the Odyssey, where Hephaistos catches his wife Aphrodite and her lover Ares in an invisible net. The story of the Return of Hephaistos was narrated in a poem of which not a word remains, but which can be reconstructed in its main outlines from brief allusions in ancient writers and with the assistance of vases, especially the François vase, which gives far the most elaborate representation of the subject.[14] Hera, disgusted with her son Hephaistos because he was an ugly cripple, threw him out of Heaven, and he would have been in great distress had he not found refuge with Thetis. Hephaistos forgave his mother, and made her a present of a masterpiece of his craftsmanship, a magnificent throne, but when she sat in it she could not rise. Only Hephaistos could free her, and he had disappeared. Ares, her son, boasted that he would fetch Hephaistos back by force, but Hephaistos beat him off with firebrands—he was the inventor of artillery—and Ares retired discomfited. At last Dionysos, through the power of wine, induced Hephaistos to return. There was a special inducement; Zeus, it seems, had gone so far as to promise the hand of Aphrodite to whoever should fetch Hephaistos back. So Hephaistos had Aphrodite to wife, but Hera, to reward Dionysos, persuaded the gods that he also should be admitted to Olympus.

In the left half of the picture, conflicting emotions and a charged atmosphere. Hera sits on the throne, with impatient hands. Zeus sits by her, an unhappy king. Aphrodite recoils at the sight of her future husband. Behind, Ares sits on a low block, crestfallen; another expressive figure, with his right leg drawn back. He is one of those tall, long-backed fellows. Athena is jeering at him, and the sort of language she must be using may be gathered from Homer, where the Olympians do not spare their tongues, and Ares, in particular, seldom gets a good word from any of them. Three other gods hasten up, Artemis, Poseidon, and Hermes. In the right half of the zone an extraordinary procession approaches. Dionysos—he has the best head in the whole picture—leads the mule on which Hephaistos rides. It is a mule this time, not a donkey. The lameness of Hephaistos is not rendered so forcibly as in early non-Attic pictures, where his legs are cruelly deformed: the shanks are shapely, but the attachment is defective, and the toes point left and right. Three satyrs, or silenoi as they are here called—both names fit these horsemen—follow, the bodyguard of Dionysos; and four nymphs, their companions. The first satyr pants under the weight of a wineskin full to bursting; the second is the flute-player who was an essential part of a Greek procession; the third has caught up a nymph in his arms; of the second nymph only the hand remains, and the third is also fragmentary; the fourth plays the cymbals, an orgiastic instrument hitherto unheard in heaven.

This is an early representation of Dionysos; it is strange that there are none before the sixth century.[15] Satyrs, too, first appear in the early part of the sixth century.[16] Kleitias' satyrs are most unusual; it is not only that they have horses' legs and not merely horses' tails and ears—so have other satyrs in black-figure,—but their whole aspect is lean and equine, and unlike most black-figure satyrs they have nothing of the pig. The heads of Kleitias' satyrs, with their roomy aquiline noses, and the hair towering over the forehead, are very like the heads, as we shall find, of his centaurs, but if anything wilder and more terrifying.

Thus the two gods who had to be content with a humble place at the wedding of Peleus are exalted at the expense of all the others.

The third zone on the body is devoted to animals. These, as we have seen, are not merely decorative in early Greek art, but significant of terror and power. There are six groups. In the middle of the front, though off centre, a pair of sphinxes with a stylized plant between, which they are perhaps thought of as guarding; a time-honoured Oriental composition consists of two animals guarding a sacred tree. To left of them, a panther attacking a stag; to right of them, a young bull attacked by a panther. On the other side of the vase, a pair of griffins with a plant between. To left of them, a boar attacked by a lion; to right of them, a lion attacking a bull. All these strong creatures have a new elegance, and there are many novel or original traits. Griffins are not nearly so common in Attic art as in early Greek art elsewhere; and these are the earliest griffins on Attic vases.[17] Seldom do these bird-headed creatures have such fine sets of teeth as here. The panther, raising both fore-legs, grasping the stag's neck and biting it, is by no means a stock figure; and there is no parallel to the attitude of the paw in two of these groups. In other animal-groups the paw is either seen from the back (as in the panther to the right), or from the side (as in the panther to the left); here it is seen with the claws up, as if to deal an upper-cut. Kleitias can never have seen a lion, and must have got this piece of realism from observation of one of the lesser felines.

On the upper zone of the neck, on the front of the vase, the Hunting of the Calydonian Boar. The splendid description of the hunt in Swinburne's *Atalanta in Calydon* is founded on Ovid, who had a good Greek original before him, probably the *Meleager* of Euripides, and was wise enough to follow it closely. Euripides, in his turn based his narrative on an earlier poem, perhaps the same that Kleitias or his learned adviser used. Artemis, angry with Oineus, King of Calydon, sent a monstrous boar to ravage his country, and picked men from all Greece were needed to overcome it. Chief among the hunters were Meleager and Peleus, and Peleus and Meleager are shown in the front place. Peleus is beardless: this adventure is thought of as taking place when he was quite young, before his marriage. Next to these two was the virgin Atalanta, who with an arrow drew first blood. Here she has shot already, and is now wielding the spear, but her quiver is at her shoulder. She is dressed in a short tunic, and is the only figure on the vase to wear a wreath. The action is very orderly and symmetrical. The boar in the middle, pierced by four arrows, two from the left and two from the right; a hound on the back of the boar, another at its rump, a third disembowelled. Under the boar, Ankaios lies dead. The hunters attack in pairs, with short spears, long javelins, and stones; archers also, wearing exotic Oriental hats—Kleitias is interested in hats,—and two of them with Oriental-sounding names. The hounds are named, as well as the hunters. One ancient writer tells us that Atalanta's hound, Aura (Breeze), was killed on this occasion, but Aura is not among the hounds named by Kleitias.

Hunting boar without firearms is a different matter from the modern boar-hunt; and hunting it on foot, from pig-sticking on horseback. The stage of action chosen by Kleitias is the same as in most ancient representations of boar-hunts:[18] it is when, after the preliminary attack with missiles, the hunters close in on the boar at bay. "The toughest and most experienced man in the field," to quote Xenophon's instructions in his treatise on hunting, "now approaches the boar from the front, looking it in the eye, left foot advanced, holding the spear with both hands, the left hand higher up on the shaft, and the right lower down—the left hand having to guide the spear, while the other thrusts."[19] That is the attitude of Meleager and Peleus on the François vase.

In Xenophon's time the boar was usually driven into nets, but in sultry weather, he says, hounds could run him down without the use of nets; for, strong as the boar is, he loses his breath and tires.[20] This was dangerous work; but so Meleager and his comrades must have hunted, without nets.

The upper zone of the neck: on the reverse. A ship, and a dance. (The picture is continuous here; the modern draughtsman has divided it, repeating one figure.) The subject is taken from the legend of Theseus. The Athenians were forced by King Minos of Crete to send a tribute of seven youths and seven maidens to be exposed to the Minotaur in his maze fastness the Labyrinth. Theseus sailed to Crete, threaded the maze with the help of the ball of thread given him by Ariadne daughter of Minos, slew the monster, rescued the fourteen, and worked his way out of the Labyrinth. Then, we are told, he and the fourteen celebrated their deliverance by a dance, in which they mimed the process of their exit hand in hand. This is what we see in the right half of the picture—one of those long, winding dances still to be witnessed in Greece. Theseus, in a festal robe, leads the dance, playing the lyre. Ariadne, facing him, holds up the ball of thread, rolled up again; and she is chaperoned by her small nurse, whose name is recorded by Plutarch, Korkyne, but Kleitias calls her simply "nurse," θροφος. Now the left half of the picture. This has often been misunderstood, and some have assumed that Phaidimos, the last of the fourteen, is thought of as having just landed from the ship. This is not so. The dance is just beginning, and he is the last to join in—a device of the painter to add a touch of life and variety to the beautiful formal delineation of the dance. As to the ship, there is no literary record to help us, and we have to explain it from the picture itself. The explanation is that the ship of Theseus, after landing him in Crete, near Cnossos, must have sailed off, with instructions to return after a given time; it was not safe to remain moored. Returning as ordered, not knowing whether they would ever set eyes on him again, they see the dance forming up, and perceive with joy that the enterprise has been successful.[21]

The ship is a long, low, open rowing-vessel, with a single sail. We notice the stem-post and the foredeck; the railing; the stern curving round and ending in a pair of swan's heads, strengthened by a timber with a strut. The steersman, warmly dressed, sits at the stern with the two steering-oars. The mast has been lowered—the only representation of this in antiquity, although the process is often described in Homer. There is great excitement and delight. Some of the rowers rise from their seats, and one of them throws his arms up in joy. Another man has jumped overboard and swims to land, with a trudgeon-like stroke. Sixteen rowers are preserved, and there were probably thirty—the vessel was a triakonter. Part of the ship is missing; the prow has a beak in the form of a boar's head.

This is a very rare subject; indeed, the only other examples we have of it are by Kleitias himself. Small fragments of two splendid vases found on the Acropolis of Athens come from pictures of the dance on a larger scale than in the François vase (pl. 12, 4 and 5). From one vase, parts of the dancers.[22] From the other, the face of a woman and the back of a head, with the inscription [Eur]ysthenes, the name of the fifth dancer from the left on the François vase.[23]

The lower zone of the neck: on the front of the vase, a chariot-race. It is the chief event at the funeral games held by Achilles in honour of Patroklos, described in the twenty-third book of the Iliad. Achilles stands at the post, and the prizes are tripods—bronze cooking-pots on three legs—and bronze lebetes, or, as we now call them, dinoi—large round mixing-bowls. The prizes are used to fill the voids under the horses, an old convention. The five drivers wear the regulation long robe, and hold, besides the reins, the goad. One of them looks back. Oddly enough, Kleitias departs widely from the Homeric account;[24] of his five charioteers only Diomed, in Homer, takes part in the race, and he, the winner, runs third in Kleitias. Two of the five, · Damasippos and Hippothoön, are not even mentioned in the Iliad. The others are Odysseus, who leads—but in Homer did not compete,—and Automedon. These are all good heroic names, but Kleitias, left to himself, did not remember the field, and could not find anyone who did; his learned friend was not at hand.

As a work of art the picture is traditional. There is some variety, but not so much as might have been expected: one chariot is very like another. Kleitias could have varied them; but what he wished to give was for once the beauty of swift, unimpeded movement in one direction, contrasting with the slow procession of the chief zone, the knots and staccato elsewhere.

The lower zone of the neck: on the reverse, a centauromachy. In early art it is usually Herakles who fights the centaurs; and until recently this was the earliest representation of the Thessalian Lapiths in battle with them; but an episode in the Thessalian centauromachy, the death of Kaineus, appears on a seventh-century bronze relief found not long ago at Olympia.[25]

Nestor, in the Iliad, mentions the Thessalian centauromachy, but only briefly, as a tremendous conflict; it is also described in the *Shield of Herakles*, but not at length; there must have been an epic, now lost, which told the story in full. Kleitias' picture is composed of seven groups (all now fragmentary) with a good deal of overlapping. On the left, Theseus and a centaur (Theseus, though not a Lapith, took part as the sworn friend of the great Lapith warrior Peirithoös). Then Antimachos and a centaur. Next, Kaineus is rammed into the earth by the centaurs Agrios, Asbolos, and Hylaios. Kaineus is one of the most picturesque figures in the legend. The maiden Kainis asked Poseidon to change her into a man, and Poseidon did so, adding the gift of invulnerability. Kaineus, as he was now called, was proof against bronze and iron; but the centaurs were armed with more primitive weapons, branches and boulders, not swords and spears, so that Kaineus was no better off against them than an ordinary man, and after many valiant deeds he disappeared, rammed into the ground. Hoplon and Petraios. A Lapith, probably Peirithoös (who cannot have been omitted), and Melanchaites; a second centaur, Pyrrhos, lies on the ground. A sixth group, of which little remains. Lastly, Dryas and Oroibios, who founders and begs for quarter.

The pictures on the handles. They are the same on both handles, with minor variations. First, Artemis, winged, holding (on one handle) two lions, (on the other) a panther and a stag. This is the type of figure which the moderns call Potnia Thērōn, Queen of Wild Beasts, from a title of Artemis in Homer. The goddess, nearly always winged, usually standing still, grasping a pair of wild beasts or birds—that is a favourite figure in seventh- and sixth-century Greece;[26] in Attica, however, it is not common, there are only nine examples in all, the earliest late seventh-century,[27] and later it became so unfamiliar that Pausanias could write, in his account of the Chest of Kypselos, "I do not know for what reason Artemis has wings on her shoulders, and holds a panther in one hand and a lion in the other." We must ask why the Potnia Thērōn appears on the François vase at all. It was Artemis who sent the boar to Calydon, but that is not why she is here. We must rather think that the Potnia Thērōn belongs to the same realm as the sphinxes, griffins, and contending animals in the third zone on the body of the vase, and the sphinxes flanking the neck in front, and is here for the same reason as they; or rather, *they* belong to *her* realm; she is their queen.

The group of Ajax and Achilles (pl. 11, 2), the earliest Attic representation of the subject, is part of the Peleus-Achilles cycle, and is the concluding episode in the eventful heroic history that began with the wedding of Peleus and the divine Thetis.[28] A curious note is struck, as Payne observed,[29] by the juxtaposition of the hieratic figure of the goddess with the labouring Ajax and the rigid body of Achilles. It is not by chance that the one brings out the other, whether the artist's action was intentional, or instinctive, or on the border between.

Above the head of Artemis the handle curves rapidly round and down, and the third handle-picture, a Gorgon, is on the part of the handle that faces inwards. Viewing the vase from the inside, the only decoration one sees is the pair of Gorgons, and if the vase were filled with wine they would look as if they were flying over a sea. The Gorgons of Kleitias are part of a story; they are Stheno and Euryale, sisters of Medusa. The complete scene is already familiar from earlier works, and we have a fragment of a full representation of it by Kleitias himself. The sherd in the Pushkin Museum at Moscow (pl. 12, 3),[30] which may be from the neck of a column-krater (rather than a volute-krater like the François vase), gives the right-hand corner of the picture, with Perseus flying and Athena following to protect him; then Hermes must have come; then the two sisters of Medusa, the dead Medusa herself, and possibly other figures.

Kleitias has left two gorgon-heads besides those of Stheno and Euryale. One, damaged, is the device on Hector's shield in the Troilos scene on the François vase; the other, which ranks among the finest of archaic gorgoneia, is the chief ornament (pl. 11, 3) of a tiny stand-like object of uncertain use in New York which bears, like the François vase, the double signature of Ergotimos and Kleitias.[31]

Lastly, on the foot of the vase, small, Pygmies and Cranes. The war between cranes and pygmies is mentioned in the Iliad,[32] but the picture on the François vase is the earliest representation of it as well as the finest and most elaborate. The pygmies are midgets—small but not deformed, perfectly made; and so they are in nearly all the early pictures of them.[33] Part of Kleitias' picture is missing, but the general composition is clear. In the middle, three groups of pygmies, using clubs and crook-handled sticks— "hockey-sticks." In the middle group of the three a pygmy has hooked a crane round the neck with his hockey-stick and is clubbing it; his companion,

hat on, lies dead on the ground. In the left-hand group another pygmy has
hooked a flying crane; his companion grasps the neck with his left hand
and with his right hand raises his club to strike. In the right-hand group
two pygmies have hooked a flying crane; one kneels, pulling it down. These
three groups are flanked by a pair of cavalry scenes. The pygmies are
mounted on splendid goats, and use slings. We hear of pygmy cavalry, long
after, in Pliny, and even of its strategic use:[34] "it is reported," he writes,
"that when spring comes, the pygmies, mounted on rams or goats, and
armed with bows and arrows, go down to the sea in force, and in a three
months' campaign destroy the eggs and young of the cranes; otherwise
they would be unable to cope with the numbers. They bring home feathers
and eggshells and use them, mixed with mud, to build their houses."

In the left-hand cavalry group one pygmy has fallen, and a crane pecks
at his eyes.

Beyond the cavalry there is more infantry; here a crane is down, and a
pygmy despatches it with a knobkerrie.

One source of the fable of the pygmies battling with the cranes was, of
course, the reports of travellers about dwarfish races living at the ends of the
earth, but another was, nearer home, the yearly struggle of the Greek farmer
with the birds. The crane was one of his chief enemies, and there are many
references in Greek literature to its destructiveness. Remember Aesop's
fable of the farmer who caught a stork and was about to kill it. "But I am
a stork," it protested, "not a crane." "I can't help that," says the farmer;
"I found you among the cranes."[35] The weapons of the pygmies in Kleitias,
and their tactics, are taken from real life in Greece; they are those used by
the farmer—and the farmer's children—to protect the crops from birds,
including cranes.

The Battle with the Cranes on the François vase has always been popular,
and a great archaeologist has claimed that "in invention as well as drawing
it gave the painter more opportunity to display his powers than the solemn
procession of deities in the chief frieze."[36] Without wishing to underrate the
qualities of the Battle with the Cranes, we must say, I think, that the high
style of the chief frieze, and the varied, vivid narrative of the others, are
even more excellent achievements.[37]

IV

LYDOS AND OTHERS

MOST of the vases dealt with in the last two chapters were of no great size.
The François vase was large, but the figures were comparatively small.
For a more monumental style of drawing we must turn to other artists,
such as the Painter of Acropolis 606, or Nearchos, or Lydos. Two of these
three belong to the second quarter of the sixth century and are contemporaries, roughly speaking, of Kleitias; the career of the third, Lydos, begins in
the second quarter, but lasts well into the third. The Painter of Acropolis 606
takes his name from a large and fairly fully preserved dinos found on the
Acropolis of Athens (pl. 13, 1–2, and pl. 14, 1).[1] The shape is known to us
from the earlier vase by the Gorgon Painter in the Louvre, as well as from
two fragmentary vases by Sophilos; and the system of decoration is the same,
several zones running round the vase and covering the whole surface. The
chief picture is a battle-scene; not a contemporary battle, for the fighters
have driven up in chariots and by this time the chariot had ceased to be used
in Greek warfare, but a battle thought of as taking place in the heroic past.
There are eight chariots. The drivers pull the horses up, and most of the
warriors have alighted; only one has a foot still in the car. Two pairs of
warriors have already met. One pair attacks; others resist, but one of their
companions is down on his face. The larger-scale reproduction gives only
part of what is preserved; more is shown, on a smaller scale, in the general
view. This is at last a picture that for size, grandeur, and vehemence may
rank with the masterpieces of the Nessos Painter and his fellows. The eager
forward faces; the fierce twirl of the moustaches; the bold lines of the helmets, which would delight an armourer; the wrenched body of the fallen
hero; the superb horses, which have shed the old-fashioned rocking-horse look
of the seventh century and the early sixth—all these and much else combine
to make this one of the best battle-pieces in archaic art. The photograph
(pl. 14, 1) reproduces an unpublished portion, the last driver and warrior
on the right of the picture, and part of the last warrior on the left, supple-
menting the able modern copy. It does not give the original colours so well;
the hair of the driver was dark red, and so was the warrior's helmet, except
the edge, which was black with white dots. On the other hand the incision
is seen to be more sensitive than one could tell from the copy, especially in

---

[1] For numbered notes to chapter iv see pages 109–111 below.

the drawing of the driver's face. The dark thing to right of the driver is his
shield, then comes the double crest of the warrior. Above the chief zone there
is a band of floral pattern, and below it another floral band, thick, and even
more formal; below that, a narrower picture-zone with a cavalry-engage-
ment, only part of which has been published. The riders are small, their
horses big and powerful. One party consists of Greeks, wearing short chitons
and brimmed felt hats, and hurling javelins by means of a thong; their
opponents are mounted archers, wearing short chiton, boots, and flapped
hats of Oriental fashion; quivers at their backs. One javelin-man is down,
with an arrow in the brain, and his horse rushes off without him. There is
fury in this picture too. Below it a floral band, and then a zone of animals
aligned in groups of two and three. These, although one would hardly have
expected it, are a little mannered in style. The artist has made an experiment
in grouping, and the animals, instead of keeping their distance, overlap
freely; this may not seem remarkable, but it is against the time-honoured
rule of the animal frieze, according to which animals are either locked in
combat or keep their distance. The innovation did not find favour. Another
floral band follows, a wreath of myrtle, and the bottom of the dinos has a
handsome design, based on the whirligig which had long been a popular form
of circular decoration.[2] Six foreparts of animals, alternately lion and horse,
are set round a thick red band like handles on a ship's wheel, or like an
idealised carrousel. The idea of speed is admirably conveyed, and is enhanced by the whippy plants in the spaces between. Finally, a second
animal-frieze adorns the top-side of the mouth: here there are no innovations, and the animals keep their distance.

Another aspect of the painter is illustrated by two amphorae in Berlin
and Tübingen.[3] In the very large Berlin amphora the foot is modern, and
as the Tübingen vase shows, should be restored with more curve. This is
one of the amphorae in which the general aspect is especially austere. In the
sixth century the decoration of the amphora soon comes to be confined to
a large panel reserved on each side, the rest of the vase, except the space
for rays at the base, being painted black; but usually there are several figures
in the panel, and it has a floral border above. Sometimes, however, there is
no floral pattern, and only a single large figure, either a horse's head or a
horseman. Other subjects are rare in this austere variety of the amphora;
and we can speak of "horse-head amphorae" and "horseman amphorae."
The horseman often leads a second horse; and in the Berlin vase two men
ride side by side, and tell as a more complex single. The hither man wears
helmet and greaves, carries a shield and spear; all that is seen of his companion is the face and the front of the brimmed felt hat. As often, a bird
flies beside the riders, this time with a serpent in its beak, doubtless a good
omen; as often, an animal runs beside—in one picture a hound, on the other

a hare,—an undersong to the main theme. This very large vase—it is nearly thirty-two inches high—may have stood as a monument on an Attic tomb, as some at least of the *horse-head* vases certainly did. Horse-head or horse-man will have borne witness to the station or tastes of the dead—either a knight, or one interested in horses.[4] The Tübingen vase is smaller (twenty inches high) and has only a single warrior on each side; the eagle has no serpent, but hound and hare are as before.

Fierce fighters like those on the Athens dinos, and by the same hand, appear on a fragment in Odessa which has historical interest (pl. 13, 3);[5] it was found at Theodosia in the Crimea, and is the earliest piece of Attic pottery as yet discovered in South Russia, which imported not a few vases from Attica in the later part of the sixth century and in the fifth, and in the fourth century became one of the chief markets.

The name of this painter has not survived. The name of Nearchos, however, is known from five signatures.[6] His most important works are fragments of two large kantharoi found on the Acropolis of Athens. The best-preserved of the four pictures decorating them represents the harnessing of Achilles' chariot.[7] It is the earliest Attic example of a subject—harnessing a chariot—which became very popular, as will be seen, in the middle and the second half of the sixth century.[8] The only harnessing-scene before Nearchos' is much earlier, again on a Corinthian work, a Protocorinthian aryballos from the second quarter of the seventh century in Berlin.[9] The pole-horses, and the hither trace-horse, are already harnessed; and Achilles himself, bearded and long-haired, stands in front of them, holding the head of the trace-horse to keep it quiet (pl. 14, 2). The fourth horse is being brought up by an old man who holds it by the forelock. The horses are named; two names, Chaitos and Euthoias, remain, and probably the beginning of a third name, the *pi* under the bellies; these are not the names of Achilles' horses in the Iliad. The artist has signed, between Achilles and the trace-horse, Νεαρχοσμεγραφσενκα[ποιεσεν], "Nearchos painted and made me." Achilles wears corslet and greaves; a female stands behind him, holding his helmet, spears, sword, and his shield, which is of Boeotian type and charged with a gorgoneion. One would expect this to be the mother of Achilles, Thetis; but if the letter to the right of the sword is the beginning of her name she may be another Nereid, Ch[oro], for example, a sister of Thetis. The photographs show that the drawing was carried out in brown before the final black was applied; there are also many traces of a careful incised sketch not only for the figures but even for the inscriptions. The untidy appearance of the pattern-bands above and below the picture is due to an experiment which, from our point of view at least, has not succeeded: the red-and-black tongue-pattern was painted on a white ground instead of on the surface of the vase itself, and the white has not resisted. It is the earliest Attic example of that *white ground* which had a certain vogue in later black-figure and became very important in the red-figure period. Another abnormal feature is in the white horses; the white, as is usual by this time, was painted on a black undercoat, but a thick black line is left to mark the white more clearly off from the background. In spite of much minute detail there is a largeness of style and a gravity of tone in the picture that point forward to Exekias in the third quarter of the century.

The other Nearchos kantharos, or one side of it at least, is devoted to the Gigantomachy, the Battle of the Gods and Giants;[10] the subject suddenly becomes popular in the second quarter of the sixth century, and more will be said about it when we come to Lydos. Nearchos as a miniaturist is known from a small round aryballos (oil-flask), in New York, which represents the Battle of Pygmies and Cranes.[11] Nearchos' picture is not to be compared with Kleitias', but the group of the pygmy capsized by the crane is not bad, and the pygmy struggling along with the dead bird on his back is the earliest example of a group that was appreciated in the fifth century. The other nooks and corners of the little vase are decorated with a scurrilous group of three satyrs; with a pair of Tritons; and with single figures of Perseus and Hermes. Nearchos here signs as potter only, but the style shows that he painted the pictures as well as fashioned the vase. He also made cups, and was the father of a famous cup-maker who will occupy us later, Tleson.*

The name of Lydos is known from two signatures:[12] one on the fragment of an early and undistinguished work, a hydria, in the Louvre,[13] the other on a fragmentary masterpiece of his prime, a dinos, from the Acropolis in Athens.[14] The hydria represents the Death of Priam, and the inscription runs HOⲖVΔOϚ:EΛΡϚEN "painted by Lydos"; the fourth and fifth letters of the verb (αφ) were omitted by mistake. Three interpoints separate it from the name. The dinos has a double signature incised on the side of the mouth; the first half of it is incomplete and all that remains is the end of the verb, . . . ϚEN. The second half reads HOⲖVΔOϚⲌ E[Λ]ΡΑФϚ[EN with the last two letters lost. There are four interpoints, or rather interstrokes, between ὁΛυδος and ἐγραφσεν, and there must have been three or four others after the first verb; there is a break here, but a trace of the upper interstroke remains in the break. More than one supplement has been proposed, but far the most natural, on the analogy of other double signatures, is: So-and-so *epoiesen* ("made it"), *Lydos egrapsen* ("Lydos painted it"). The *maker* may have been Lydos himself, or may have been someone else. These rather dull particulars are necessary to justify the use of the name Lydos for the painter of the dinos and of the vases, in the same style, which will occupy us for the rest of this chapter.

---

* See below, pp. 55–56.

The dinos did not fire perfectly; much of what should have been black turned brown, and became lighter in tone than the added dark red; most of the white, too, has faded, this also probably because of defective firing. What with that, and the fragmentariness, the vase is not very easy to study, but as a central piece it is worth an effort. The chief zone is dedicated to the Gigantomachy, the Battle of Gods and Giants. In the zone below there are two subjects, one a procession—animals being led to sacrifice,—the other a hunt on horseback. The third zone has animals. The large fragment (e) gives, in the uppermost zone, parts of four figures; other pictures of the Gigantomachy, contemporary and later, help one to interpret the remains. First, *Zeus* is probably standing with his left foot in the chariot-car and his right foot on the ground, holding the reins and goad in his left hand, and the thunderbolt raised in his right. Second, *Herakles*, on the farther side of the chariot, has one foot in the car, and sets the other on the pole of the chariot; in this precarious position he draws his bow. He wears, besides the short chiton, the lionskin which is not given to Herakles in Attic art until the second quarter of the sixth century.[15] Third, *Ge*, Earth herself, stands to left on the far side of the chariot. Without the other pictures it would have been impossible to interpret the little of this figure that remains; in those she is seen bending forward, taking Zeus by the beard and forehead, beseeching him to spare the giants her sons. Fourth, again on the far side of the chariot, *Athena* strides to right, attacking with her spear. The three, Zeus, Athena, and the mortal Herakles without whose aid the giants could not be defeated, form the kernel of Attic gigantomachies.

The leg on the right of fragment o may belong to Zeus, wearing short chiton and cloak. On the left, a *goddess* (her peplos leaving her shank bare) overtakes a fleeing giant, sets her foot on him, and drives her sword down through his corslet into his breast. He turns, falls, but the fingers still grasp the shield-grip; the right arm was extended. On the extreme left of the fragment is the greaved shank of another *combatant* rushing to left. Fragment t has parts of *Apollo* and *Artemis*; Artemis, who draws her bow, looks at first glance like a Herakles, for she wears a lion's skin over her peplos. Apollo's arm is raised (not as in the modern copy), probably using spear or sword. The female feet on fragment u may be Artemis', and the shod foot Apollo's; at their feet as they run is a fallen *giant*. Fragment q shows *Hermes* in conflict; a *giant* attacks him with his spear. The device on the giant's shield is a splendid satyr-head in high relief, with upturned nose, open mouth, white teeth, and hair swept back from the brow. *Hermes*, armed with helmet and shield (device a gorgoneion), thrusts his spear into the throat of a second *giant*, who falls, but tries to draw his sword. The giant wears thigh-armour as well as greaves. *Aphrodite* is seldom seen to take part in the Gigantomachy (although she fights in the Iliad, if without success), but on fragment *r*, crowned with myrtle, she wields spear and shield against the giant *Mĭmos* (perhaps written by error for Mimas), whose device is a large bee. In the next fragment Dionysos, ivy-crowned, attacks to left, with shield and spear, assisted by a lion, and perhaps, as on many vases, by other animals as well. Fragment *h* has the greaved leg of a warrior running to left, and part of the giant *Athos* fallen prone, his left leg drawn up so that the shin rests on the ground. Fragment *a* has the upper part of a *warrior* attacking to left. Fragment *b* has part of the giant *Perichthonios*, and some uncertain vestiges (long hair, chiton, and goad?). In fragment *s* the giant *Aristaios* attacks *Hephaistos*. Above, a piece of the floral border. In fragment *c* the giant *[Hopl]adamas* is down on one knee. Fragment *i* gives the hand of *Poseidon* holding the island of Nisyros which he broke off from the island of Cos and hurled upon the giant who opposed him. On the right is a hill—perhaps figuring the island of Cos—which continues on fragment *k*, with plants and a startled hare and fox; then comes the chariot of one of the gods.

In the second zone, three animals are led to sacrifice: a cow, a sow, and a ram or sheep. It is a *trittys* or *trittoa*, an offering of three different animals, corresponding to the Roman *suovetaurilia*. The men conducting them carry branches—always in place at religious ceremonies—and one of them is shown to be the slaughterer by the set of knives he carries in a case slung round his neck; the short garment of white linen which he wears round his waist has an incised pattern on it looking like diaper. The second scene on this zone is a hunt on horseback, with hounds and hare. Lion, panther, boar, sphinx, and siren are among the sturdy animals in the third zone.

The dinos of Lydos must be nearly contemporary with the kantharoi of Nearchos, shortly before the middle of the sixth century. The drawing is not less elaborate than in Nearchos, but a little broader.

Somewhat earlier than the dinos in Athens and of everyday quality is the column-krater by Lydos at Harvard.[16] The shape, as was said above, occurs in Attica as early as the period of the Nessos Painter,[17] but was probably Corinthian in origin. The main design on the obverse of the Harvard vase, the chariot seen from the front, may have been Corinthian to begin with, but reached Attica early in the sixth century and is already found on a vase by the Gorgon Painter.[18] There is only one person in the car, the driver, in long robe and brimmed hat. Flying birds fill the spandrils between the horses' heads, and on each side of the chariot there is a group of warriors fighting, one attacking and one turning tail; in the right-hand group the attacker leaps upon his opponent, who is borne down on one knee. The device on the shield is the forepart of a threatening snake in the round. We have already seen a picture, on the dinos by the Gorgon Painter in the Louvre, in which two warriors fight in the middle, while to left and right their drivers, who have brought them to the field, hold the chariots in readiness to take them back or transfer them to other ground.* Here the painter has inverted the accent; the chariot is in the middle and has become the chief part of the design, while the combatants are relegated to the sides. The back of the vase is decorated with a symmetrical group of three animals, a sphinx between two lions with reverted heads. The holes in the middle of the obverse mark the place of rivets; the vase, like many others, is seen to have been mended in antiquity.

A second column-krater by Lydos was recently acquired by the British Museum (pl. 15, 1).[21] The picture on the back is the same as in the Harvard vase, a sphinx between two lions. On the front the story of the Judgement of Paris is related in much the same way as on the C Painter's pyxis in the Louvre† and several other Attic vases of the period. Hermes leads the three goddesses forward; as usual in earlier pictures, the three look very like one another, and the observer cannot help thinking that Paris will have a difficult task. So thinks Paris also, and bolts in alarm. Paris' reluctance to act is known to us from later writers such as Lucian, but it was probably described in the original epic narrative, in the *Cypria*.[20] One touch in the picture will not have come from the epic, but from a painter, whether Lydos or a predecessor: Paris' dog feels his master's alarm and shows sympathy. To left of the major group, Lydos has added a minor group of three figures, a woman between two men; they are hard to name, but two of them recur in the Judgement of Paris on an ovoid neck-amphora in Florence.[21] The figure-scenes on the Florence vase, and the animals on the neck, might be by Lydos himself, but the animals below the figure-scenes are not in his style and must be by a collaborator. There is no dog in the Florence picture, but between the legs of Hermes there was room for an owl.

A column-krater in New York,[22] finer than the other two, is almost on the level of the signed dinos in Athens. The red is well preserved, but most of the white has faded. The picture, which runs right round the vase, represents the Return of Hephaistos. Kleitias, on the François vase, told the story in full, with all the characters, and much contrast of emotion between one character and another. Lydos concentrates on the riotous procession of satyrs and maenads, which formed only one end of Kleitias' picture; and the only real contrast is between the solemn figure of Dionysos, standing or moving slowly, and his excited followers. If Kleitias' picture is like a symphony, Lydos' is like the blast of a trumpet.

Dionysos is near the middle on one side of the vase, holding vine, ivy, and drinking-horn; Hephaistos on his mule has been separated from Dionysos (whom he is usually shown as following) and shifted to the middle of the other side to make a centre-piece. The procession is headed by a satyr playing the flute; then satyrs and maenads dance or scramble along, holding

---

* See above, pp. 16–17.
† See above, p. 24.

branches of vine and ivy, wineskins, drinking-horns, and one satyr grips a large snake; snake-taming forms part of religious revels in many places. Under the first handle, and near it, the satyrs and maenads turn or look back towards Hephaistos; a satyr lays his hand on a maenad's shoulder, and she grasps him by the tail; under the second handle, a satyr and maenad embracing bring up the rear. Three of the satyrs vary the profile order of the procession by turning their faces towards us. The cloaks of Dionysos and Hephaistos have three-dimensional folds, which appear from time to time in the second quarter of the sixth century, one of the initial steps towards the more complex treatment of drapery in the late archaic period. A careful floral design adorns the mouth of the vase; the top-side of the mouth is alive with animals; and there is a gorgoneion on each handle-plate.

The Dionysos of the New York krater recurs, smaller but with little change, on a vase in the British Museum.[23] In shape it is an amphora, but adapted to serve a special purpose. There is a spout, and the wall is double; the wine was poured into the inner receptacle, and cold water into the space between the outer and the inner wall. The water could be changed and the wine thus kept cool; the vase is in fact a "psykter-amphora." The composition on one side is conditioned by the spout, which for some reason is not in the middle. Under the spout, a small satyr bends and plays with a hare, just as the satyrs bend to clear the handles on the krater in New York. The satyrs and nymphs are so like those of the New York vase that one can scarcely help thinking of this as part of another Return of Hephaistos, and is surprised to find that the picture on the other side of the amphora does not give the continuation, with Hephaistos mounted on his donkey or mule, but the subject is the young Theseus putting the Minotaur to the sword. The monster, forced down, grasps the sword-arm of Theseus, and has picked up a stone, but Theseus catches him by the wrist. Four youths look on, two of them naked, two clothed; they are part of the tribute to the Minotaur, the fourteen Athenian youths and maidens whom Theseus now saves.

There are three-dimensional folds in the cloak of one youth, as in the himation of Dionysos. Theseus wears a loin-cloth pulled up between his legs and ornamented with a rosette. His cloak, as often in this scene, lies on a boulder seen between his legs. The slaying of the Minotaur by the Attic hero was a favourite subject with Attic vase-painters from the middle of the sixth century onwards, and occurs already in the second quarter; the earliest representation, however, is not Attic, but probably Corinthian, on a gold band of the seventh century found at Corinth.[24] Before leaving the London vase we notice that the floral decoration above the pictures is in the same style as on the New York krater. The group of Theseus and the Minotaur is repeated, with slight variation, on an amphora by Lydos in Taranto,[25] but the design is changed by reducing the onlookers to two and placing a female figure, Ariadne, in the very middle of the picture. It is the same sort of shifted accent as in the Harvard vase. Theseus wears the same unusual garment as before,[26] but the stone between his legs is replaced by an Attic owl. The subject of the other picture is an old favourite, Herakles and the Centaur, doubtless Nessos; the centaur has a stone in his hand, but as on the much earlier Nessos vase in Athens, he founders, stretching out an imploring hand towards the hero's beard. Herakles, as on the signed dinos in Athens, wears the lionskin which was still wanting in earlier Attic pictures. The subordinate figures play the same part in the composition as in the Theseus scene—an onlooker standing on each wing, here a man, and a woman, no doubt Deianeira, standing in the middle. The white portions have faded; only the mattness of the surface shows that the heads, arms, and feet of the female figures were once white. The red also is not perfectly preserved and the left calf of Theseus is damaged, but these are minor matters; the drawing, as nearly always in Lydos, has a certain ease and warmth which are lacking in much black-figure. A third amphora by Lydos, in a private collection at Basle, is fragmentary (pl. 16). The subject on one side is again Theseus and the Minotaur, but the composition is somewhat different: the monster has turned to flee. The onlookers are two youths and two maidens, representing both sections of the tribute to the Minotaur. The maidens hold their mantles out in front of them with both hands: this gesture—which makes them into what may be called "penguin-women"—is extremely popular in the first half of the sixth century, but does not survive the middle, and must mirror a passing fashion in life. On the other side of the vase a horseman sets out, leading a second horse; a woman ("penguin"), a small girl, and two youths look on. The head of the left-hand youth with its tilted chin has an engaging candour. The vase is perhaps a little earlier than those in London and Taranto. On an amphora in the Cabinet des Médailles, Paris, Herakles tackles the Nemean lion.[27] Like Theseus, he has laid his cloak on a rock, which serves to fill the space between the lion's hind-legs. The man and the two youths looking on have no justification in the legend; they are spectators and no more. The last amphora we shall look at is a very large vase in Naples.[28] For subject the artist reverts to the old group of two mounted men side by side, and even the bird is there, but he has added a floral band above the picture, and he has inverted the stress: the nearer rider, seen at full length, is the young squire, while the master, bearded, and fully armed with corslet, helmet, and shield, is the off figure, visible only in part. The group is repeated, with slight variations, on the other side of the vase. There are more amphorae by Lydos, but these will suffice; by this time the one-piece amphora is becoming the leading black-figure shape, and most of the vases we shall be considering henceforth will belong to a few classes: amphorae, neck-amphorae, hydriai, and cups.

A hydria by Lydos is recomposed, on paper, from fragments in Göttingen and in the Cabinet des Médailles.[29] The chief picture, on the body, is a chariot-scene, one of many on hydriai. The occupants of the car are missing, but the lower part of a draped man remains, standing behind the chariot or rather beside it, and no doubt addressing them. His himation has a three-dimensional fold. The horses are just like those on the amphora in Basle. The secondary picture (pl. 17, 2), on the shoulder of the vase, represents a foot-race—four young sprinters (of the fourth the left arm is all that is preserved), and spectators (or rather, perhaps, the judges)—two men and a youth. The small scene has much charm. The athletes are contrasted with the heavily clothed observers in face as well as in body; and while all four seem to be fast, the leader does look a little faster than the rest. This type of runner, striding hugely, with the toes of the back foot touching the ground, with the forward leg extended and raised right up from the ground, with the arms spread-eagled, with left arm and left leg moving together, and right arm and right leg—that is one of the most characteristic figures in archaic vase-painting, but it cannot be said to appear until the second quarter of the sixth century. That right arm and right leg should move forward together is not in nature; but in this type of figure the notion of speed is admirably expressed.*

The long line of Panathenaic prize-amphorae begins in the time of Lydos, and a small fragment of a Panathenaic amphora by him is preserved in the University of Chicago;[30] it comes from the back of the vase, and has parts of two sprinters in the same style as those on the hydria, but less careful. Speed is well rendered in the flying figures on a plate by Lydos in the Robinson collection at Oxford, Mississippi.[31] The round space is decorated in a manner already familiar from the cups of the C Painter and others with a pair of winged figures side by side, whose outstretched limbs form a whirligig design. Both are youthful, and they are accompanied by a hare and a serpent. It is not certain who they are; most likely the winged sons of Boreas, Zetes and Kalais. A similar pair on a fine cup-fragment, of the same period but by another painter, from the Acropolis of Athens, have the beginning of an inscription beside them, the letters *Ke* . . . , but this is difficult to complete, and the name may be that of the artist rather than of the persons represented.[32]

Lydos painted cups as well as pots. His cups of Siana type are slight and not very interesting. More important is a fragmentary cup found in the cemetery of the Ceramicus at Athens and now in the Ceramicus Museum.[33] It is not of Siana type, but is either a merrythought cup†—the greater part of the handles is missing—or of some similar form. The subject

---

* On the motive see below, p. 90.
† See above, p. 23.

shows it to have been made for funeral use: on one half we see the prothesis, a dead man lying on the bier, with women beating their heads, and male mourners as well, a man and a little boy; on the other half the valediction (pl. 15, 2), youths and men—one of them very old—in two groups, making the gesture of farewell, and chanting the lament. The theme is ancient, goes back to the Geometric period, but it is nowhere else found on a drinking-cup; it is treated in a somewhat unusual manner; and there is passion and reality in the figures.

Lydos has left other work besides vases. The Vlasto collection at Athens contains fragments of rectangular clay plaques, parts of a set that decorated a sepulchral monument at a place called Spata in Attica.[34] Portions of several such sets have reached us: of an early set, for example, by Sophilos; of a later, by Exekias. The Vlasto plaques are nearly fourteen inches high, the figures very large—a foot high—and very careful. The best-preserved fragment (pl. 19) gives the left-hand part of a valediction scene, men raising their arms and chanting as on the cup from the Ceramicus. This is Lydos at his best. The other fragments show a youth in the same attitude, a woman tearing her hair, a man grasping his head in distress. The context will be clearer when we come to the sepulchral plaques by Exekias, which are more fully preserved.

The plaques and all these vases by Lydos belong to his middle or later period, the years round about the middle of the sixth century, but there are a good many vases from an earlier stage in his career. One of them is a hydria in the Villa Giulia at Rome, which has the earliest Attic picture of the conflict between Herakles and the three-bodied Geryon.[35] The subject was a great favourite with Attic vase-painters in the second half of the century; the earliest representation of all is Corinthian of the seventh. In shape, the Villa Giulia vase is plain and squat, the lines less tense than in later hydriai. The figures are extremely short and sturdy. Herakles, wearing the lionskin, draws his bow. Geryon consists of three complete warriors thought of as joined at the waist. One of them, pierced through the eye with an arrow, stumbles, and the head falls back; the other two press on with spears levelled. The devices on the shields, incised, are a tripod and the forepart of a lion. Eurytion, the herdsman of Geryon, with his goatskin cap, lies dying on the ground. On the shoulder, a siren between two lions. The reproductions hardly do justice to the grandeur of this rugged work, and the original itself has suffered; the surface of the vase has become dull, the contrast between light and dark is obscured, and the incised lines do not show up as brightly as they should. This is not only the earliest, but the best geryonomachy in Attic black-figure, and the only one that will compare with the Chalcidian in the Cabinet des Médailles, or the red-figured by Euphronios on his famous cup in Munich.

A still earlier phase of Lydos appears on two hydriai, one of which is in Munich, the other in the Louvre. The shape is the same as in the Villa Giulia vase. On the Munich hydria, two men, fully dressed, lead horses, and a short "penguin-woman" stands between them.[36] The men are naturally not grooms, but owners. Three massive animals adorn the shoulder, a swan between two panthers. The Louvre hydria, which is not quite so early, is also concerned with horses;[37] once more a youth rides one horse and leads another, while three men and two "penguin-women" watch his departure. Between the horse's legs a goose is seen preening itself. On the shoulder, a fawn between two panthers; on both hydriai the old-fashioned filling-ornaments are retained in the animal-pictures on the shoulder, just as they were in the animal-zones on the François vase.

Besides the vases that can be assigned to Lydos himself, many others are so closely related to him that they must have been made in the same workshop. It is important, in justice to Lydos, to distinguish these from the work of his hand. Several minor artists, assistants of Lydos, can be traced; we cast a glance at one of them only, the Painter of Louvre F 6. The distance between him and Lydos can be measured by comparing the column-krater in Harvard, which is by Lydos, with a column-krater in Oxford and a hydria in Rhodes which are by the Painter of Louvre F 6.[38] It would plainly be unfair to Lydos that he should be burdened with such inferior pieces. The difference is not between the same man when he is himself and when he is not quite himself, but between the artist and the mechanical imitator.

V

THE HEIDELBERG PAINTER— LITTLE-MASTER CUPS—AMASIS

In our second chapter we spoke of a type of kylix to which we gave the conventional name of "Siana cup."* We saw that this was the dominant type of cup in the second quarter of the sixth century; that there were two ways of decorating the exterior—what we called "overlap" and "double-decker"; and that the chief artist was the C Painter. The Heidelberg Painter,[1] so called after two cups in Heidelberg, also specialised in Siana cups, and has left some sixty of them, fragmentary or complete. When I first wrote about him, I was impressed by the resemblance he bears to a great artist of the middle and third quarter of the sixth century, the Amasis Painter, of whom we shall speak presently, and I had to consider the possibility that the two might be the same, that the cups of the Heidelberg Painter were simply the early work of the Amasis Painter. I now perceive that this is impossible; the two artists overlap, but the resemblance remains, however it is to be accounted for, whether the Amasis Painter was taught by the other, or whether they learned from the same teacher, or whatever the reason. On the other hand it is likely that the Heidelberg Painter was at one time a colleague of the C Painter and was supplied by the same potter.

A cup in Florence is an early work of the Heidelberg Painter.[2] The figures are shorter than in his later cups, quainter and more old-fashioned. Outside, the decoration, which is the same on both halves, is of overlap type. It is one of those scenes in the palaestra which become common in the second quarter of the sixth century, here wrestling (pl. 20, 1). A man sinks on one knee and throws a youth. A piece is missing on the left, but both hands of the youth are visible; he shows no distress—wrestling is rich in peripeteiai, and the tables are often turned. The referee, wand in hand, stoops and peers. This vivid group of three is flanked by four figures of officials, shouldering their wands. There have been such onlookers before, but they are more frequent in middle and later black-figure than in early. Sometimes their presence is more or less justified by the subject, as here; at other times there is really no excuse for them so far as the subject goes, as when Herakles wrestles with the Lion, or clubs the Centaur, and they merely serve to make

---

* See p. 21 above.
[1] For numbered notes to chapter v see pages 111–112 below.

a short strip into a long one, or, let us say, to give a deadly struggle the appearance of a sporting event. Some artists are more partial to spectators than others; the Heidelberg Painter likes them, and so does the Amasis Painter. Very formal artists naturally tend to use them more than others do.

Inside the Florence cup, Ajax retrieves the body of Achilles from the battlefield. The tondo is incomplete, but one can see that Ajax runs with his burden instead of toiling under it as in the earlier and more solemn group on the François vase.

On a cup in Munich (pl. 20, 3),[3] the kernel of one half consists of a warrior arming. He lifts his leg to put on the greave; it is a characteristic attitude, and this is the moment in the process of arming that is most frequently represented in the archaic period.[4] The helmet on the ground serves to fill the gap below the lifted leg. From each side a youth walks up, one bearing the shield, emblazoned with a serpent, which is partly in the round, the other raising a hand in encouragement. There are four onlookers, two on the left, two on the right. The other subject is taken from the palaestra, but the athletes have been reduced to one, and all the other figures are spectators. A youth steps forward, preparing to throw the discus; unexpected so early is the foreshortening of the discus, which is seen in three-quarter view.[5] This is a late work of the Heidelberg Painter. The drawing is more elegant than on his early athlete cup in Florence, less quaint but also less spirited; he has come under the influence of the new ideal of which Kleitias was among the first representatives.

A cup in Würzburg is also from the painter's later period.[6] One of the outside pictures is formal, Dionysos, seated, receiving the homage of men and women. The other is more lively. The subject is the same as on the seventh-century masterpiece in Berlin, Peleus bringing his infant son to Chiron. This is usually a quiet episode; here the artist has chosen to quicken the pace, he has produced the appearance of excitement, and an amusing contrast between the hasty, heated males and the serious females; but of course he has sacrificed the ethos of the legend. The woman behind Peleus may be thought of as his wife, the goddess Thetis.[7] The three behind Chiron are the centaur's womenfolk, who, according to Pindar, took a large share in the education of Chiron's pupils. Pindar speaks of the boy Achilles as "staying in the house of Philyra,"[8] and in the great scene in the fourth Pythian ode, the young Jason, when he makes his soft and beautiful answer to the insulting words of his uncle Pelias, begins: "Chiron was my teacher. I come from the cave, from Chariklo and Philyra, where the holy daughters of the centaur reared me," παρ Χαρικλοῦς καὶ Φιλύρας, ἵνα Κενταύρου με κοῦραι θρέψαν ἁγναί.[9]

It is a far cry from the poet at his most pellucid to the humble and even somewhat misguided work of the early vase-painter, but the women are the family of Chiron. It is possible that the artist could not have named them, but it is also possible that he intended the foremost of them for Chariklo, Chiron's wife, the second for Philyra, Chiron's mother, and the third for a daughter of Chiron and Chariklo.

There is some modern repainting in the figures, and it is well therefore to look at the incomplete picture of the same subject on the fragment of a somewhat earlier cup by the same painter in Palermo (pl. 20, 2).[10] The eager pair Peleus and Chiron are here accompanied by Hermes, who has guided Peleus to the habitation of the centaur on Mount Pelion. This trio forms the heart of the design. A vestige of the Thetis, if Thetis it be, is preserved behind Peleus, and the greater part of Chariklo behind Hermes.

Towards the middle of the sixth century a shape of cup was invented which took the place of the Siana cup as the dominant type in the middle and the third quarter. This is the Little-Master cup. It is of very light make, with an offset lip and a tall stem. It is descended from the Siana cup, but it is a new model. Its immediate forerunner is the "Gordion cup" practised by the artists of the François vase, Ergotimos and Kleitias. A little cup of delicate fabric, bearing the double signature of these two artists, was found far in the East, at Gordion in Phrygia, and is now in Berlin.[11] It is neither a Siana cup nor a Little-Master cup, but may be thought of as one of the experiments that led to the creation of the Little-Master cup. There are a few other kylikes of this type by various potters, and one calls them "Gordion cups."[12] Outside, the lip is black, and apart from a palmette at each side of the handles the only decoration consists of the artists' signatures in fine letters. Inside is a small picture of two dolphins and a fish, which is surrounded by a broad band of simple patterns—tongues, dot-bands, lines—like the borders on Siana cups. It is not unnatural for an artist to treat the inside of a bowl, or part of it, as if it were a round pond, lake, harbour, or sea. Pour in liquid and the likeness increases. Kleitias has thought of a round piece of water, with sea-creatures in it. It is encircled by vegetation—what we call "tongue-pattern" was still leafage to him,—forming, with its cinctures, a waterside. There was a "round harbour" (λιμὴν κυκλοτερής) on the *Shield of Herakles* in the poem: "On the shield there was a harbour with safe haven from the raging sea, circular, made of refined tin, and seeming to heave with waves: two silver dolphins, spouting, were (chasing?) the mute fish."[13]

Reconstructors of the *Shield* lay no stress on the word κυκλοτερής, "circular," but there is a representation of a λιμὴν κυκλοτερής, with a dolphin in it, on archaic coins of Zancle, Messina.[14] Before Kleitias, a round water appears, with dolphins in it, and fish swimming towards a plant (water-lily) in the middle, on the finest of all Laconian vases, a cup in Taranto;[15] and similar seascapes or water-pieces on two other Laconian cups.[16] A much earlier work reminds one of the Laconian cup. The golden bowl in the Louvre given by the Egyptian king Thothmes III to the priest and general Dhowti[17] forms a round lake (λίμνη τροχοειδής) with a rosette—a plant—in the middle, a row of lotus-flowers round about, and fishes swimming between the two. Later Egyptian bowls of blue faience[18] have similar subjects and help to bridge the gap between the fifteenth century B.C., the time of Thothmes, and the beginning of the sixth, the date of the Laconian cup. Lastly, out of countless later works, let us recall an early mediaeval colour-piece, also in the Louvre, the patine of Saint-Denis, where in a sea of dark green serpentine golden fishes swim.[19]

Ergotimos is not known to have made Little-Master cups, but cups by his son Eucheiros are very nearly of that type.[20] There are two species of Little-Master cup, the lip-cup and the band-cup.[21] In the lip-cup the lip is tooled clearly off from the bowl, and the outside of the lip is reserved (pl. 21, 3). In the band-cup the lip is not tooled off, but passes into the bowl with a gradual curve, and is black outside as well as in. A minor difference between the two is that in the band-cup, but not in the other, there is often a small fillet, usually painted red, at the junction of bowl and stem. The reason for this difference is that the lip-cup is "punctuated" twice, between bowl and lip and between stem and bowl; whereas the band-cup is punctuated once only, between bowl and stem, and the potter feels that he must strengthen the single punctuation—a colon against the two commas of the lip-cup. This insistence on διάρθρωσις, distinct articulation, is Greek. One example: Aristotle, it will be remembered, points out that the female body is less beautiful than the male because the several parts are less clearly marked off from each other; it lacks διάρθρωσις. In many lip-cups and in nearly all band-cups the interior is plain, painted black, except for a small reserved disc in the middle, containing a circle and its centre. A good many lip-cups, however, have a round picture inside; in this they keep the tradition of the Siana cup alive, and help to hand down the round picture to the great red-figure cup-painters. Outside, the figure-decoration of the lip-cup is on the lip, and consists of a small brief picture in the middle of each half: one, two, sometimes three figures, animal or human—what Payne has called "spot-light" treatment.[22] The only decoration of the handle-zone is an inscription, though even that is sometimes omitted, and there is often a small palmette at each side of the handle. In the band-cup the lip is black, and the decoration is in the handle-zone, which it usually fills with many figures. In general effect the lip-cup is a bright vase, one sees much of the clay surface; the band-cup is a dark vase, with little of the clay surface allowed to show, just as the amphora is a dark vase, while the neck-amphora is a bright vase. Lastly, the quality of the lip-cup is in general higher than that of the band-cup.

It is in the small, often tiny, designs on the Little-Master cups, more than anywhere else, that the true miniature style of drawing, perfected by Kleitias, is continued. We speak of the Little-Masters, although some of the decorators of lip-cups and band-cups painted full-size pictures as well. Perhaps the finest of Little-Master cups is the lip-cup with the signature of the potter Phrynos in the British Museum (pl. 21, 1–2).[23] Unfortunately it is incomplete; the foot is alien, so that one does not get the full effect of the vase as a whole. The handle-zone has the usual row of letters between the handle-palmettes: on one half, *Phrynos made me, hail*; on the other, *Hail and drink me, yes.* These are far the commonest kinds of inscriptions on Little-Master cups: the signature of the potter or a salute to the drinker. It will be noticed that the inscription is not, as in most sorts of vase, an explanatory adjunct to the picture, but an integral part of the decoration as a whole.[24] The handle-zone is bordered above by a thin black band, stressing, once more, the articulation of the cup. One might have expected the band to come immediately below the offset of the lip, but it is always well below, and one sees why: if it were right under the picture on the lip it would tell too strongly, would kill the inch- or two-inch-high miniatures.[25] The subject on one side is the Birth of Athena, which we found represented, for the first time in Attica, on the C Painter's pyxis in the Louvre.* Here the painter has reduced the scene, rendered elsewhere with many figures and much circumstance, to the three principal characters. Zeus sits on his throne, brandishing the thunderbolt in his excitement. Athena bursts from his head; Hephaistos, who has cleft the skull, moves off, axe in hand, and looking back raises his hand, whether in surprise, as in earlier vases, or as if satisfied with his work. The Zeus, sitting with his legs well forward and his arms in full action, is very different from the passive, almost cowed creature in the C Painter's "Birth of Athena" and many others. In the second and slightly more elaborate picture two of the characters are the same; Herakles arrives in Olympus and is introduced by Athena his protectress to her father, and his, Zeus. The hero, on him all he owns—white shirt, lionskin, bow, arrow, quiver, and club,—is led smartly forward by the eager goddess; Zeus, sceptred, extends a hand. For vigour and movement, for terseness, finish, and narrative power, these two small pictures are black-figure at its best. The drawing is alive in every line; even what is inanimate has life—the lionskin, the thrones. The figures are very short, with large heads: this is regular in Little-Master cups: the picture-space is so shallow that if the proportions were normal the figures would be too tenuous.

Phrynos signs as potter, Φρῦνος ἐποίησεν, and we do not know whether he painted the cup as well as fashioned it. We call the artist "the Phrynos Painter," and can point to other, unsigned works by the same hand. A lip-

* See pp. 23-24.

cup in the Vatican[26] has no figures outside, only a greeting, *Hail and drink*, between the handles. The chief decoration is a round picture inside, and the theme is familiar from the François vase or the cup by the Heidelberg Painter in Florence,* Ajax rescuing the body of Achilles (pl. 22, 1). Here the body is naked, which is unusual in this subject, but the inscriptions rounding out the design show that the artist means Ajax and Achilles, and no others. Much energy, though not the grandeur of the Kleitian group. There is a little repainting in the middle of the picture.

The most typical, perhaps, of the Little-Masters is the Tleson Painter, who decorated most if not all of the sixty-odd cups that bear the signature of the potter Tleson, son of Nearchos.[27] The father's work has been spoken of already. Many of the Tleson cups have no decoration beyond the signa- ture between the handles; others have a brief picture on the lip, others a round picture inside, and a few both. The subject is commonly an animal, and the tondo of a Tleson cup in Castle Ashby, with the time-honoured design of two goats confronted and a plant between them, is an exquisite example of the painter's animal-style.[28] Goats in Castle Ashby and Boston, cocks in Castle Ashby and Berlin, swans in Nicosia (pl. 21, 3),[29] will serve as specimens of the external decoration on his cups. His animals are as characteristic as other artists' people, and are readily recognised even when, as on his few band-cups, the usual signature is suppressed. Thus the goat of the lip-cups reappears on the unsigned band-cup in Munich,[30] and on the other half of it the cocks of the lip-cups, only with their hackles up, confront each other in the presence of their hens. The sirens flanking the goat are the same as in other signed works. No less personal are his sphinxes and lions, stags and swans. On another band-cup by the Tleson Painter, in the Cabinet des Médailles, Paris, the goat is replaced by a stag, and the sirens spread their wings.[31] Not many of the cups signed Tleson have human figures, but the lively cup in London with the Return of the Hunter (pl. 22, 2)[32] should doubtless be assigned to the same hand as the animal pieces, although there happen to be no hounds, horses, or foxes on them to compare.

We have looked at one band-cup and assigned it to the Tleson Painter. A larger and more elaborate band-cup, in Munich, bears the signature of two potters, Archikles and Glaukytes;[33] how they shared the work is not known. On each half of the exterior a symmetrical composition of many small figures fills the handle-zone. The Hunting of the Calydonian Boar is treated in the same way as on the François vase, though of course with less variety and much less art. The hunters are all naked, and each man, with one exception, wields two weapons. The hounds are named, as in Kleitias, as well as the hunters. On the other half, Theseus slays the Minotaur in presence of a goodly company. Athena stands on one side holding the hero's

---

* See p. 50.

lyre, ίΥΡΔ, which he will need, as we know from Kleitias, in the victory dance; on the other side stands Ariadne, holding, as in Kleitias, the skein which had threaded the Labyrinth, and a wreath or crown. Behind her is her nurse, the τροφός, again known from Kleitias; being of humbler origin than the rest, she has less self-control, and roots vigorously. There was not room for the fourteen sons and daughters of Athens, but there are full seven on the left side, if only five on the right. The painter has inadvertently given one of the youths a beard; it is suggested that he was thinking of King Minos,[34] who is sometimes present at the death of the Minotaur, and the figure is named Simon, which is, after all, an anagram of Minos. All the girls have the old-fashioned "penguin" look. The handles are flanked by sphinxes; they have no connexion with the Hunt or with Theseus—each pair forms a picture by itself,—but they cannot help looking round at the main scenes. No other work by the painter has been identified; and the same must be said about some of the best band-cups: the arming fragment in the Vatican;[35] the pleasing fragments with spidery men and women dancing, in Samos; and above all the cup in New York which has the Return of Hephaistos on one half, and Dionysos with Ariadne on the other (pl. 24, and pl. 25, 1–8).[36] Hephaistos, mounted on a handsome mule, is led by Dionysos and escorted by a satyr. The figure in the very middle of the picture is not either of the principals, but the satyr, who turns his head into full front view and glowers at the spectator. A satyr playing the flute, and a satyr and two maenads dancing, head the procession; and five satyrs and maenads, all dancing, bring up the rear. In the other picture, Ariadne stands still, in the middle, with Dionysos facing her; satyrs and maenads, five on one side, six on the other, rush up, hop, dance, all except the hindmost satyr, who labours under the weight of a huge wineskin. There are many gay pictures on Little-Master cups, but none more amusing than these, and one would like to know other works by the same hand. The nearest approach is a fragment of a band-cup in Boston, with a warrior about to leave home (pl. 25, 9);[37] two men look on (there must have been others); and the old father raises his voice in a passionate last address; the dog looks up at him.

Our last Little-Master shall be a band-cup in the Louvre,[38] on which the picture of Dionysos and Ariadne in the midst of capering satyrs and maenads bears a real resemblance, in conception and composition, to that on the cup in New York, and the two pictures must have been influenced by a common original. The Louvre cup, however, is not by the same painter as the other. It is one of four fine band-cups by a well-known artist who was not primarily a decorator of cups, the Amasis Painter. The second picture on his cup in the Louvre is a battle-piece, with cavalry in action as well as hoplites (pl. 26, 2). One of his other band-cups represents a Return of Hephaistos which has something in common with the second picture on the New York cup.[39]

This is indeed the place to speak of the Amasis Painter,[40] for the ground has been prepared, first, by what was said of the Heidelberg Painter, and secondly, by our study of Kleitias. He has much in common with the Heidelberg Painter, surpassing him, however, in all respects; a good deal also of Kleitias, if not the finest part, has passed into him—lightness, elegance, and precise technique. The name of Amasis occurs on nine vases (including a small fragment without figures), always followed by the verb *epoiesen*, "made"; Amasis was the potter. Looking at the decoration we see that the style of drawing is the same in all; the vases must have been painted by one man. He may well have been the same as the potter, but as this is not certain we call him the Amasis Painter. Many unsigned vases can be attributed to him. A great part of the pleasure one receives from the vases he decorated, whether signed or unsigned, is due to the potter-work, the shape and surface-finish, in fact to Amasis, and the potter Amasis is as clearly defined a personality as the Amasis Painter; he has his own idea of shape, and goes his own way, keeping apart from the majority.

The signed vases are three neck-amphorae of a special model, four jugs of the shape known as olpe, a cup, and a sort of small bowl. The signed neck-amphorae are of the broad-shouldered, short-necked class that replaces, in the middle of the sixth century, the ovoid neck-amphora of the second quarter. The best-preserved of the three is in the Paris Cabinet des Médailles.[41] The two chief pictures are equally careful. In the more interesting of them, Dionysos stands or moves slowly, holding his kantharos in one hand and raising the other to greet a pair of maenads who dance towards him, closely linked, their arms round each other's shoulders. Both hold sprigs of ivy, and a pet animal—a hare, a small deer. The nearer one wears a panther-skin over her peplos, and both have necklaces and handsome ear-rings. The female flesh, instead of being white, is reserved, left in outline; this technique is common in early black-figure, unusual later. It occurs, however, from time to time, in other vases by the Amasis Painter, in Lydos, and elsewhere. The picture illustrates both the strength and the weakness of Amasean drawing. The lines, both in the figures and in the pattern-work, are admirably sure, but they are less sensitive and expressive than in Lydos, or, as will be seen, in Exekias. Hands and feet, for example, are not the painter's forte, and neither the movement nor the grouping of the linked maenads is convincing. There is repainting, by the way, in their faces—very little, but just enough to make them look more vacuous than they really are. The picture on the other side is a simple meeting-scene; Athena greets Poseidon. The flesh of Athena is in the usual technique, the disadvantage of which is that the white is not perfectly fast; here it had fallen in parts, and the modern restorer felt bound to refresh it. The most attractive piece of drawing on the vase is the small battle-piece on the shoulder; the Amasis Painter is an excellent miniaturist. The combination of large- and small-scale figure-work on the same vase is common in black-figure. The more regular part of the conflict is on the Dionysos side of the vase, five single combats, with little variation; on the left, an unarmed man blows the horn; on the right, an archer flees.[42] On the Athena side, two single combats are flanked on the one part by the pursuit of a warrior who has turned tail; on the other, by a group of three—a warrior falling, a companion to the rescue. The heraldry, as always in our painter, is excellent.

The finer of the two signed neck-amphorae in Boston[43] is incomplete, and the foot has been restored after the other Boston vase. A young warrior receives his armour, while an old man looks on. It is a common subject, but here the persons are named: Achilles, his mother Thetis, and his aged friend Phoinix. This is the original armour of Achilles, the suit which he lent Patroklos and lost, not the replacement suit described in the eighteenth book of the Iliad; and the scene is doubtless laid at Phthia in Thessaly, not at Troy.[44] A snake supports the crest; a ram's head adorns the cheekpiece of the helmet; the large device on the shield is a lion felling a deer. Leather corslet, greaves, and sword are already worn; a pair of spears completes the outfit. A small fragment of a similar amphora in the Merlo collection at Los Angeles has part of a head which is almost a repetition of Thetis's, with a piece of the rare spiral-border above it.[45] The fragmentary picture on the other side of the Boston vase represents the Struggle for the Tripod of Apollo, which Herakles attempts to carry off, while Apollo resists, and Hermes interposes. This is a favourite subject in Attic vase-painting, red-figure as well as black, of the late sixth century and the early fifth; the earliest representation of it, as we have seen, cannot be later than 700,* but it does not become common till long after. The more complex drapery and the more substantial figures show that the Boston neck-amphora is later than that in the Cabinet des Médailles. Indeed, the drawing of the muscular bodies would point to a date not earlier than the twenties or teens of the sixth century, contemporary with the Leagros Group and the red-figured work of Euphronios and his fellows; in any case this is a very late Amasis Painter. An unusual feature of both Boston vases is that the feet of the figures stand free instead of resting on a ground-line. In the other vase a faint incised line runs round the vase at this point, but it can only have been meant as a guide-line and not to be seen.[46] The omission of the ground-line was perhaps intended to lighten the figures by withdrawing them from the pull of the base.

The slender jug (olpe) in the Louvre may be chosen as an example of the smaller and slighter signed vases.[47] The shape is not new; it had been much used by the Gorgon Painter and his companions. The picture is one of many

* See above, p. 7.

processional or encounter scenes in the work of the Amasis Painter; on the
Louvre vase Herakles is escorted by Athena and Hermes, one would have
expected into the presence of Zeus, but instead of Zeus there is Poseidon.[48]
We leave the signed cup for the present, and look at some of the unsigned
pots. An unsigned amphora in New York, a handsome specimen of the
canonical shape, has an arming-scene on each side.[49] The moment chosen is
the same as in the cup by the Heidelberg Painter* and scores of other vases,
the adjustment of the greave. The warrior has slung his sword round him;
his helmet is at his feet; the shield, emblazoned with the forepart of a lion,
is held ready by a youth, and another youth holds a wreath, perhaps to
crown the helmet. There are several spears about, but it is plain that, as in
the arming-scene by the Heidelberg Painter, the warrior's spears are the pair
held by the woman and youth in front of him, the others merely serving as
staves in sixth-century fashion. The variant on the other side of the vase is
less well preserved; the surface is fretted in places and has been retouched.
The person facing the warrior is a woman, who holds one of his spears, and
also an aryballos, a small round oil-flask. The second spear, and the shield,
are held by a youth who stands behind the woman. The helmet is there
again, but no sign of a corslet in either picture. This is an early work of the
painter, and a good example of his most formal style. The pattern above
the picture deserves a word: the painter's floral bands are rather less desic-
cated than in most of his contemporaries.

The one-piece amphora of this type was invented, as we saw, late in the
seventh century, and it lasted into the fifth, but about the middle of the
sixth century a somewhat more elaborate variety of it was introduced and
soon came to be used for most of the finer work. This is what is called
"amphora type A"; in essentials it is the same as the older "type B,"
differing only in the slightly more complex forms of handles and foot. Amasis
made amphorae of type A, but he had his own idea of it, and his version
differs from the accepted one. The masterpieces of the Amasis Painter are
on three vases of this shape, all unsigned: one in Berlin, one in Würzburg,
and small fragments of a third in Samos. The subject on one side of the Berlin
vase (pl. 23, 1)[50] is again a warrior receiving his armour. A woman faces him
holding the spear and the magnificent shield, which is of Boeotian type and
is charged with a gorgoneion surrounded by foreparts of horses and lions,
the same kind of design as appeared much earlier on the dinos by the Painter
of Acropolis 606.† The woman's flesh is not white, but reserved like that of
the maenads on the neck-amphora in Paris. The head is charming, and so are
the sandalled feet. A young man stands beside her, and a warrior follows.
On the left, a third warrior is in conversation with a curly-headed youth
fully dressed. Although one group consists of four persons, and the other of

* See above, p. 51.
† See above, p. 38.

only two, they are so arranged as not to break up into a two and a four. There are no inscriptions, and one cannot be sure that the warrior is Achilles, the woman Thetis. Above the picture there is a small frieze in miniature. Dionysos is in the middle, listening to a satyr who plays the flute; Ariadne stands behind the satyr. Or rather, Dionysos and Ariadne are thought of as standing together, and the satyr facing them. Satyrs and maenads dance round the trio; we have seen such figures before, but they are always welcome. The minor theme becomes the major on the other side of the vase. Dinoysos stands in the middle, satyrs and maenads trip towards him; on each side a couple, satyr and naked maenad with their arms round each other's necks, then a single maenad, clothed. The left-hand woman holds a wreath and a pet hare. The upper part of the right-hand one is missing, but she may have held a pet animal too. The subject recalls the signed vase in the Cabinet des Médailles, but the style is ampler, and there is more life. The flesh of the females is again reserved, not painted white. The small picture above is athletic: boxing, jumping, throwing the javelin.

The amphora of the same shape in Würzburg (pl. 23, 2) is less well preserved;[51] parts of the surface are damaged and have been repainted. The whole vase is consecrated to Dionysos. There are many ancient representations of the vintage, and sometimes the vintagers are mortals, more often they are satyrs; and here it is satyrs of Amasean breed, fat, hairy, and swine-like, with huge necks, who strip the vine, shoot the grapes into the vat, tread them, water the must, and supply the music. In the small picture above, Dionysos sits, satyrs and maenads dance. The other side of the vase represents, one might say, the first taste of the new wine. Dionysos dances, holding sprigs of ivy, and a kantharos which a satyr fills from a wineskin, looking round at us proudly. A satyr plays the flute, and two others hasten up, their arms round each other's necks, with drinking-horns, one drinking. This is the earliest picture in which Dionysos himself joins in the dance, instead of standing motionless amid the tumult. There is more dancing in the small frieze, with a pair of satyrs in the middle particularly active. The left half is unfortunately in bad condition.

A third amphora, in Samos, must have been of this type and was at least equal to the Würzburg, but only two fragments remain.[52] On the larger we see two groups of satyr and naked maenad (pl. 26, 1). One of them is a version of the Amasean group of two figures interlocked; the maenad holds a kantharos in her right hand and with her left grasps the satyr's wrist. At first one thinks of a sprigged skirt, but it is a vine-branch held by the satyr, making a pleasant pattern against the background of the woman's body. The female flesh is again reserved. Behind this couple a satyr lifts a maenad in his arms and embraces her; it is the same sort of group as in the pictures of the Return of Hephaistos on the François vase and on a Caeretan hydria

in Vienna.[53] Not the least interesting part of the fragment is the huge
column-krater standing on the ground in front of the first couple. It is
adorned with a group of two figures in incision. Only the legs are preserved,
but they suffice to show that this is an example, the earliest known, of a
motive that became popular later and inspired some of the masterpieces of
red-figure—the satyr stealing up to assault a sleeping nymph.[54] The second
fragment of the Samos amphora is from one of the miniature friezes that
crowned the pictures. We should have liked more of it. A satyr, who holds
a kantharos, has taken a companion on his back and is persuading a donkey
to dance; a third satyr, grasping a drinking-horn, encourages him, and a
maenad dances a fling.

It seems a long way from this Dionysiac side of the Amasis Painter to the
trim, polished compositions of which we have had examples already and
which constitute the greater part of his production. We return to these for
a moment with an oinochoë in the British Museum which may be chosen
as a specimen of the smaller unsigned vases.[55] The time-honoured symmetrical design of the four-horse chariot seen from the front, here with a
young driver standing in the car and holding the goad, while a man and a
naked youth look on. The same design is repeated with variations on the
fragment of a small bowl by the same painter in Palermo,[56] and twice on
the two sides of his fragmentary amphora in Bonn.[57] The artist is fond of
the formal yet strange old composition, and in the Bonn vase he has retained
an early trait which must count as a deliberate archaism: the long dank
manes of which we have spoken so often were no longer fashionable either
in art or in life.

We began our study of the Amasis Painter with a cup and we conclude it
with a few others. Several band-cups of his remain, but no lip-cup. His early
cup in the Louvre,[58] with riders and youths, and at the handles lions, has the
upper part of a lip-cup, but the thick-stemmed foot is of Siana type, while
the position and character of the figure-work—many figures, and in the
handle-zone—points forward to the band-cup. It is an experimental piece,
and might even be called a hybrid. Another cup in the Louvre, with courting
scenes, has something of the band-cup, but belongs to a special class of which
only a few remain.[59] A curious late cup in Boston (pl. 26, 4)[60] is of the new
type A (which will be discussed in our next chapter), except that the thick
fillet between bowl and stem is omitted. The decoration on one side, a siren
with the body in the form of a large eye—or a large eye stuffed out to make
a siren—occurs occasionally elsewhere, but taken with the effrontery of the
picture on the other half, not shown here, it almost makes one fancy that
the artist is parodying the new type of cup. More attractive are the signed
cup in the Vatican and two unsigned of similar form in Oxford (pl. 26, 3)
and Florence.[61] In these Amasis has almost achieved the beautiful cup of

'type B' which was invented in the late sixth century and became the dominant type in red-figure painting. The bowl, lipless, passes into the stem with a gradual curve; move the punctuating fillet from the base of the stem to near the edge of the foot-plate and you have cup B. The foot-plate of the Vatican cup is as in type A, but in the Oxford cup it is already of torus form as in type B. The external decoration consists of a single figure in each half (in the Vatican cup flanked by eyes), and a floral motive at each handle. As in the Boston neck-amphorae, the figures have no ground-line to stand on: further, the whole stem is reserved instead of being black. A very light-coloured cup. Inside, the Vatican cup has a small gorgoneion, the Oxford cup is black save for a small circle and dot. It is not so much the figures and patterns, pretty though they are, that make these cups so pleasant, as the fine shape and proportions, the colour and satin-like sheen of the clay—the work, in fact, of the master-potter Amasis.

VI

EXEKIAS

THE NAME of Exekias is found on eleven vases,[1] usually followed by the word *epoiesen*, indicating that Exekias was the potter, but twice by the two verbs *egrapse kapoiese*. The iambic trimeter 'Εξηκίας έγραψε κἀποίησέ με indicates that Exekias not only fashioned the vase but also decorated it. We must now ask whether the eight vases which the inscriptions state to have been *made* by Exekias were also *painted* by him. In five of them the decoration is so slight that one can scarcely be sure; the two best are in the same style as those with the double signature, and must have been painted, as well as fashioned, by Exekias. The eighth vase remains, an amphora in the Louvre which is earlier than the rest and hardly by the same hand.[2] It belongs to the large group of vases, mostly amphorae, called "Group E."[3] The pictures on the Louvre amphora might conceivably be early work by Exekias, painted before his characteristic style was formed, but it is better kept apart. Group E, however, to which it belongs, is the soil from which the art of Exekias rose, the tradition which he absorbs and transcends.

The vases of Group E were made in the middle of the sixth century and the earlier part of the third quarter. The same subjects are repeated again and again with minor variations: the Birth of Athena; Theseus and the Minotaur; Herakles and the Lion; Herakles and the three-bodied Geryon. The geryonomachy on the Louvre amphora with the signature of Exekias as potter is more careful than the ten other geryonomachies of Group E, for instance those in London or in the Roš collection at Baden in Switzerland,[4] but the composition is the same, and the difference in quality is insignificant. Contrast the same subject on the early hydria by Lydos in the Villa Giulia.* It might perhaps be maintained that the picture on the Exekias vase was more natural in one point. In Lydos, Herakles was shown close to Geryon, yet drawing his bow as if he were a good way off. In the Exekias vase, being at close quarters, he uses the sword, but this is a matter of no importance; the Exekian picture is in every way inferior. One or two particulars may be noted. The farthest of Geryon's heads is one of the repainted parts. The shield-device is a very stiff gorgoneion. Eurytion draws his cutlass, but an arrow has pierced him through the eye and brought him down. Lastly, be-

---

[1] For numbered notes to chapter VI see pages 112–114 below.
* See p. 48 above.

sides the potter's signature, and the names of the persons, there is a third kind of inscription, *Stēsias kalos*, "Stesias is fair." These kalos-inscriptions begin in the middle of the sixth century and persist through the fifth. The other picture on the vase is a chariot-scene. The hero Anchippos—the name occurs on another vase,[5] but nothing is known about him—stands with his driver in the car. A human-headed bird is seen in the air, doubtless a good omen. The horses, all named, Kalliphora, Kallikome, Pyrrhokome, and Semos, are the best part of the picture. In general type they differ little from those of Lydos. The off trace-horse sinks its head, tugging at the reins. At present the vase carries a lid, but there is no reason to suppose that it belongs.[6]

An early work by Exekias himself is the vase in Berlin which bears the double signature "Exekias painted and made me."[7] It is a neck-amphora of the broad-shouldered, short-necked, precise, and powerful shape that succeeds the slenderer ovoid neck-amphora of the second quarter of the sixth century. Herakles wrestles with the Nemean Lion.[8] To the right is Athena, shield on arm; to the left Iolaos, one hand laid on the other in a gesture of suspense. The composition does not differ much from some of those in Group E, but the figures are more compact and substantial, the incised detail finer and surer. The style is bare and rigid. Meagre, the picture on the back of the vase: two warriors leading their horses, shouldering spears, their shields hung behind them. The horses are named, Phalios and Kalliphora, and so are the horsemen; they are Attic heroes, Demophon and Akamas, the sons of Theseus. There is some restoration, especially the muzzle of Phalios, part of his breast and of the rump of Kalliphora, parts of the helmets. The kalos-name is Onetorides. The floral ornament is as hard and metallic as the figures.

The neck-amphora in the British Museum[9] is distinctly freer, both in shape and in drawing. It is also better preserved, and one can enjoy, undisturbed by restorations, the warm polished clay and the lustrous deep-black glaze. Only the white has suffered; it was repainted, but has now been cleaned. Exekias here signs as potter only, but the drawing is evidently his as well as the potter-work. The subject on one side is the death of the Amazon Penthesilea (pl. 27, 1). Achilles thrusts his spear into her throat, and she falls. There have been many pictures of amazonomachies before this: in Attica from the second quarter of the sixth century onwards; many groups, also, of a warrior turning to flee, too late; but here the group has attained a classic form—black-figure can hardly go beyond this. The word ἀκρίβεια comes into one's mind, the "accuracy" commended, in their simple, matter-of-fact way, by ancient critics of art; and one cannot help thinking of bronze statues. There is much fine detail, especially in the chiton, pantherskin, and helmet of the Amazon, but it does not detract from the simple

rightness of the total effect. On the other side of the vase stands Dionysos
holding sprigs of ivy, and a kantharos which a boy, his son Oinopion, offers
to fill; it is a restrained picture, and the figure of the god is without the dae-
monic quality which it has in Kleitias and Lydos. The floral bands below the
pictures, compared with those on the Berlin vase, are unobtrusive; the floral
design at the handles has been stripped of leaves and reduced to a wintry,
almost mathematical, design of large and slowly winding spirals.

The most famous of Exekias' vases is the large amphora in the Vatican.[10]
It bears the double signature, "painted and made," in a verse on the rim,
and the potter-signature is repeated on the front of the body. We have
already mentioned the shape known as "amphora type A,"* a somewhat
more elaborate variety of the traditional amphora: the handles, instead of
being round and plain, are flanged and adorned with ivy, the foot is in two
degrees, and a fillet is added between foot and base. The neck and shoulder
of the vase are longer than before, the belly less tense, and the picture begins
lower down. The story figured on the front of the vase is not recorded in
extant literature, and our knowledge of it is gathered from works of art
alone, chiefly vases, some of which are more circumstantial than this.[11] The
ingenious hero Palamedes (this we do know from the poets) invented various
games to while away the long hours at Aulis; one day at Troy the two chief
champions of the Greeks, Achilles and Ajax, became so absorbed in their
board-game that they did not hear the alarm, and before they looked up
the Trojans were in the Achaean camp. Exekias gives the two principal
figures only. The names are added, in the genitive. Achilles and Ajax sit
on block-seats at a third block. The game was a sort of backgammon, combining skill with chance. Dice were first thrown, and the cast entitled the
player to make certain moves; the skill consisted in making the best possible
use of the cast, whether it was high or low. Achilles here says *tessara*, four:
that is, he has thrown a three and a one, or a pair of twos, and proceeds to
make his move accordingly. Ajax says *tria*, three: that is, he has thrown a
two and a one. Euripides may have been referring to this episode in the line
quoted by Dionysos in the *Frogs*: "Achilles has thrown two pips and a
four."[12] Both heroes are on duty, ready-armed, holding a pair of spears,
dressed in short chiton, leather corslet, greaves, and richly ornamented
cloak. A small piece of realism is the bulge made by the stiff flaps of the
corslet through the cloak below the waist.[13] Their shields lean behind them;
Achilles wears his Corinthian helmet, Ajax's is laid on top of his shield.
Another realistic touch is the crest swaling over on this side of the helmet.
Achilles bends a little less than Ajax, and his helmet forms the apex of the
triangular design: he is a little the grander (γεραρώτερος) of the two. Both
wear the old-fashioned thigh-guards, but Achilles has a rarer piece of armour

* See p. 59.

as well, the rerebrace.[14] The shields, too, are of the old-fashioned Boeotian type, and have magnificent devices; Achilles bears a satyr-head in high relief, between a snake and a panther, Ajax a gorgoneion between two snakes. Ajax has a longer beard than the younger Achilles. In this picture, with its profusion of minute incised detail in hair, armour, and mantles, the black-figure *technique* reaches its acme, or even passes it; the other side of the vase, with more moderation, is more pleasant as a work of art (pls. 28–29). A young man, Castor, stands in the middle, dressed in a chlamys, carrying a spear over his shoulder, and holding his horse Kyllaros. He looks round at his mother Leda, who offers him a flower with one hand and holds a pair of sprigs in the other. His father, Tyndareos, stands at the horse's head and strokes its face. A small boy carries a seat on his head, with a folded garment laid on it; a small aryballos, oil-bottle, is tied round his forearm. At the other end of the picture Polydeukes, naked, bends to caress the dog which leaps up towards him. It is sometimes thought that Castor is setting out, while his brother Polydeukes has returned from an outing.[15] It is perhaps rather more likely that both are returning home, but Polydeukes arrived first, put his horse in the stable, and stripped, while Castor, arriving a little later, is welcomed by his father and his mother, who offers him a flower to smell, and fragrant sprigs of fresh myrtle. In either case the seat, the change of clothes, and the oil for anointing are intended for Polydeukes.

Comparing this vase with those in Berlin and London, one becomes aware that the artist has found his way into a freer world. Where there was rigidity, there is now a blend of austerity and charm. Exekias is less interested in violent action than his predecessors, more in quiet unhurried movements and small though not insignificant activities that last for some time. His persons, more than others, are felt to have breeding and character, ἦθος. The scene in the house of Tyndareos is not so much a scene from everyday life, to which the artist has added heroic names, as a scene from heroic life when at its simple everyday level. All Greece is in Homer; and the tone of Exekias' picture is the same as in many parts of epic, in the Telemachy for example, or in that part of the Iliad where Nestor and Odysseus come to the house of Peleus, find him sacrificing in his courtyard, with the assistance of Menoitios and Patroklos, and are invited in by Achilles.[16] Exekias, with the limited means of an art hardly out of its childhood, has achieved something of the same simple grace as Homer with his incomparable resources.

The physique and bearing of these men and women bring them into line with the kouroi and korai of sixth-century sculpture, and with the figures in low relief on the sepulchral stelai of archaic Attica. The horse in the middle is already of late archaic type, far more sensitively drawn in all its parts, from head to hooves, than in the Berlin Exekias. Another small touch of realism is the ruffled tail. The thick peplos of Leda is foldless, but the chlamys of Castor and the himation of Tyndareos have many folds, and a three-dimensional lower edge; they are late archaic drapery at an early stage. The modern draughtsman[17] has miscopied the lower part of the chlamys, which is really red like the upper; this is of some importance as binding the central figure together. On the other hand, the surface of the vase is not well preserved and the white has faded; the modern drawing gives the white as it originally was.

Cups came from the workshop of Exekias as well as pots.[18] Of the four cups signed by him as potter, the two Little-Master cups, and a sort of belated variation on the Siana cup, are insignificant. It is not clear, of course, that they were decorated by him, but in any case Exekias may have required, like Lydos, a larger field to work on; in spite of his minute detail, he is not really a miniaturist. The fifth cup, in Munich, is important (pl. 27, 2).[19] It is an early example of the shape of cup, known as type A, which, near the end of the third quarter of the sixth century, began to displace the Little-Master cup.[20] Type A is a massive model, with lipless bowl and short stout stem well marked off from the bowl by a thick fillet. This was the new kind of cup in vogue when the red-figure technique was invented, and most of the earliest red-figured cups are of type A. Cup A is regularly an "eye-cup"; on each half of the exterior it bears a pair of large eyes, which were apotropaic in origin and were sometimes thought of as gorgon's eyes. The interior of cup A is often decorated with a small round gorgoneion. Outside, a vine may fill the space at the handles; between the eyes there is often, as here, a nose. There are many variants of this decoration. A figure or figures may take the place of the nose, and there may be figures at the handles instead of vine. The decoration of the Munich Exekias cup is unusual in several respects. Eyes and nose are normal, but figure-work at the handles is not very common; still less common, that a large picture should occupy the whole of the interior. The technique, too, is abnormal: the exterior pictures are ordinary black-figure, but the black-figure design inside is painted not on the surface of the vase itself but on a fine lustrous coral-red slip with which the whole picture-space was coated before the figures were begun. This coral-red is of the same nature as the black glaze, and was obtained either by protecting the colour from reoxidization in firing, or by the addition of some ingredient. Later artists, both black-figure and red-figure, used it on occasion. The exterior of Exekias' cup is quadripartite: two eye-areas, two handle-areas. The centre of interest, which is usually in the eye-area, has been shifted to the handle-areas with their figure-scenes. The subject in both is a fight over the dead body of a warrior. The body fills the space under the handle; in one picture the dead man, lying on his back, is already stripped; three warriors fight for the body on each side of the handle; one of them bends to take hold of it. This might possibly be the struggle for the body of Patroklos. At the other handle, the warrior, fallen prone, is still armed, but without spear, sword, or shield. The drawing of the "bronze men" is less detailed than in the larger vases. The chief picture is inside the cup. It is an unusual scene: Dionysos, holding a drinking-horn, sails over the sea; the water is not rendered, but indicated by the dolphins that play about the vessel. (The face of Dionysos is restored.) The vessel is of the same kind as in the François vase: the prow in the form of a boar's head much stylized; the stern ending in the head of a swan; rail, ladder, and steersman's hutch all given. A tall vine grows beside the mast.

Cup A held more than the Little-Master cup and was less flimsy. In decoration, it must be said, black-figure cups of this type are not very successful. The reason for this does not lie in the intractability of the big eyes, which break the surface and dwarf the rest of the design, for Chalcidian potters contrived to harmonize them with the rest of the decoration and with the cup as a whole, and in Attica itself the *red-figure* cup of type A is a success.

We now pass to some of the vases that are seen from the style to have been painted by Exekias, although they bear no signature; we begin with amphorae. Four fragments in Leipsic come from an amphora which had the same two subjects as the Vatican vase, but less elaborately executed.[21] The surface is beautifully preserved. One sees the shanks of Achilles, his block-seat, the tip of his cloak, part of his shield, with the tail of the feline emblazoned on it, and the shield of Ajax, with a gorgoneion between a snake and a lion or panther. From the other picture the fingers of Polydeukes remain, with part of the white hound, held on a leash. An amphora-fragment by Exekias in the University of Lund (pl. 27, 3)[22] might seem at a hasty glance to come from the same vase and to give the head of Tyndareōs, but the name is inscribed, and it is Theseus. What can the scene be at which Theseus is present, bearded and fully dressed? Perhaps his sons Demophon and Akamas were leading their horses, as on the neck-amphora by Exekias in Berlin. A fine amphora in Philadelphia,[23] a late work of Exekias, has a battle-scene, taken from the epic *Aithiopis* (pl. 30). After the burial of Hector, with which the Iliad concludes, two champions came to help the Trojans. First, Penthesilea the Amazon, daughter of Ares, and after her death at the hands of Achilles, Memnon, son of Eos, goddess of the Dawn. Memnon slew Antilochos, who died to save his father Nestor. Then Achilles slew Memnon. Soon after, Achilles himself was slain by Paris. On the Philadelphia vase, Ajax drops his spear, bends, and lifts the dead body of Achilles; on the left of this group, Menelaos slays one of Memnon's negro henchmen, here named Amasis, who is armed with club and wicker targe (*pelta*). On the other side of the vase, Antilochos lies, slain by Memnon; and three Greeks, two in hoplite armour, the third an archer, chase two naked men, doubtless negroes, away from the body, which they may have been attempting to despoil. There may be a mistake in the naming; one of the Greeks is called Euphorbos, and the Euphorbos known to us was a Trojan. But it is possible that there was a second Euphorbos in the epic, a Greek.[24] In another point, however, Exekias has made a confusion, or at least has made it possible for us to make a confusion. The negro followers of Memnon can hardly have remained on the battlefield after the death of their master; Menelaos is not driving them away from the body of Achilles, but from the body of Antilochos while their master is still alive. Two episodes, of one day, but not simultaneous, have been divided unequally between the two sides of the vase, the Antilochos episode occupying one side and half of the other, the Achilles episode the remaining half. Both subjects are unusual: Memnon's negroes are figured elsewhere, but seldom in battle; and while there are many pictures of Ajax carrying the body of Achilles, there is only one other in which Ajax is hoisting the body from the ground.[25] Exekias has chosen the moment preceding the usual one. Achilles wears a cloak of the same kind as in the Vatican vase, thigh-armour, and a leather corslet; Ajax's corslet is of bronze. His device is a group of a panther attacking a deer; the other devices are a raven, and a dog gnawing a haunch. A pleasant detail is the gorgoneion in relief on the knee of the greave; bronze greaves with this decoration have been preserved.[26] The club is the traditional weapon of the negro; according to Herodotus, the Ethiopians in the army of Xerxes were armed with clubs.[27]

Fragments of another amphora by Exekias, of the same period, also in Philadelphia,[28] give the greater part of the designs on both sides of the vase (pl. 31). The general theme recalls the old "horseman" amphorae, but the subject is new, and unique in archaic art. The horseman has dismounted to graze his horse. On one side he is in hoplite armour with crested helmet, shield (the device again a raven), cloak, and spear. The cheekpieces of the helmet are adorned with a ram's head in relief. On the other side of the vase he is an archer, in Oriental costume (sleeves, trousers, hat with long flaps, bow and quiver). Both of them let the lead out and wait, again an action that takes quite a while.

So also in the Boulogne amphora with the Death of Ajax (pl. 32, 1).[29] The theme is well known from the Sophoclean tragedy, which is nearly a hundred years later, and it was often treated in archaic art from Protocorinthian times onwards—Ajax either riving himself on his sword, or fallen about it. Exekias is alone in showing not the dead hero, or the moment of his death, but the slow preparation for the final act—Ajax, his resolution taken, methodically fixing his sword in the ground. Behind him, a palm-tree; in front of him his spears, helmet, and the famous shield. The face—and this is rare in black-figure—is furrowed with grief. The other picture on the vase is a very conventional chariot-scene; the artist has put all his power into the Ajax.

Of the unsigned neck-amphorae, the most interesting, though not the best, is perhaps that in Boston with the harnessing of a chariot.[30] The shape is the same as in the signed neck-amphorae, but above and below the chief pictures there are small ones: above, cock-fighting; below, lions, boars, and a bull. The treatment of the harnessing-scene is unique. The subject is divided between the two sides of the vase. Usually, as in Nearchos, the pole-horses have been harnessed and one of the trace-horses is being led up. Here one pole-horse is harnessed, a man holds the reins and goad, and a naked man stands at the horse's head holding it by topknot and muzzle to keep it quiet. The second pole-horse is being put into place, but resists and rears; the man leading it has been pulled off his feet and now comes down with knees bent. Two women watch unmoved. The trace-horses are on the other side of the vase; one of them is held by a fully armed warrior who re-calls the Demophon and Akamas of the Berlin Exekias, while a man who recalls the Theseus of the Lund fragment stands at the horse's head and cautiously pats its nose. A woman holds the warrior's spear. The second trace-horse is seen from the front,[31] and a man takes it by the nose. The execution of the pictures is not equal to the conception—is hardly worthy, indeed, of Exekias. One feels that the painter must have treated the subject in the same manner, but with more care, in a work that has not survived.

We now come to a vase that shows Exekias in a better light, the great calyx-krater in Athens, found in the American excavations on the north slope of the Acropolis.[32] This is the earliest and an exceptionally solid and massive example of what soon became one of the leading shapes in Attic vase-painting; many masterpieces of red-figure are calyx-kraters. It is possible that Exekias invented the shape. The handles are missing, except the stumps, and parts of the picture. The kalos-name Onetorides is the same as in the Berlin neck-amphora and the Vatican vase. On the front, a chariot-scene. The occupants of the car are missing, but the end of Herakles' name is preserved, and the spear of Athena; it is her chariot, in which she is con-ducting the hero to Olympus. Five deities attend her: Apollo playing the cithara; Artemis; Poseidon; a goddess who is not named or whose name has not been preserved—perhaps Aphrodite, or Amphitrite; and Hermes. The picture on the other side of the vase is the fight for the body of Patroklos. One might have expected this to be a common subject, considering how im-portant it is in the Iliad, but there is only one other certain example of it on a vase, on the early red-figured cup by Oltos in Berlin. The body, stripped, lies on the ground, with three warriors contending for it on each side: on the Greek side, two heroes whose names are missing, perhaps Ajax and Mene-laos, and a third, Diomed; on the Trojan side, Hector and two others, per-

haps Glaukos and Aeneas. Diomed is joining his companions, and so, it may
be, was the corresponding figure at the other edge of the picture. The areas
of the handles are treated separately: at each, a vine, and a seated maenad.
The lower part of the vase is decorated on each half with an animal group,
two lions attacking a bull, but the stretches of this zone that lie between the
handle-roots go in subject with the handle-areas; a small satyr runs, looking
back.

Exekias, like Sophilos and Lydos, has left other works besides vases.
Fragments in Berlin, with some scraps in Athens,[33] come from a set of clay
plaques, each about 37 cm. high by 43, which decorated a sepulchral monument, probably of sun-dried brick, and, ranged side by side, formed a kind
of frieze; the plaques seem not to have been continuous, but to have stood
a little away from each other; they are thus very like what is commonly
understood by a "picture." Each picture is complete in itself, but they are
all concerned with the funeral and the mourning for the dead. Two of the
fragments are from a representation of the prothesis, the lying in state, a
favourite theme in sepulchral art, as we saw, from the Geometric period
onwards.* The dead woman, clothed and wreathed, lies on a couch which
stands on a platform; a woman with one foot on the platform and the other
on a stool, bends, and adjusts the cushion under the head. Another woman
stands on the extreme right. Part of a name is preserved, ending in . . .χαρις
—Timocharis or the like. A table stands beside the couch. A column marks
the scene as taking place indoors; it is painted in a yellow or light-brown
colour obtained by mixing diluted glaze with white. The middle of the plaque
is missing; on the left, one sees the top of a second column like the first, a
woman with loose hair beating her head, and an old man, named Aresias,
lamenting. The yellowish-brown pigment reappears on a fragment, probably
not of the same plaque, in which one mourning woman is darker than the
other; the use of "two whites" or "a white and a yellow" occurs on vases,
but is rare. Other plaques represent the funeral procession—men, youths,
young boys, women, walking; men and youths riding and driving in chariots.
In a group of walking figures the leader turns his head full-face towards us.
A young boy in a dark-red himation raises his hand, probably in the gesture
of greeting and farewell which appears in many other funerary pictures. An
almost complete plaque shows a man standing in a chariot; a woman stands
facing the horses, and bordering the design off on the right; three girls
accompany the chariot, two of them beating their heads. There were several
chariot plaques, and on one of them the names of two horses are preserved,
Semos and Kalliphora, both familiar from vases; here again a woman stands
facing the horses. On another plaque a cart drawn by a fine pair of mules
is making ready; a small servant has just finished harnessing, and is with-

* P. 3 above.

drawing the pole on which the heavy mule-collar has rested during the process. Once more a woman stands facing the animals at the end of the picture; her name is Sime. Another woman stands on the far side of them, holding branches: her name ends in . . . *is*. The mules are Phalios—the name of a horse on Exekias' Berlin vase and elsewhere—and Mylios. Another fragment probably gives the occupant of the mule-cart, a woman sitting with a wand in her hand: the mule-cart also formed part of the funeral procession. Lastly, the rarest of the plaques (pl. 32, 2). The scene is laid in the women's quarters. The woman sitting with loose hair and her head veiled by her mantle is the chief of these mourners. She raises her left hand so that the chin rests on it lightly. It is the first hint of those many pensive or sorrowful attitudes, in which the chin is propped on the hand while the arm rests on the knee or on the other arm, which reach their full development in the second quarter of the fifth century and are familiar from many tombstones of the fifth century and the fourth. Two women sit beside her, one laying an arm upon her; two others sit facing her; one of these, whose feet are on a stool, bends her head in sympathy; the right arm is raised, and the chin must have rested on the hand much as in the chief mourner. This is the foreground; in the background, three women stand and pass the infant son, the orphan, from one to another. It is a well-planned three-figure group; the woman in the middle takes him from the arm of the woman on the right, and the woman on the left prepares to receive him in her mantle. The boy is tiny, but his features are already formed, with shapely chin and aquiline nose. The drapery is the same as in the Vatican amphora, foldless peploi of thick material, many folds in the softer himatia. The drawing of the different kinds of chair is attractive. We have used the phrase "chief mourner"; if the picture were alone we should probably call her the widow, but unless the building which the plaques adorned was intended for more than one person, which is always possible, the dead was the woman with whose prothesis we began. This is Exekias at his most characteristic: measured composition, gestures and attitudes potent from their very restraint.

◇   ◇   ◇

Exekias and Amasis have long been regarded as the two chief names in the black-figure of the mid-sixth century and the years succeeding. Lydos, older than they, must be added to make a third. A fourth name has often been bracketed with Amasis and Exekias: Nikosthenes.[34] This is partly due to the great number of vases that bear the signature, and largely to a lack of discrimination. Nikosthenes always signs as potter, never as painter. The name, followed by the word *epoiesen*, "made," occurs on about a hundred black-figured vases, and on eight red-figured. The red-figured vases, which were decorated by several painters, are outside our present province; a word may be said about the others. Among the earliest of them is a small neck-amphora in the British Museum;[35] it is an accomplished piece of pottery, and the drawing is neat and lively. Of the four pictures on body and neck, two are of wrestlers and two of boxers. The athletes are not youths, but portly men, and the wrestlers are either getting bald or have cropped the hair of the forehead. The boxers, as in most Greek pictures of boxing, stand foot to foot and hammer at each other's heads; not unnaturally some blood flows. This is the most impressive side of boxing to the simple mind, and that might account for its popularity with the more unsophisticated among the painters of vases, but it appears from ancient descriptions of boxing matches that the Greeks did not fully appreciate the value of the body-blow.[36] These are pleasant enough little pictures, with some bite. Unfortunately none of the other vases with the signature of Nikosthenes are certainly by the same hand. It can be traced, however, in a good many unsigned vases, both pots and Little-Master cups; a lip-cup with Theseus and the Minotaur, in the British Museum, and a band-cup with a battle-scene, in Berlin, will serve as examples.[37] The artist may be called the BMN Painter, short for "the Painter of the neck-amphora with the signature of Nikosthenes, number B 295 in the British Museum." The great majority of the vases signed Nikosthenes were decorated by another man, who may be named "Painter N." Most of them are neck-amphorae of a very odd shape which is peculiar to Nikosthenes. It has a long neck, a thin flaring mouth, a high foot, thin band-like handles, and two raised fillets, about an inch and a half apart, round the middle. Sometimes the midband—the zone between the two fillets—is decorated with a floral pattern, or even with small figures; but Painter N admired the overlap type of decoration which was by this time dying out in cups, and often runs his picture right over the raised fillets. The style of drawing in all these Nikosthenic neck-amphorae is slovenly and dissolute, but it is worst in those that have overlap decoration. More could be said about Nikosthenes, but it would probably be in the same strain.

Able painters of the second rank were active in the middle and the third quarter of the sixth century. Their work equals or surpasses most of the vases in Group E, although it does not reach the level of Exekias at his best. We glance at two of them only. The Painter of Berlin 1686[38] is named after an amphora with a picture of a procession in honour of Athena, a humble forerunner of the frieze of the Parthenon.[39] The goddess herself stands at her altar, armed, and raising her spear. Her priestess stands in front of the altar, holding a bunch of sprigs; a man and a youth approach, and a youth leading a cow to be sacrificed. The musicians on the other side of the vase, two flute-players and two citharodes, also belong to the procession. All these figures have a remote and hieratic air. The Minotaur amphora by the same painter in Oxford is less careful, but the photograph shows the shape better than the reproductions of the Berlin vase, and the quality is equal to the average of Group E.[40] One of the artist's best works is a large amphora of type A in the Faina collection at Orvieto, which has a good harnessing-scene on one side, and on the other Herakles struggling with Triton in the presence of Nereus and two Nereids.[41] Of the slighter pieces, we must be particularly grateful to the artist for his small amphora in Berlin, with its well-known picture of a chorus of Knights,[42] a valuable record of the masquerades which contributed, when the time came, to the rise of Attic comedy.

The picture with which we conclude this chapter is on an amphora in the Vatican (pl. 33).[43] In a wooded place a woman mourns for a dead warrior, her husband or her son. The body lies naked on a bed of branches. Fir-trees and planes, and on one of the firs a bird. The hero's armour, greaves, helmet, and shield. The artist had intended to draw the usual floral border above the picture and had ruled the lower line of it, but thought better. The woman has been taken to be the goddess Eos, mourning for her son Memnon, but one cannot be sure. The other side of the vase is disappointing, a trifling picture of Menelaos threatening Helen after the fall of Troy.[44] The mourning scene is worthy of Exekias. It is easy to say that the artist must be copying a work by someone else; it may be so, but there is no evidence for it. One would wish to find other vases by this painter; he is not very far from Group E, but cannot be counted as belonging to it. I see a resemblance to the prothesis on a fragment of which part is in Bonn, the other part lost.[45] The lesson is that fine work may be found on vases which cannot be assigned to any of the noted artists.[46]

VII

LATER BLACK-FIGURE

WE NOW reach the point of time, momentous for the art of black-figure, when the new technique of red-figure was invented. For a while the older manner held its own, but before long it was forced into the second place, and by the end of a generation nearly all the finer work was being done in red-figure. It is not certain who invented the red-figure technique, but the claim of the Andokides Painter is strong.[1] *Andokides* was a potter; his signature appears on eight vases, always followed by the word ἐποίησεν or ἐποίει: "made by Andokides." Four of the eight were decorated by one artist, who may or may not have been Andokides himself; it is to this artist that the conventional name of the Andokides Painter is given. He must have been a pupil of Exekias. Two were decorated by another artist, whose name is known, Psiax; one by a third, the famous red-figure painter Epiktetos; and one, the earliest of all, a small black-figured amphora which came to light a few years ago and is now in California, by a fourth artist.[2] A good many other vases can be assigned to the Andokides Painter besides the signed ones, and the list of his works is very varied; it includes black-figured vases, red-figured vases, vases half in black-figure, half in red-figure, and one vase in a unique, experimental technique—like red-figure, but the figures reserved on a white ground instead of on the native hue of the vase.

In "bilingual" vases—that is, those in which part of the decoration is in black-figure, part in red-figure—the division varies. In a cup, the inside is usually in black-figure, the outside in red, but in the cup with the signature of Andokides, one half of the exterior is in the one technique, the other half in the other; in heraldic language, the design is counterchanged. In the bilingual amphorae, the picture on one side is in black-figure, the picture on the other in red-figure, the subject being sometimes the same and sometimes different. The unsigned amphora in Munich[3] is one of those that have the same subject on both sides: Herakles resting, visited by Athena. In the black-figure version the artist has added two figures: Hermes, and a boy cup-bearer. The round krater, the dinos, at which the boy is busy, is of the same shape as the much earlier vase by the Gorgon Painter, and has a similar stand. Herakles, dressed in a himation, reclines on a couch, holding a kantharos, under a vine; bread, meat, and another drinking-vessel, a cup,

---

[1] For numbered notes to chapter vii see pages 114–116 below.

75

are on a table beside him. His bow, quiver, and sword are hung up. On the red-figure side, only the two chief figures are given, and the attitudes are not quite the same as in the black-figure picture; Herakles holds his knee, and Athena, like the Leda of Exekias, offers a flower. The black-figure picture does not show the painter at his best; the composition is nerveless, the figures of Herakles and the boy languid, as if the artist had lost interest for the moment in the old technique. The red-figure version is better, but neither here nor in his other red-figure pictures does the Andokides Painter use the possibilities of the new technique to the full; that was reserved for younger men, Euphronios and his companions. In red-figure the Andokides Painter remains a fairly able forerunner, just as in black-figure he remains a commendable successor of Exekias.

An all-black-figure amphora, of the somewhat simpler type B, in the Rothschild collection, Paris,[4] is especially close to the Munich vase, less ambitious but more satisfactory. On the front, Herakles, kneeling, strangles the lion, while his nephew and squire Iolaos stands by, taking care of his master's club, and Athena steps out of range. The hero's bow, quiver, sword, and garment hang in the field, and do something to fill the void space above the main group, but the composition is still somewhat loose. On the reverse there is the old contrast between Dionysos, who stands solemn in the middle, holding vine, ivy, drinking-horn, and the satyrs dancing one at each side.

A novel aspect of Herakles is shown on an amphora in the Villa Giulia at Rome.[5] Herakles, holding a cithara, mounts a platform, between Athena and Hermes seated on campstools. This is one of many black-figured pictures from this period and somewhat later in which Herakles is seen playing the cithara or about to play it, with the gods themselves for audience. It seems a strange rôle for the man of action, especially when the instrument is not the simple lyre, which boys learned to play at school, but the elaborate cithara, which could only be played by a virtuoso. This new conception of Herakles must be due to a poem that has not come down to us, in which he was depicted as not only brave, and patient of toil and hardship, but the friend of the Muses as well.[6] A late reminiscence of this Herakles is preserved in the *Herakliskos* of Theocritus,[7] where he is said to have been taught music by the famous Eumolpos; the words used show that the instruction went far beyond the elementary stage; Eumolpos made Herakles into a bard (ἀοιδὸν ἔθηκεν), and the instrument named is the boxwood phorminx (πυξίνᾳ ἐν φόρμιγγι), which must mean not the simple lyre, in which there was not much wood, but the elaborate cithara. There is an echo of Exekias, as often with our painter, in the scene on the other side of the vase. A youth wearing a woollen blanket-like cloak, with a petasos, carrying a pair of spears over his shoulder, and leading a horse, approaches an old man; a woman offers a wreath. The question again arises whether the youth is returning or setting out. The rendering of Herakles on the Villa Giulia vase connects it with a larger and finer amphora in Boston (pls. 34–35),[8] which has the same subject on both sides, once in black-figure and once in red-figure, Herakles driving a bull to sacrifice. In the Munich bilingual there was a good deal of difference between the two sides; here they repeat one another without much change. The bull wears a woollen fillet in token of consecration, and is held by a rope passing round the horns. Herakles strides forward with his club in one hand, and in the other, besides the rope, a bundle of spits (secured by slides), on which the meat will be roasted after the slaughter. Sword and quiver are at his side, and a pair of wineskins, containing wine for libation and consumption, hang from his shoulder. The space above the bull's back is filled by a tree. It is a simple, bold design, without the hesitation apparent in some of the painter's work.

The neck-amphorae of the Andokides Painter, in point of form, are based on those of Exekias, slightly simplified. This version of the shape became extremely popular in the later archaic period, and the neck-amphorae of our artist stand at the head of a vast series in the late sixth century and the early fifth. The neck-amphora in Oxford[9] shows Dionysos in the familiar guise, standing still, holding kantharos and vine. He looks round at Hermes who approaches; a maenad, seated on the back of a satyr, plays the flute; another satyr completes the composition, which is again a little loose. On the reverse of the vase the artist takes no risks; he chooses the old, highly decorative design of the chariot seen from the front. On the better-preserved neck-amphora of the same shape in the British Museum[10] the chief picture is of Athena standing in her chariot with Herakles beside her, bound for Olympus, or arriving there, attended by Dionysos, Apollo, and Hermes: the same subject as on the calyx-krater by Exekias. The other picture is a rather lifeless version of the Ajax and Achilles on Exekias' amphora in the Vatican. Echoes again. Even the handle-spirals are commonplace adaptations of an Exekian motive. The shape, however, is majestic; and there is a drop of Exekian solemnity in the chariot-scene.

The third great shape of vase in late sixth-century black-figure is the hydria. One of the Andokides Painter's best vases is a hydria in the British Museum (pl. 36, 1).[11] Dionysos, kantharos in hand, reclines on a couch, with food on a table beside him, as Herakles did on the amphora in Munich; ivy takes the place of vine. Two couples trip towards the couch, one at the head, one at the foot. Hermes seizes the kantharos to fill it (Hermes as cup-bearer is known from other sources, for instance from a fragment of Sappho).[12] A woman, whether Ariadne or a nymph, sets an ivy-wreath on Dionysos' forehead; there are other pictures of the crowning at the beginning of the party.[13] At the foot of the couch, a satyr and a nymph dance up, the satyr with his arm round the shoulder of the nymph, whose arms are both extended. Right in the middle of the picture is the music; between couch and table, a powerful satyr plays the cithara. Lastly, at the left edge, Hephaistos arrives, his hammer over his shoulder. This is a unique representation, and not easily explained. It is not one of the usual episodes in the Return of Hephaistos, but perhaps a place may be found for it in the narrative all the same. Let us suppose that Dionysos finds Hephaistos busy in the workshop and persuades him to be his guest. Hephaistos—here we remember the somewhat similar situation in the eighteenth book of the Iliad[14]—asks for time to put his tools away carefully, wash, and dress, and tells Dionysos not to wait for him. When Hephaistos at last arrives in the house of Dionysos he finds that the god has already lain down on the couch and is being entertained with music and dancing. Overcome by the festal splendour, the simple Hephaistos raises his hand in wonder.[15]

◇ ◇ ◇

Two of the remaining vases with the signature of the potter Andokides were painted by one artist, a black-figured neck-amphora in Castle Ashby and a bilingual amphora in Madrid; neither bears the name of the painter, but two small red-figured vases are by the same hand as they, and are signed by the painter Psiax.[16] Psiax was another artist of the transition, who painted black-figure vases, red-figure vases, and vases combining the two techniques; further, black-figured vases on a white ground, black-figured vases on a coral-red ground,[17] and vases in a sort of imitation red-figure, the design being in added colour, not reserved. The finer of the two pieces with the signature of Andokides, in Castle Ashby,[18] is a neck-amphora of a special model, one of three such vases. The body is black, and the decoration consists of two small pictures on the neck: a frontal chariot, between two boys, and Dionysos with two dancing satyrs. The subjects are old, but they are lightly carried out in a miniature style of much charm, and the vase as a whole is a happy creation. The pictures on the large bilingual amphora in Madrid[19] are delicately executed, but much less successful. The black-figure picture shows Dionysos with satyrs and maenads; the red-figure, Apollo with Leto, Artemis and Ares. The rather unstable figures have a child-like appearance, which would be better suited to small vases like the alabastron in Leningrad with Dionysos and a maenad, and a maenad and a satyr, in black-figure on a white ground.[20] Among the best of Psiax's large-scale works is the picture on a hydria in Berlin (pl. 36, 2).[21] The subject, the harnessing of a chariot, is a favourite at the time, and we saw earlier and abnormal versions of it* on vases by Nearchos and Exekias. The pole-horses are almost ready. A youth named Simon stands behind the car holding reins and goad.

---

* See pp. 40, 70 above.

The actual harnessing is done by a man who stands on the far side of the horses. He wears the long robe of a charioteer and is the expert. These two persons, one holding the horses steady, the other, the older, engaged with the harness, are regular in pictures of the subject. There is normally, too, a third person at the horses' heads, often soothing them by holding or stroking their faces, here stooping and lending the expert a hand. Lastly, a youth leads up the off trace-horse, which is muzzled. At the shoulder of the hither pole-horse, and below it, one sees the ends of the yoke, the yoke-pad, the bridle of the second trace-horse, and a small cross, set with prickles, to discourage boring.[22] An Athenian named Simon was the author of a standard work on horsemanship to which Xenophon acknowledges a debt, and one would like to think that this was an ancestor, but the name is common. The drawing is dainty, the incisions fine—the major lines thin, the minor lines still thinner. The small picture on the shoulder represents a fight, in three traditional groups; and, as often in hydriai, there is a still smaller picture, a predella, in lieu of a pattern-band, below the chief one: lion and bull, panther and ram, panther, the felines slender, the other animals almost drooping.

❖   ❖   ❖

The Antimenes Painter,[23] so called after the name of a youth on his hydria in Leyden, may be thought of as the brother of Psiax. There is no means of saying whether they were actually related, but their styles are so alike in important respects that the expression may serve. The number of his vases is very large: he is one of the chief painters of the standardised neck-amphora and hydria which are two of the three leading shapes in the black-figure of this time; the third, the amphora, was used by him, but less often. Besides his own vases, there are many in his manner by other artists, some of whom can be distinguished. He might have been expected to employ the red-figure technique on occasion, like Psiax, and he has much in common with early red-figure vase-painters, but no red-figure work by him has reached us. A certain kinship with Lydos suggests that he may have been a pupil of the older artist.

The relation of the Antimenes Painter to Psiax may be illustrated from his perfectly preserved hydria in London (pl. 38, 3),[24] which has the same subject as the Berlin Psiax (pl. 36, 2), the harnessing of a chariot. The elements of the composition are the same. The pole-horses are joined, a youth behind the car holds reins and goad, an older man, dressed in a long chiton, is busy with the harness, a youth stands at the horses' heads, another brings up one of the muzzled trace-horses. Here the youth with the reins plants one foot in the car, and this is more frequent in such scenes than standing with both feet on the ground. The youth at the horses' heads, too, is more normal: instead of bending with his head concealed by the horses, as in Psiax, he holds the face of one horse with both hands; but the former motive, bending with head concealed, occurs on other harnessing hydriai by the Antimenes Painter. The execution is less refined than in Psiax; there is less detail, and the incised lines are of a uniform thickness; but the movements are freer and better, the style broader and more natural, without the mincingness to which Psiax is prone. On the shoulder, a vigorous battle-scene, superior to Psiax's; as predella, a boar-hunt, with some of the hunters on horseback.

A favourite subject on hydriai, water-pots, of the later archaic period is appropriately the communal fountain, and there are several "fountain-hydriai" by the Antimenes Painter and his associates. One sees part of the fountain-house, women filling their hydriai at the spouts, others approaching with empty hydriai on their heads, others returning, their hydriai filled. So for example on two vases by the painter in London and in the Vatican.[25] A very unusual fountain-picture is on the hydria in Leyden from which the artist takes his name (pl. 38, 1–2).[26] The scene is laid in the palaestra. In the middle is the fountain, seen from the front. The porch is supported by three Doric columns, over which there is a light architrave and a pediment decorated with a disc between two serpents. The raking cornice curls up into a volute at each end; the side-acroteria are in the form of prancing horses. At the panther-head spouts, a man and a boy are enjoying a shower. The boy seems to be Antimenes, at least the name is written beside him, with the word *kalos* above. On each side of the fountain there is a tree with clothes hanging on the branches, and two figures under it. On the right, a youth pours oil into his palm to anoint himself; a boy waits impatiently for his turn with the oil-flask. Under the other tree a youth takes down the oil-flask from the branch where it has been hanging, and a boy waits. The figures are comparatively small, and the picture comes a little nearer to being a real landscape than in the many vases where the figures dwarf the buildings. On the shoulder, a chariot-scene; in the predella, a hunt, as in the London hydria, but the quarry is a stag.

The prettiest of many neck-amphorae by the Antimenes Painter is in the British Museum.[27] Herakles, who has taken off his lionskin and hung it over his club, is welcomed by the centaur Pholos. The centaur carries the usual fir-branch over his shoulder, with his quarry tied to it—a fox, a hare, a bird,—and is accompanied by a pet fawn. Hermes, who has guided Herakles, now takes a seat. The other side of the vase gives a glimpse of ordinary life, of the olive-harvest. Three trees are shown: a boy has climbed into the biggest one and strikes the boughs with a stick; two men also beat the tree, and a boy picks up the fallen olives and stows them into his basket. The boys and one of the men wear the hats of wool or goatskin often seen in pictures of countrymen. The figures are again comparatively small and the picture begins to approximate to landscape. There is only one other rendering of this subject, and that is also by the Antimenes Painter.

◇   ◇   ◇

The Leagros Group[28] represents a somewhat later stage of vase-painting than the work of the Andokides Painter or Psiax and his "brother." The name of Leagros, usually followed by the adjective *kalos*, is inscribed on a great many late sixth-century vases, mostly red-figured, but half-a-dozen of them black-figured. Five of the six are hydriai, not all by one hand, but evidently from one workshop and closely interconnected in style; they, and a very large number of other vases that go with them, form the Leagros Group. It is the black-figure counterpart of what is called the Pioneer Group in red-figure—the works of Euphronios, Phintias, Euthymides and others, some of which were probably made in what may be called the Leagros workshop. The vases of the Leagros Group are not equal to the best contemporary red-figure, but they have great vigour and power (sometimes even a touch of brutality), and, set beside them, much work by the Andokides Painter or the Antimenes, not to mention Psiax, seems tame.

The favourite shape is the hydria. A perfectly preserved vase in the British Museum may introduce the Leagros Group (pl. 39, 1–2).[29] The chief picture, in the large rectangle on the body, represents a quarrel between two heroes. It is a frequent topic in later archaic vase-painting, both black-figure and red-figure. The quarrellers are often Ajax and Odysseus. After the death of Achilles, his armour was to go to "the best of the Achaeans"; the Achaeans awarded it to Odysseus, and Ajax flew at Odysseus, who was forced to draw in self-defence. Here, however, while the man on the left might well be Ajax, his opponent is a youth, and Odysseus could not have been depicted as a youth. Either, therefore, the painter has made a mistake, which is not very likely in a work of this quality, or he has no particular heroic quarrel in mind, but takes pleasure in the contrast between the youth and the middle-aged man, or he thinks of another quarrel, one of the many that took place before Troy or in other places. In Scheria, the bard Demodokos sang of a famous quarrel between Odysseus and Achilles,[30] but in any quarrel one would expect Achilles to be the aggressor,[31] and that would not be so here, where the young man is evidently the attacked. There are just seven figures in this and many other quarrel-scenes on archaic vases; perhaps they are the Seven against Thebes.[32] Friends hold the two back, and a man interposes. It is a well-composed and expressive crisscross, with much overlapping; the large figures, muscular and thickset, cover much of the background. The handsomest heads are those of the two disputants, the older man with a grand aquiline nose, the other of youthful comeliness. They do not shout, the others shout. Little white is used, and not much red; it is a very black picture. A solid platform for the figures is furnished by a border of thick palmettes; the predella picture, with its miniature, is discontinued in the Leagros Group. There is a small picture on the shoulder, Dionysos and Ariadne seated facing each other, with satyrs, maenads, and Hermes, but here also the drawing is broader than in most earlier shoulder-pictures.

The majority of the subjects in the Leagros hydriai are taken from the life of Herakles and from the Trojan War. Some of them are novel; others, while traditional, have novel elements, or show a new spirit. On a hydria in the British Museum (pl. 39, 3),[33] Herakles attacks the three-bodied Geryon at close quarters, seizing the crest of one helmet and raising his sword. There is nothing unusual in the chief group, but the attitude of the dying Eurytion, kneeling, eyes closed, spears in hand, as if turned to stone, makes a new centre-piece. Behind Herakles, Athena and Hermes stand side by side, she raising her hand, he turning his head away, not so much from squeamishness as to balance the outer, doddering head of Geryon at the other edge of the picture. Herakles has the long trunk-like nose which is often found in this group, especially in the work of one painter. On the shoulder, a hero carries off a woman; his comrade holds the chariot ready; the victim extends her arms towards her mother or guardian, and a sister or companion runs up, raising her skirt from her ankles. This is a small black-figured counterpart to the contemporary scene on the great red-figured amphora by Euthymides in Munich,[34] and here also the hero may be Theseus carrying off Helen. His left leg, frontal and foreshortened, is in the taste of the late sixth century, as shown in the Euthymides amphora and in many other red-figured vases; the figures begin to break the profile rule freely and to turn large parts of their bodies towards the spectator.

The figure of Herakles on another Geryon hydria of the Leagros Group, in Munich,[35] is typical of the new policy towards the third dimension (pl. 40, 2). Herakles draws the bow; that is traditional; but his attitude breaks with tradition: the right leg is seen from the front, with the foot extended and viewed from above. The torso too is in front view, and the anatomy of the parts between chest and groin, long neglected by artists, is more fully carried out than before. It is the beginning of that systematic study of anatomy which, together with the new conception of the figure in its relation to space, transforms Greek drawing in the late archaic period. The new art finds its purest expression in red-figure, but something of it is seen in late archaic black-figure also, notwithstanding the weight of tradition in the older and less flexible technique. The archer in the attitude of our Herakles is one of what might be called the programmatic figures of the new movement; a good example in contemporary red-figure is the Herakles on a neck-amphora, close to Euphronios, in Leningrad (pl. 40, 1).[36]

Two of Geryon's three bodies are knocked out in the Munich hydria; one falls forwards, the other back. The white shield plays the same part in the design as on the London vase. Eurytion lies writhing on the ground. Athena stands behind Herakles, with his club resting against her thigh. The shoulder-picture is taken from the Iliad, and represents the dragging of Hector's body, a subject which comes in at this period and forms the chief decoration of another hydria in the group.

On a hydria in the British Museum, Herakles is matched with Acheloös,[37] the combat best known from the description in the *Trachiniae* of Sophocles. The composition of the two figures recalls the Herakles and Nessos on the early vase in Athens. Herakles overtakes the bull-bodied, bull-eared, man-faced river-god and breaks off one of the magic horns in which his strength resides. Deities watch—Athena, raising a large hand, Ares, and Hermes.[38] Mortals also—the aged Oineus, and perhaps his daughter Deianeira. On the shoulder, Theseus and the Minotaur. The onlookers are not immediately recognisable as a selection of the fourteen youths and maidens, but that is what they are.

A subject that first appears at this time is the slaying of the giant Alkyoneus in his sleep by Herakles. On a hydria in the British Museum, Alkyoneus sleeps in his cave, still grasping his enormous club;[39] Herakles strides up with his sword; Athena sits outside the cave, and part of a chariot-team, possibly thought of as belonging to Herakles, is seen at the edge of the picture. The half-seen chariot-team is a favourite motive in the Leagros Group. The horses have animated faces with large muzzles and open mouths. Another popular detail in the group is the huge wreath worn by the giant. A second adventure of Herakles not depicted until this period is the struggle with the gigantic Antaios, which appears on a hydria in Munich.[40] Both wrestlers have caught each other by the ankle; Antaios is under, and Herakles presses the head down. Athena and Hermes support Herakles; the two other persons must belong to the party of Antaios. This vase is one of those that bear the kalos-name of Leagros. Another is the Munich hydria with Herakles and Kyknos.[41] Kyknos has fallen on one knee, and Herakles attacks him with a big stone. In this scene the chariots of the two combatants are regularly represented; here, characteristically, half of each team appears, with Athena partly visible behind the team of Herakles.

We now turn to some of the Trojan pictures. A hydria in the British Museum illustrates an episode in the legend of the boy Troilos.[42] Achilles has slain him on the altar of Apollo, and in his fury cuts the head off and hurls it at the rescue party; there are earlier pictures of this brutal act, which must have formed part of the epic narrative. Here, as often before, the distance between the figures is not actual; the foremost Trojans—Hector and Aeneas are the names given in the earlier pictures—are naturally some way off. On the left is the usual half-chariot-team, one cannot be certain whose; Achilles has not arrived in a chariot; it may belong to the rescuers. The left hand of Achilles was originally open; then the painter closed it and made it hold a pair of spears. He may have painted the open hand out, but if so, any over-paint has now disappeared. On the shoulder, athletes: boxers, javelin-throwers, a discus-thrower, and a pair of runners.

A previous moment in the same legend is depicted on a hydria in Munich.[43] Achilles, at the altar of Apollo, has laid his spears by and holds Troilos by the ankle, as if about to dash him on the steps, or rather perhaps to hurl the whole body, not only the head, at the enemy.[44] Athena stands bolt upright, as if to protect Achilles' rear. The rescue party issues from the city gate: a chariot, half seen, at the gallop, a warrior in hoplite armour, an archer. Priam sits or crouches in the middle, grasping his neck in a gesture of despair.[45] The tree in front of the gate reaches into the picture on the shoulder, which for once forms part of the main scene. It represents the wall of Troy, with the battlements manned; two warriors are visible, and an archer who turns and draws his bow at Achilles; a third warrior rises and refreshes himself from a horn. There is also an old man, and three women stretch out their hands towards the cruel scene or beat their heads. It is clear that the apparent distances are not to be taken literally. Priam is not in the precinct of Apollo, but just outside the city gate (as on the François vase); that is to say, a wide gap is to be imagined—if it were necessary to translate the picture into actuality—between the left-hand portion of the picture, including Priam, and the group on the right; the painter has set the two side by side without thinking it necessary to consider the distance.

An excellent picture on a hydria, inscribed with the name of Leagros, in Würzburg, is taken from the Sack of Troy (pl. 41).[46] Neoptolemos slays the aged Priam on the altar of Zeus. The group is framed by two figures of women. Female figures are traditional in this scene, sitting or cowering near the altar in attitudes of despair; here they stand upright, and seem to be invoking divine vengeance, which did indeed follow: "for," in the words of Pindar, "Apollo swore that he who slew the aged Priam on the home-altar, should not return home himself, or reach old age."[47] Two half-chariot-teams once more close the picture at the sides. On the shoulder it is the familiar episode of Achilles and Ajax at their game. Athena warns them, and two warriors, with an archer, eke out the strip to the requisite length. The heroes are not quietly absorbed as in Exekias, but so excited that they have almost left their seats.

A hydria in Munich figures another episode from the Sack of Troy, Aeneas carrying his father Anchises to safety on his back;[48] this is a popular scene in the late sixth century, forming a kind of pendant to the group of Ajax retrieving the body of Achilles. Aeneas is accompanied by his young son, two fully armed warriors, and an archer. Part of the left-hand figure is missing, which obscures the composition; the figures in the middle were framed, as in the Würzburg vase, by the upright figures of two women, making lament;[49] they form the background of sorrow to the hopeful foreground. This hydria has a special interest because of the rare glimpse it gives, in the picture on the shoulder, into the potter's workshop:[50] a potter fashions a large vessel on the wheel, which is spun by a boy; another vessel is being carried away to dry; a big porter brings fuel to the furnace, which a workman rakes out; a painter, unless it be an inspector, holds an amphora on his lap; in the middle is the white-haired master himself, very like Anchises, and holding a sceptre as Anchises does.

The latest Trojan scene, in order of the story, is on a hydria in Berlin.[51] Neoptolemos leads Polyxena to the tomb of Achilles at which she is to be sacrificed. The tomb is a large white mound in a lonely place; a hare is seen beside it, and one of those large snakes that are often shown in the neighbourhood of graves. In the air above is a small winged warrior flying; it is the ψυχή or είδωλον, the soul or shade, of Achilles. On the left, two warriors stand side by side as if on guard, and a chariot-team is half seen, with a third warrior behind the horses.

A hydria in Munich presents a familiar pair.[52] Ajax kneels and takes the body of Achilles on his shoulders. A small figure of a warrior is seen in the air, the spirit of the dead Achilles. Ajax has planted his two spears in the ground, to resume them when he has adjusted his burden. The spears bound the kernel-group on the left; the uprights of the spears are repeated by the line of Achilles' legs, and by his long hair falling over in front, a traditional element in the design. In the background the battle goes on: on the right, a Greek warrior—perhaps Menelaos or Odysseus; on the left, two Trojans facing him. A chariot-team, half seen, gallops up. This is a very black vase; the figures cover nearly the whole surface. The theme is old, but rendered as if it were new, and the sense of weight and effort is well given.

A rarer counterpart to the time-honoured group of Ajax with the body of Achilles appears on a hydria in the British Museum.[53] A Greek warrior has hoisted the dead body of an Amazon on his back, and, dropping his shield, carries it out of the battle. The pair are usually taken to be Achilles and Penthesilea; others have thought of Theseus, with the body of the Amazon Antiope, who went over to his side and fell fighting against her own people. A warrior and an archer precede them, while another warrior rushes back into the fight, scrambling over a wounded Amazon who lies on the ground. This, like the last, is a memorable picture.

We have confined ourselves to the *hydriai* of the Leagros Group. The average quality is high; and if one is looking at photographs of vases, or even at vases themselves, there is something to be said for a picture that keeps still while one looks at it and does not need to be chased over a series of receding curves. The pictures being all of the same shape, and most of the subjects taken from one or other of two cycles, the deeds of Herakles, and the tale of Troy, we have had, more than elsewhere, the same feeling as when we look over a set of illustrations on a wall or in a book. In style, all these hydriai have much in common, and they must have been painted in the same workshop, but they are not all by the same hand. One would have expected that it would be fairly easy to parcel them out among the various artists, but it proves to be difficult, and has not yet been done. A few personalities, however, can be distinguished from the rest, and we may conclude with a glance at one of them, the Acheloös Painter,[54] so named after a neck-amphora in Berlin.[55] Herakles overtakes the terrified river-god and breaks off his horn. Hermes sits watching and adds a touch of caricature to the scene: this painter has a comic vein and never shows the deep seriousness that characterises the Leagros Group as a whole. A shrub provides the branches which are almost obligatory in late black-figure backgrounds. The inscriptions are meaningless.

Serious, so far as the subjects allow, is the treatment of two Heraclean adventures on a neck-amphora by the Acheloös Painter in the collection of the Marchesa Isabella Guglielmi in Rome (pl. 42). Herakles, armed with club and bow, rushes after the Erymanthian Boar. The same tree as before, but no inscriptions. The woman-headed bird, a siren, is probably a good omen. The other picture is unique; Herakles, having won the golden apples of the Hesperides, runs with them over rocky country.[56] That rough terrain is indicated, and not, as one might think, water, is shown by other vases and by the rendering of the rock on a neck-amphora by the Acheloös Painter in Dr. Wilfred Hall's collection at Tynemouth (pl. 43, 1). On each side, elderly revellers, one of them lifting a girl on to his shoulder. The same revellers appear on other vases by the painter, for example a volute-krater in Taranto which, like most early vases of the shape, is decorated on the neck only, the body being painted black. The upper zone of the neck has chariots, with the drivers mounting; in the lower, men and youths recline, holding long branches, while a woman sits on the couch and offers a flower; at each end of the couch a naked man dances; the dog has her bone. That finishes the group, which repeats with slight variations. The reclining man appears again, on an amphora in New York;[57] another man plays the flute, and the dancers are women. A special revel is depicted on one of the painter's largest vases, an amphora of Panathenaic shape in the British Museum (pl. 43, 2).[58] Herakles, playing the flute, is preceded by Hermes playing the lyre and singing, and followed by the faithful Iolaos. Hermes is accompanied by a goat, Herakles by a lowing calf. There is a good deal of noise in the picture. Big wreaths, and the usual tree. One sees the painter's sinewy, middle-aged, rather sophisticated figures, with mobile necks, hog-eyes, trunk-like noses, and receding foreheads.

The Leagros Group is the last great group of Attic black-figured vases. Large numbers of full-size black-figured neck-amphorae were still produced in the first quarter of the fifth century, but most black-figured vases were now small. Among these the lekythoi are important; they have much interest of subject, and the drawing, though slight, is usually lively and sometimes charming. Miss Haspels has given an admirable account of them in her *Attic Black-figured Lekythoi*. The last of them belong to the middle of the fifth century. The old technique continued to be used for the Panathenaic amphora, and this will be the topic of our concluding chapter.

VIII

PANATHENAIC AMPHORAE

WITH THE Leagros Group we reached the last decades of the sixth century, and we found black-figure still competing, not unsuccessfully, with the new red-figure technique, but red-figure rapidly gained the upper hand; black-figure was more and more restricted to small, slight, or rough vases, and by the middle of the fifth century it was almost extinct. With one great exception. The prizes at the Great Panathenaic games, held once every four years, were amphorae of the famous Attic oil, and for these official vases the old technique was retained. Hundreds of Panathenaic amphorae, if we count fragments, have come down to us, the earliest belonging to the second quarter of the sixth century, the latest to the Hellenistic age. They enable us to recapitulate the history of black-figure vase-painting, not from the beginning, but from the period of Kleitias or early Lydos; and to continue the history through the fifth and fourth centuries down to a time when the red-figure technique had long ceased to exist.[1]

The shape of the Panathenaic vase, with its swelling body, short thin neck, pinched base, small foot, remains the same, in essentials, all the time, although its character is gradually transformed to suit changing taste. The subjects of the pictures remain the same. On the front a figure of Athena, in warlike attitude, between two columns surmounted by cocks, with the inscription τῶν Ἀθήνηθεν ἄθλων, "a prize from the games at Athens." On the reverse, a picture of the type of event in which the victor was successful. The style of the reverse is "straight"; in other words, apart from the old-fashioned technique, the drawing is in the natural manner of contemporary art. The style of the obverse, the Athena between the columns, is straight during the archaic period, but not after it; in the period of freer art it remains traditional and "archaic," just as Athenian coins do—not, of course, true archaic, but a mannered mixture of old and new.

Athletic contests are reported to have been introduced at the Panathenaea in the year 566, and it is natural to connect this date with what from the style are seen to be the earliest of our Panathenaic amphorae. The Burgon vase in the British Museum,[2] so called from the scholar who found it, was not awarded for an athletic contest, but for an equestrian; it might therefore be earlier than 566.[3] The style shows that it cannot be much earlier, and it

---

[1] For numbered notes to chapter viii see pages 116–118 below.

is likely enough that the custom of giving amphorae as prizes came in simultaneously for all events.

Neck-amphorae of this general form had long been made in Attica, can be traced back to the Late Geometric period,[4] and it is probable that they had long been used to contain oil. The Burgon vase is stout and squat; let us compare it with some later Panathenaics, all in the British Museum, and see how the shape develops.[5] For the present we consider the shape only. In London B 134, by the Euphiletos Painter, about 530, the neck is shorter, the body longer, and the whole vase gives a deeper impression of collected power (pl. 49, 1–3). In London B 133, by the Eucharides Painter, about 480, the shape is even stronger and more compact; the shoulder is higher, the handles closer to the neck, the mouth and foot straighter, and there is distinctly more incurve at shoulder and base. In London B 606, of about 400, the incurve at base and shoulder has increased, and the line has slackened. London B 604 (pl. 46, 4), of about 366, has a new elegance: the curve of the neck swings right up into the flaring mouth, which is now concave instead of convex; and as if to make up for the slighter "punctuation"* between neck and mouth, the foot is given a lip at the top. In London B 611, of 327 B.C., the elegance is exaggerated; the neck and handles are longer, the base slenderer, the proportions spoilt.

To return to the Burgon Panathenaic. Like the vase itself, the Athena is short and stout. Her garment, a peplos, is simple, and no folds are indicated. The helmet, as in all the earliest Panathenaics, is no more than a skull-cap with a high crest attached. The aegis is a sort of large bib, covering the breast only, set round with a few big snakes. The device on the shield is a fat dolphin. In several respects the decoration is not yet canonical. There are no columns to left and right of the figure; there is no band of tongue-pattern above it; the neck of the vase has a siren on one side and an owl on the other instead of the floral design that soon became obligatory. The picture on the reverse represents a horse-race of a special kind, the συνωρίς, which differs widely from the chariot-race; a pair of horses is driven by a young man who sits in a light cart with his feet resting on a board suspended from the pole. The wheels are cart-wheels, and the horses' collar is like the mule's collar as we saw it on the plaque by Exekias.† Besides the goad, the driver holds a long rod curving round at the end and furnished with a pair of what seem to be dangling metal plates intended to encourage the horse. The same instrument appears on a cup in the Louvre in the neighbourhood of a pair of mules.[6] In the few later pictures of this event chariot-wheels are substituted for cart-wheels, and the driver is content with a goad.[7] The style of the Burgon vase is contemporary with the earliest work of Lydos, but

---

* See p. 53 above.
† See pp. 71–72 above.

is rather more uncouth; the nearest approach to it is on a prothesis plaque in the Louvre.[8]

The fragmentary Panathenaic in Halle is contemporary with the Burgon or little later, but of much better quality.[9] The inscription is not preserved, but there can be little doubt that this was a prize-vase. Not much of the Athena remains, but we have the greater part of the picture on the reverse, three sturdy sprinters, a youth and two men (pl. 17, 1). Above them is part of an inscription, the end of the word ἀνδρῶν, "of men."[10] This is a splendid early example of the running attitude which first appears at this time:[11] the forward leg raised so that the thigh is horizontal and the foot well advanced, the arm of the same side of the body raised, both upper arms horizontal, and the forearms at right angles. (Here the back leg too, as often, is raised from the ground.) The suggestion of thunderous speed is even stronger than in the later runners by Lydos on the shoulder of his hydria (pl. 17, 2).* The Halle Panathenaic has been attributed to Lydos himself, and it has much in common with him, but is not certainly, I think, his. The design on the neck of the vase is floral, but not yet of canonical type.

From the other Panathenaics of this earliest period only fragments survive. Good part of a very early Panathenaic has been found in the American excavations of the Athenian Agora.[12] The Athena is of the same build as on the Burgon vase, and, as there, the sole of the back foot as well as the front one is planted firmly on the ground, which gives a very earthbound effect. The aegis is again bib-like, with fat semicircular frontal-headed snakes. The shield bears a large flower, a kind of marigold, a common device at the time.[13] This amphora was one of the prizes for the pentathlon, for the second picture alludes to three of the five events: the javelin, the discus, the long jump with weights, haltēres, in the hands. A fourth man, facing the other three, may have been either another javelin-thrower or the judge with his wand. The inscription is missing, but this too was doubtless a prize-vase.

Good fragments from the Acropolis of Athens give glimpses of short Athenas and thickset athletes,[14] but the next complete vase is in Florence (pl. 18).[15] It has several unusual features. There are no columns yet: the inscription, τῶν ᾽Αθήνηθεν ἄθλων, is on the back of the vase instead of on the front, and runs horizontally instead of vertically, and on the front of the vase a naked man stands facing Athena with a fillet in his hand.[16] The vigorous picture on the reverse shows that the event was the chariot-race. The driver in Greece was sometimes the owner and sometimes not.[17] In any case the man on the front of the vase must be the victor, that is, the owner. One might not expect the victor in the chariot-race to be shown naked, but there does not seem to be any other explanation; the man has the same nudity as a marble kouros. Athena still has the cap-helmet and the large

---

* See p. 47 above.

round aegis-snakes; but one heel is ever so slightly raised from the ground, the long aegis covers back as well as breast, and, as often later, two garments are worn. The shape is now canonical, and the floral band on the neck is of the accepted type. The painter is in all probability Lydos: the style of drawing is very like him, especially as he is seen in a late and eccentric work, the oinochoë in Berlin,[18] and there we find the same profusion of sharp folds at the lower edge of garments. We have already mentioned part of a later Panathenaic amphora by Lydos, the fragment with sprinters at the University of Chicago;* we cannot be sure, of course, that it was inscribed.

A Panathenaic amphora in the British Museum (pl. 49, 1-3) is interesting for two reasons.[19] First, in subject as well as shape it is at last canonical: Athena raises one heel from the ground, which gives the figure swing; wears an aegis covered with scales and trimmed with smaller serpents; and is flanked by two columns surmounted by cocks. The columns perhaps refer to her temple, but possibly they are only there to support the cocks. The cocks are there as symbols of the fighting spirit; the cock, in the words of the poet Ion, "smitten in body and both eyes, forgets not his courage; though fainting, he crows":

οὐδ' ὅ γε σῶμα τυπεὶς διφυεῖς τε κόρας ἐπιλάθεται ἀλκᾶς
ἀλλ' ὀλιγοδρανέων φθογγάζεται.[20]

Secondly, the artist is the first who is known to have painted *many* Panathenaics; it is plain that he specialised in them, since we have ten by him, including two fragments. He has come to be called the Euphiletos Painter from the inscription Εὐφίλητος καλός which surrounds the chariot-wheel here emblazoned on the shield (pl. 49, 1).[21] It may seem odd to find a kalos-inscription on an official prize-vase, but a century later, if the story is true, Pheidias himself wrote Παντάρκης καλός on the finger of his Zeus at Olympia. The Athena of the Euphiletos Painter is an energetic figure, still short in the leg; there are many folds in the two garments; and the cap-helmet has been replaced by a less simple form with frontlet, neckpiece, and floral ornament on the skull. The detail photograph shows the nutcracker features and the quiff (pl. 49, 2). The vase was a prize for the pentathlon, three events of which are indicated in the second picture, the javelin, the discus, and the jump with haltēres. The athletes are taller and leaner than before, and there is a mixture of liveliness and stiffness in their attitudes (pl. 49, 3). The Panathenaic by this painter in Leyden is also a pentathlon vase.[22] The events are the same as in the London Panathenaic, but the attitudes of the jumper and acontist are even more violent, while the discus-thrower is in the contorted posture that follows the one depicted on the London vase. The shield-device, partly repainted, is a lion attacking a deer. One of the other

* See p. 47 above.

Panathenaics by the Euphiletos Painter represents the chariot-race, and four of them the foot-races, long distance and short. The best of our artist's sprints is on his Panathenaic in New York;[23] the movement is less tempestuous than on the early vase in Halle, although our painter was probably not thinking either of a longer distance or of a less crucial moment in the race. The drawing of the faces is mannered. The parts between breast and hip are still rendered in the summary fashion of early times. The date of these vases should be about 530.

A good foot-race by another artist of this period is on the Panathenaic in Copenhagen;[24] the date should be about 525, contemporary with work by the Andokides Painter. The Athena is slenderer and less emphatic than the Euphiletan. The shield-device is a large eye. The foot of the vase seems wrongly attached.

A fine Panathenaic in Nauplia is not far from the Andokides Painter himself;[25] the artist, the Mastos Painter, was one of his companions. The Athena is not completely preserved. Device, a triskeles. The picture on the reverse of the vase is one of the most attractive on any Panathenaic (pl. 37). The victory is in a horse-race and the winning horse is being led in. Jockeys were small boys in Greece, as they sometimes are today. They were not always professionals: Pausanias saw at Olympia the statues, by a noted fourth-century sculptor, Daidalos of Sicyon, of one Timon and his son Aisypos, a boy on horseback; Timon had won not only the chariot-race, but also the horse-race with his son up.[26] On the Nauplia vase the boy holds a pair of long branches; the man beside the horse passes one hand between the reins and the horse's clammy neck, and with the other adjusts a fillet on the reins. Thus the horse too receives recognition. (We remember the praise of the race-horse Pherenikos in Pindar and Bacchylides, the statues of race-horses recorded by Pausanias and in the Anthology,[27] and the fourth-century marble reliefs, in Athens and in the British Museum, in which a horse is being crowned.)[28] A man stands in front of the horse, patting its face and holding a wreath and branches. A youth stands behind the horse holding out a branch. I am inclined to think that the man beside the horse is the trainer; but the owner is the man who pats the horse; and the youth, his son.

The picture likest this in subject is on a vase of somewhat earlier style in the British Museum.[29] The shape is Panathenaic, although the proportions are different, but this cannot have been a prize at the Panathenaea. A boy, wearing a short chiton, and mounted on a horse, is followed by a youth who carries a wreath, and bears on his head a tripod, the prize; a man stands in front of the rider and announces that "the horse of Dysniketos wins" (the proper name is badly misspelt). Athena appears on the front of the vase in the prescribed attitude, but she is accompanied by Hermes and another male figure. The prize, not oil but a tripod, shows that the games referred to are not the Panathenaea. The artist is the Swing Painter, a curious minor painter, and this is one of his less comic works.[30]

There are no inscribed Panathenaics by the Antimenes Painter; there are uninscribed, unofficial ones, and a prize-vase in Boulogne is by a painter related to him.[31] The athletes are wrestlers, and illustrate the beginning of the throw known as the cross-buttock. There are two onlookers; one is the judge or trainer with his wand, the other a spectator leaning on his stick. The wrestlers are of heavy build, and one of them like many wrestlers has his hair shaved in front.* The shield-device, partly repainted, is an anchor.

We are now nearing the end of the sixth century, and there are three good Panathenaics from the Leagros Group. The Athena on the New York vase[32] has changed costume, and wears a chiton instead of a peplos. The rim of the shield is no longer red, but black with red dots. The shield-device in all three Panathenaics of the Leagros Group is a siren, and henceforth each painter tends to confine himself to one device. On the reverse, one of our best pictures of the horse-race (pl. 44, 1). Three jockeys, on powerful horses, pass the post. (The head of one boy is missing, except the hair of the forehead.) They use long cut sticks instead of the usual whip. They ride, of course, without saddles or stirrups; spurs were sometimes worn, but are not represented on Panathenaic vases. The two other Panathenaics of the same style, one in Sparta,[33] one in Taranto,[34] were awarded for the chariot-race, and the artist has chosen the perilous moment of turning round the post. At Olympia the post was turned twenty-three times, and each time there was a chance of coming to grief, as we remember, for example, from the *Elektra* of Sophocles. The wheels of the chariot are in three-quarter view, the bodies of the trace-horses foreshortened or at least diminished, the breasts of the pole-horses three-quartered and their faces frontal. The three-quarter view of chariots wheeling round comes in before this, in the period of Group E, but is especially appropriate to pictures of a race. The Leagros Group corresponds in black-figure to the red-figure work of the great pioneers, Euphronios, Phintias, Euthymides, and it has been plausibly suggested that a small fragment of a Panathenaic, found on the Acropolis, in Athens, may be black-figure by Euphronios.[35]

The next period is late archaic red-figure: the two great pot-painters of the period (as opposed to cup-painters) are the Kleophrades Painter, whose name has now been proved to be Epiktetos—Epiktetos the Second,—and the Berlin Painter, whose name is still unknown. Both of them painted black-figure prize Panathenaics, and the finest Panathenaics of the period, as might be expected, are theirs. A third red-figure artist who painted Panathenaics is the Eucharides Painter, and as a general rule the prize Panathenaics of the fifth century can be shown to be by red-figure artists,

---

* See p. 73 above.

not by a special class of black-figure artists producing prize-vases and nothing else, nor yet by any of those humble black-figure painters who were active in the first half of the fifth century. In the fourth century the same rule very likely held good, although it has not yet been found possible to assign a fourth-century prize vase to a particular red-figure painter.

There are seven Panathenaics by the Kleophrades Painter, besides some fragments, and a good many others are either from his hand or in his manner.[36] It would be natural to expect, considering the number of replicas required in the production of Panathenaic amphorae, that some of the work would be turned over to copyists, but this does not seem to have been common. Two of the Kleophrades Painter's Panathenaics are in New York. One of them has a chariot on the reverse, the other a pair of pancratiasts. The Athena on the chariot-vase (pl. 45, 2)[37] shows how much character could be imparted to the traditional figure; as one might anticipate from his red-figure work, no Panathenaic Athenas give such an impression of power as the Kleophrades Painter's. This is partly due to the sit of the figure and to the proportions, partly to the massive forms, both in body and in head; in the head the large ear and nostril and thick lips are Kleophradean. Even the lettering is exceptionally bold. The shield-device is always a Pegasus. The charioteer on the reverse is not very well preserved. The second New York vase[38] has a scene from the pancration, which was an all-in combination of wrestling and boxing. One man has kicked the other, who catches his opponent's foot, passes his hand under his leg, and tilts him backwards. A judge or trainer stands watching, holding the forked wand of his office. A third vase, in Munich, was a prize for the pentathlon (pl. 45, 1).[39] The man in the middle stands with one leg frontal, holding a pair of haltēres, jumping-weights; his companion prepares to throw the javelin; the third figure is again a judge. These powerfully built athletes are the brothers of those on red-figured vases by the Kleophrades Painter, such as his calyx-krater in Tarquinia.[40] It will be noticed that the anatomy of the middle of the body is now fully carried out. Fragments from the Acropolis give a good head of Athena by this artist, and parts of another event, the long-distance foot-race.[41]

The Eucharides Painter is an able artist of the second class, and his Panathenaics are sound.[42] His vases in London and Toronto[43] were both prizes for the horse-race. The small jockeys ply the whip, and one of them looks round, as often in ancient pictures, although the practice is said to be discouraged on the modern race-course. Athena now has a distinct sleeve. Her shield-device in both vases is a snake.

The Panathenaics by the Berlin Painter are more important.[44] His prize-vases belong to his latest period, after 480; it is as if he received the contract after the Kleophrades Painter had given up this class of work. We possess a long series of prize-vases the earlier of which are by the Berlin Painter, the later by a pupil and follower, also a great red-figure artist, the Achilles Painter. These take us well into the classic period, to 440 B.C. or even later. The earliest of the Berlin Painter's Panathenaics is in the Marquess of Northampton's collection at Castle Ashby.[45] The Athena is slenderer than the Kleophrades Painter's, with a long face and neck. On the skirt of the sleeved chiton groups of massed vertical folds alternate with void spaces as in the later among the red-figure vases of the Berlin Painter. The shield-rim is set with small, dense, red dots. The device, as always in the Berlin Achilles series, is a gorgoneion. The other picture represents the long-distance foot-race, four tall elegant figures (pl. 44, 2). The post is shown, but this is not the finish, only the turn; there is thus hope that the elderly man who is running fourth, but well within himself, will forge ahead and win after all. While three of the runners raise the forward leg, as is usual in the art of the sixth and fifth centuries, one of them raises the back leg, which is rare until the second half of the fifth.[46] Rare also, so early, that the arm-leg movement, as in nature, is diagonal; in all four figures left leg and right arm move forward together, and right leg and left arm.[47] Lastly, the three-quarter views of breast and back are well executed. All these particulars contribute to the appearance of ease and grace.

The Athena of the Panathenaic in the Czartoryski collection at Castle Goluchow[48] differs only in minor details. The reverse represents a horse-race: graceful horses with small heads; slender boys using sticks instead of whips; one of them looking back. On the Vatican Panathenaic,[49] in which there is some repainting, the subject is the boys' sprint; here again the arm-leg movement is crosswise in most of the figures and in two of them the shoulders are in three-quarter back-view. The next stage is illustrated by the amphora in Benghazi,[50] where the men's sprint resembles the boys' sprint on the Vatican vase, and the Athena differs only in being taller and thinner.

Two Panathenaics, found together in a tomb at Bologna, and now in the Museum there, are by the Achilles Painter and, as we said, not earlier than 440.[51] The Athena (device still a gorgoneion) is a repetition of that at Benghazi, and the men's sprint is much the same as there, but the hand is unmistakably the Achilles Painter's. The other Bologna vase relates to the long-distance race for boys, but the picture consists of two groups, not thought of as simultaneous. On the left are two boys running, one sprinting to overtake the other; on the right, the victor, holding branches in his hands, stands frontal and looks up at a man who may be a trainer, although he is not characterised as such. Another sprint by the Achilles Painter is on a fragmentary Panathenaic in the Robinson Collection at Oxford, Mississippi.[52] Three others, all fragmentary, in the same collection, are later, about 430, and by another artist;[53] the two Athenas that remain are even slimmer than in the Achilles Painter, and the drawing is drier and more formal. The device is Nike proffering a wreath.

The Kuban Group, so called after a vase found in that district of South Russia, brings us to the very end of the fifth century.[54] On a small vase of this group, in the British Museum,[55] the Athena is still more meagre than on the Robinson vases, and even the cocks have become scraggy. The reverse illustrates a new event (of which there are a few other pictures, all from the end of the fifth century and the early part of the fourth): javelin-throwing on horseback, the target a shield fastened to a post. It has been noticed that, entertaining as this may have been, it was not regarded as a very serious athletic performance, since we read that only five amphorae were awarded as the first prize.[56] The full-size Panathenaics of this group are more striking, if that is the word. The vase from the Kuban, in Leningrad (pl. 46, 1–2),[57] has an absurd Athena, with long legs, straight skirt, and on a long neck a tiny head. The florid ornamentation of the garments is in late fifth-century taste at its lowest. The device is a star with a small gorgoneion in the middle. The cocks are scraggy. On the reverse, the end of a boxing-match; the fallen boxer raises his finger in sign of submission. A third boxer, holding a strigil, looks on, and the judge is also present. This is the unbearably trivial style that is common at the end of the fifth century and the beginning of the fourth. In the London chariot-vase by the same painter the garments are even more ornate, and the lower edge of the chiton is decorated with a frieze of dancing-girls.[58] A third vase by the same painter, also in London, was a prize in the pentathlon.[59] The potter has allowed himself to tamper with the shape, and has given the body a melon-like form which happily was not imitated. The device on the shield is interesting; it represents the bronze statues of the Tyrant-slayers, by Kritios and Nesiotes, set up at Athens in the year 476. The same device occurs on two Panathenaics of the same period as ours, but by a different painter, in Hildesheim.[60] It has been argued that the choice of this exceptional device commemorates the expulsion of other tyrants, the Thirty, and the restoration of the democratic regime at Athens, in the autumn of the year 403; the amphorae would then have been offered as prizes at the Panathenaic games of summer, 402.

What will happen now? Will the Athena, and the cocks, grow still thinner? The answer is given by a vase in Berlin, which bears, or bore, its date upon it.[61] In the fourth century it became the practice to inscribe the Panathenaic amphorae with the name of the archon for the year. As we know, from other sources, the archons for every year in the fourth century, we can date the vases exactly. The practice must have been prescribed by a law passed early in the fourth century. It might be thought that the date would be that of the Panathenaea at which the amphora was awarded, but this is not so; the date is that of the collection of the oil.[62] The earliest fairly complete amphora with the archon's name is in Oxford; the archon is Asteios, 373/2 B.C., but a small fragment in Istanbul bears an archon's name which can be restored with certainty as Hippodamas, who held office in 375/4.[63] Now the Berlin Panathenaic also bore an archon-name, but unfortunately all the letters except the final sigma are effaced. The style shows the vase to be earlier than the Asteios amphora, and it is stated that there is space for just seven letters before the sigma, neither less nor more; if so, the archon was Philokles, of 392/1 B.C.[64] The style would suit a date somewhere in that neighbourhood, and the costume of the Athena recalls the Hildesheim vases. In any case the figure is a reaction from the exaggerated Athena of the Kuban Group; the proportions are normal, and the drapery plain. What of the cocks? They were past revival, and have been abolished. Their place on top of the columns is taken by a small design often reproducing a statue; here a figure of Agathos Daimon on the left, and of Agathe Tyche on the right. The "symbols," as they are called, change from year to year, and may be compared, roughly, to the "symbols" on coins. The picture on the reverse of the Berlin vase is again javelin-throwing on horseback, but here the youths wear helmets. The foot of the vase is modern.

The small fragment of 375/4 in Istanbul gives, besides the archon's name, the name of a potter Bakchios,[65] a member of a family about which something is known. Another member of it was the potter Kittos whose signature appears on a Panathenaic in the British Museum (pls. 46, 4 and 47, 1).[66] It is unusual in not bearing the name of the archon—it may have been a competition sample,—but the style of the Athena shows it to be not far from the archonship of Polyzelos, in 367/6 B.C., from which several Panathenaics have been preserved.[67] We have already spoken of the elegant shape, with the innovations, accepted henceforth, in mouth and foot; another novelty is that the traditional rays at the base have disappeared. The costume of Kittos' Athena is very plain, with simple folds; the helmet and crest are more fanciful. The device is a star, and the columns are surmounted by figures of Triptolemos. The inscription, for the first time, is written *kionedon*, the letters horizontal instead of lengthwise. On the reverse, pancration; one youth has the head of the other in chancery. The drawing is accomplished, and elegant to excess: a more unsuitable style for a picture of what was a slightly regulated rough-and-tumble cannot easily be conceived. In the London Panathenaic with the name of the archon Polyzelos, 367/6 B.C.,[68] the goddess resembles the Athena of Kittos, and the shield is the same—device a star, sparse white dots on the rim. The layout of the wrestling-scene on the reverse is much as in the Kittos vase, and the two might go back to a rough sketch by one artist; the style, however, is as different as can be. There is no elegance here; the wrestlers are short, heavy, and unprepossessing.

Sometime between 359 and 348 B.C., a change was made in the Panathenaic Athena, it is not known why, and a new series begins.[69] The goddess now faces right instead of left. The inside of the shield is now shown instead of the outside, and we are deprived in consequence of the shield-device. A good example of the new Athena, though not one of the earliest, is on the Panathenaic in Harvard (pl. 48, 1) which bears the name of the archon Theiophrastos, 340/339 B.C.[70] The skirt is longer; the aegis is reduced to a mere cross-cord with a small gorgoneion (here faded) in the middle, and the garment clings to the breasts as well as to the rest of the figure. A swallow-tailed wrap is worn over the shoulders: this is not a novelty, as it appears on a Panathenaic in Eleusis of the year 363/2 B.C.[71] The swallow-tails are echoed in the lower edges of the over-garment above the knees, and at the ankles in a rudimentary train. The edges are stressed by thick white borders. The swallow-tails do not really correspond to anything archaic, but they become a feature of archaistic work at the beginning of the fourth century and remain so throughout antiquity. Is it quite by chance that this Athena reminds one of early twentieth-century fashion plates? Or may not a Paris designer at his wits' end, desperately turning the pages of a dictionary of art in search of a new and hideous idea, have hit upon a woodcut of a fourth-century Panathenaic amphora, and suddenly warmed at the sight of antiquity at its worst?

This Athena was stereotyped, and was repeated on all Panathenaics from the introduction of the rightward turn. Thenceforth the reverses varied greatly in style, but the obverse was drawn to pattern.

The reverse of the Harvard vase has a very unusual representation (pl. 48, 3). Two boxers are seen, not fighting, but receiving instructions from an official before the match (rather, I suppose, than being warned for infringing the rules). On the left is a female figure leaning on a pillar, looking round towards the athletes, with her face in three-quarter view. The himation is drawn tightly round the whole body, and, as often in the fourth century, covers chin and mouth. An inscription informs us that this is Olympias, the personification of the athletic festival at Olympia. It is surprising to find Olympias depicted on a prize awarded at another sports meeting, the Panathenaea. It can only mean that the victor in the boxing contest at the Panathenaea stands a good chance of winning the still more important contest at Olympia two years later; Olympias, as it were, has her eye on the pair. Modern parallels will occur, and we think of Pindar's odes, in which the poet often contrives, as has been said, to congratulate an athlete on an Olympic victory which he might have won.[72] In his tenth Nemean ode he actually speaks of a victory at the Panathenaea as being a "prelude" to a victory at Olympia.[73] The presence of Olympias on the reverse of the Harvard vase is perhaps answered by the presence of Zeus, in whose honour the

Olympic games were held, as a symbol on the obverse: on the left column, a figure of Athena; on the right column, Zeus, sceptred, holding Nike on his hand. The figures are tall, with small heads: these are already the so-called Lysippean proportions of the late fourth century. It is characteristic, too, of that period that three of the four figures front the spectator.

The next year from which Panathenaic amphorae have survived is the archonship of Pythodelos, 336/5, four years later than the Harvard vase. On a Panathenaic with this name in the British Museum[74] the Athena is the same, but the symbols are changed: the small figure of Athena on the left-hand column holds an *aphlaston*—stern-ornament of a ship—on which an owl is perched; the other symbol is Triptolemos sitting in his winged car, with a "bakchos" beside him—the bundle of branches carried by initiates at Eleusis.[75] The reverse has a pair of boxers again, but in action (pl. 47, 2). On the left, a third boxer, perhaps the winner of the other semi-final, watches; on the right, a female figure, as in the Harvard vase: Nike, dressed in white chiton and dark mantle, holds a palm-branch. The boxers have small bullet-heads, thick limbs, and heavy, gross bodies with thick waists; this is a new ideal. There is another novelty; the boxers wear the new heavy glove, while those of the Theiophrastos amphora still wore the old light hand-covering consisting of a simple soft thong. The new glove must have been introduced at the Panathenaea between 339 and 336; at the Panathenaea, and about the same time at all the great athletic meetings, including Olympia.[76] The terrible new glove, and the changed physical type of the boxers, are both symptomatic of a certain trend in the sporting thought of the time; the aged Plato, it will be remembered, had favoured the heavy glove for the young men. On the neck of the vase, an olive-wreath is substituted for the traditional ornament. There is only one other Panathenaic with an olive-wreath;[77] the innovation did not find favour. Another fruitless experiment was made in the same year. On a second vase with the name of Pythodelos in London,[78] and another in Munich,[79] the upper part of the Athena is the same as usual, but the feet are close together, and the effect of a hobble-skirt is obtained (pl. 46, 3). On the reverse, the race in armour, four ponderous athletes in the same taste as the brute boxers. In the amphora from the year of the archon Niketes, 332/1, in the British Museum,[80] the Athena, though of the usual type, is a little simpler; the artist has pared away the train at the ankles and the projecting end at the thigh. In the pancration on the reverse, one man has again his opponent's head in chancery; he catches it in the crook of his arm and pummels it. The referee is ready to intervene if necessary, and there is a third athlete. He gazes out of the picture, and the whole composition has that frontal tendency to which we have referred.[81] A little later is the Panathenaic in the British Museum from the year of the archon Euthykritos, 328/7:[82] it is not very well preserved, but deserves a glance because it shows that even at this late period the sprinter might still be represented, as in early times, with left leg and left arm both advanced. All four runners, however, set the forward foot on the ground and raise the back leg; this scheme has at last driven out the more violent one in which the forward leg is raised. On a Panathenaic in Leningrad, the back foot is again lifted, but the arm-leg movement is diagonal.[83] The archon's name is lost, but the style is so like that of a Panathenaic which bears the archon-name Neaichmos that the date should be the same, 320/319 B.C.

The last archon's name to appear, on a small fragment of an extant Panathenaic, is Polemon, 312/311.[84] Just how much longer the practice persisted is not established; Hellenistic Panathenaics bear the names of other, minor magistrates, the tamias, the agonothetes, whose dates are seldom known.[85] The official inscription τῶν Ἀθήνηθεν ἄθλων was still used in the second century B.C. A second-century Panathenaic in Berlin, although uninscribed, was doubtless a prize at the Panathenaea (pl. 49, 4).[86] The fourth-century Panathenaics, however one may judge the style of the drawing, are handsome pieces of pottery, skilfully fashioned, technically sound, with fine colour and surface; in the Hellenistic period the technique has collapsed. In the Berlin amphora one recognises the old shape, but caricatured: the traditional Athena, but debased and furnished with a baroque Corinthian helmet instead of the Attic. Of the horses it were well to say nothing. Red-figure had long been extinct: this is the end of black-figure. We have followed its story, in the Panathenaic amphora, from the days of Peisistratos to the days of Kleisthenes, of Themistokles, of Kimon, of Perikles, of Alcibiades, of Kallistratos, of Demosthenes, of Lachares, of Chremonides, of Eurykleides, of Kephisodoros. Looking back over the distance we have travelled in earlier chapters, we see the age of Kleisthenes, beyond it the ages of Peisistratos and Solon, beyond those the seventh century, and beyond that, ages in which although almost everything is misty this small plot of ground is clear.

NOTES

LIST OF ABBREVIATIONS USED

(NOTE: in references to the *Corpus Vasorum*, for the sake of brevity, the name of the collection and the commonest rubric—III He—are omitted. If the rubric is not III He, for instance III Hf or III Ic, the necessary letters are added.)

ABC.	*Antiquités du Bosphore cimmérien.*
ABS.	Beazley *Attic Black-figure: A Sketch.*
AD.	*Antike Denkmäler.*
Adamek.	*Unsignierte Vasen des Amasis.*
AEM.	*Archaeologisch-epigraphische Mittheilungen aus Oesterreich.*
AJA.	*American Journal of Archaeology.*
Albizzati.	*Vasi antichi dipinti del Vaticano.*
AM.	*Mitteilungen des Deutschen Archäologischen Instituts: Athenische Abteilung.*
Annali.	*Annali dell'Instituto di Corrispondenza Archeologica.*
Ant. class.	*L'Antiquité classique.*
Anz.	*Archäologischer Anzeiger* (part of *Jb.*, q.v.).
ARV.	Beazley *Attic Red-figure Vase-painters*
Ashm. Rep.	*Ashmolean Museum, Report of the Visitors.*
AZ.	*Archäologische Zeitung.*
BCH.	*Bulletin de correspondance hellénique.*
Berl.	Beazley *Der Berliner Maler.*
Bieber *HT.*	*The History of the Greek and Roman Theater.*
——— *Th.*	*Die Denkmäler zum Theaterwesen im Altertum.*
Bloesch *AKS.*	*Antike Kunst in der Schweiz.*
——— *FAS.*	*Formen attischer Schalen.*
BMQ.	*British Museum Quarterly.*
Brönsted.	*Mémoire sur les vases panathénaïques.*
BSA.	*Annual of the British School at Athens.*
BSR.	*Papers of the British School at Rome.*
Bull.	*Bullettino degli Annali dell'Instituto.*
Bull. Metr. Mus.	*Bulletin of the Metropolitan Museum.*
Bull. MFA.	*Bulletin of the Museum of Fine Arts, Boston.*
Bull. Vereen.	*Bulletin van de Vereeniging tot Bevordering der Kennis van de Antieke Beschaving.*
Burl. 1888.	*Burlington Fine Arts Club. Catalogue of Objects of Greek Ceramic Art. 1888.*
Burl. 1903.	*Burlington Fine Arts Club. Exhibition of Ancient Greek Art, 1903* (published 1904).

Burl. Mag.	*Burlington Magazine.*
Buschor *Vasen.*	*Griechische Vasen.*
Caskey *G.*	*Geometry of Greek Vases.*
Cl. Rh.	*Clara Rhodos.*
CC.	Collignon and Couve *Catalogue des vases peints du Musée National d'Athènes.*
CR.	*Classical Review.*
CV.	*Corpus Vasorum Antiquorum.*
Cypr.	Beazley *Some Attic Vases in the Cyprus Museum.*
El. cer.	Lenormant and de Witte *Élite des monuments céramographiques.*
Enc. phot.	*Encyclopédie photographique de l'Art: le Musée du Louvre.*
Eph.	*Ephemeris arkhaiologike.*
EVP.	Beazley *Etruscan Vase-painting.*
FD.	*Fouilles de Delphes.*
FR.	Furtwängler and Reichhold *Griechische Vasenmalerei.*
Furtwängler *AG.*	*Die antiken Gemmen.*
——— *KS.*	*Kleine Schriften.*
Gardiner, Norman. *Athl.*	*Athletics of the Ancient World.*
——— *GAS.*	*Greek Athletic Sports.*
Gerhard *AV.*	*Auserlesene Vasenbilder.*
——— *EKV.*	*Etruskische und kampanische Vasenbilder.*
——— *TG.*	*Trinkschalen und Gefäße des Königlichen Museums zu Berlin.*
Graef.	Graef and Langlotz *Die antiken Vasen von der Akropolis zu Athen.*
Gründel.	*Die Darstellung des Laufens in der griechischen Kunst.*
Hafner.	*Viergespanne in Vorderansicht.*
Hampe *FGS.*	*Fruehe griechische Sagenbilder.*
Haspels *ABL.*	*Attic Black-figured Lekythoi.*
Hesp.	*Hesperia.*
Hoppin *Bf.*	*A Handbook of Greek Black-figured Vases.*
——— *Rf.*	*A Handbook of Attic Red-figured Vases.*
Izv. Mat. Kult.	*Izvêstiya Akademii Istorii Materialnoi Kulturi.*
Jacobsthal *ECA.*	*Early Celtic Art.*
——— *O.*	*Ornamente griechischer Vasen.*

Jb.   *Jahrbuch des Deutschen Archäologischen Instituts.*

Jh.   *Jahreshefte des Oesterreichischen Archäologischen Institutes.*

JHS.   *Journal of Hellenic Studies.*

Johansen *Iliaden.   Iliaden i tidlig graesk Kunst.*

Kl.   Beazley *Der Kleophrades Maler.*

Lane *GP.   Greek Pottery.*

Langlotz.   *Martin von Wagner-Museum der Universität Würzburg: Griechische Vasen.*

Manch. Mem.   Memoirs and Proceedings of the Manchester Literary and Philosophical Society.

Masner.   *Die Sammlung antiker Vasen im K.K. Oesterreichischen Museum.*

Merlin.   *Vases grecs.*

Metr. Mus. St.   Metropolitan Museum Studies.

Micali *St.   Storia degli antichi popoli italiani.*

Millingen *AUM.   Ancient Unedited Monuments.*

Mingazzini *Cast.   Vasi della Collezione Castellani.*

ML.   Monumenti antichi pubblicati per cura della Reale Accademia dei Lincei.

Mon.   Monumenti inediti pubblicati dall' Instituto di Corrispondenza Archeologica.

Mon. Piot.   Fondation Eugène Piot. Monuments et Mémoires publiés par l'Académie des Inscriptions et Belles-Lettres.

Mus. Greg.   Museum Etruscum Gregorianum (ed. 1842).

Mus. Journ.   The Museum Journal (Philadelphia).

Neugebauer.   *Führer durch das Antiquarium:* ii, *Vasen.*

—— *ADP.   Antiken in deutschem Privatbesitz.*

Payne *NC.   Necrocorinthia.*

—— *Protokor.   Protokorinthische Vasenmalerei.*

Pellegrini *VF.   Catalogo dei vasi greci dipinti delle necropoli felsinee.*

Perrot.   Perrot and Chipiez *Histoire de l'art dans l'antiquité.*

Peters.   *Studien zu den panathenäischen Preisamphoren.*

Pfuhl.   *Malerei und Zeichnung der Griechen.*

—— *Mast.   Masterpieces of Greek Drawing and Painting.*

Pottier.   *Vases antiques du Louvre.*

PP.   Beazley Potter and Painter in Ancient Athens.

Quagliati *Mus. Tar.   Il Museo Nazionale di Taranto.*

RA.   Revue archéologique.

REA.   Revue des études anciennes.

REG.   Revue des études grecques.

Rend. Acc. Linc.   Rendiconti della R. Accademia dei Lincei.

RG.   Beazley and Magi La raccolta Benedetto Guglielmi nel Museo Gregoriano Etrusco.

Richter *AAC.   Archaic Attic Gravestones.*

—— *Craft.   The Craft of Athenian Pottery.*

Richter and Hall.   *Red-figured Athenian Vases in the Metropolitan Museum of Art.*

Richter and Milne.   *Shapes and Names of Athenian Vases.*

de Ridder.   *Catalogue des vases peints de la Bibliothèque Nationale.*

RM.   Mitteilungen des Deutschen Archäologischen Instituts: Römische Abteilung.

Robinson and Harcum.   *A Catalogue of the Greek Vases in the Royal Ontario Museum of Archaeology, Toronto.*

Rumpf *Sak.   Sakonides.*

Schaal *Rf.   Griechische Vasen: rotfigurig.*

—— *Sf.   Griechische Vasen: schwarzfigurig.*

Schefold *U.   Untersuchungen zu den Kertscher Vasen.*

Schmidt, E.   *Archaistische Kunst.*

Smith, Cecil H. *Forman.   The Forman Collection. Sotheby, June 19, 1899.*

Süsserott.   *Griechische Plastik des 4. Jahrhunderts vor Christus.*

Swindler.   *Ancient Painting.*

Technau.   *Exekias.*

Thiersch *Tyrrh.   "Tyrrhenische" Amphoren.*

Univ. Mus. Bull.   University Museum Bulletin (Philadelphia).

VA.   Beazley Attic Red-figure Vases in American Museums.

V. Pol.   Beazley Vases in Poland.

Waldhauer *KO.   Imperatorskii Ermitazh. Kratkoe opisanie sobraniya antichnikh raspisnikh vaz.*

Walters.   *Catalogue of the Greek and Etruscan Vases in the British Museum,* ii.

Watzinger. *Griechische Vasen in Tübingen.*

WV.   Wiener Vorlegeblätter.

My own writings are quoted without surname.

NOTES

CHAPTER I
THE ROAD TO BLACK-FIGURE

[1] Payne *NC.* p. 7.

[2] Athens, Ceramicus Museum, inv. 1073: Kübler *Kerameikos iv* pl. 10, 1, whence Lane *GP.* pl. 3, b.

[3] Berlin: *AM.* 43 pl. 1 (Schweitzer).

[4] Athens 804: *Jb.* 14 p. 201; Pfuhl fig. 10; Merlin pl. 1; Buschor *Vasen* p. 14; part of the chief picture, Lane *GP.* pl. 5, b.

[5] Torr in *RA.* 25 (1894) pp. 14–27; Köster *Das antike Seewesen* figs. 21–27; Chamoux in *RA.* 23 (1945) pp. 56–97; Kirk "Ships on Geometric Vases" in *BSA.* 44 pp. 93–153.

[6] Sydney 46.41: Chittenden and Seltman *Greek Art: A Commemorative Catalogue* pl. 8; *Handbook to the Nicholson Museum* ed. 2 p. 244 (Trendall).

[7] On Late Geometric, Proto-Attic, and earliest black-figure: J. M. Cook in *BSA.* 35 pp. 165–219 and 42 pp. 139–155; also Gebauer and Eilmann *CV. Berlin 1*, reviewed by J. M. Cook in *JHS.* 59 pp. 151–152 and by R. S. Young in *AJA.* 1939 pp. 714–715.

[8] Athens 810: *AM.* 17 pl. 10, 1–2 and pp. 209 and 214 (Pernice), whence (part) Perrot 10 p. 58; CC. pl. 19, 467. Pernice observed that it led on to the Analatos hydria (below, note 11); see also J. M. Cook in *BSA.* 42 p. 146.

[9] Oxford 1935.18: *Ashm. Rep.* 1935 pl. 1; detail, *BSA.* 35 p. 182 fig. 5.

[10] London 1936.10–17.1: *BMQ.* 11 pls. 18 and 19a (Martin Robertson). On this and the last see also *BSA.* 42 p. 150 (J. M. Cook).

[11] Athens 313: *Jb.* 2 pl. 3, and pl. 4, below, r. (Böhlau), whence (part) Perrot 10, 59–61, Pfuhl fig. 79; side, Merlin pl. 17, 1; part, *BSA.* 35 pl. 38, b and pl. 39, with p. 166 (J. M. Cook); part, Buschor *Vasen* p. 36 fig. 42. On the Analatos Painter, J. M. Cook in *BSA.* 35 pp. 172–176 and 42 p. 142.

[12] The pupil of the centaur's eye is slightly damaged. The picture on B is similar, but birds take the place of the plant on the left. Below, five full-sized horses and under one of the "goat-horn" handles a small one. Fragments of a lid may belong: on the lid, lines, bands of zigzags like those below the horses, and a few small birds.

[13] Virgil *Aen.* 7, 674.

[14] Cambridge 30.2: *CV.* 2 pl. 15, 8. With this and the Elgin vase compare also the ovoid krater Berlin A 16 (*CV.* 1 pl. 7, 2 and pl. 8, 1).

[15] Louvre: *Mon. Piot* 36 pl. 2 and pp. 28–29 and 37 (Audiat), whence (A) Buschor *Vasen* p. 37.

Attributed to the Analatos Painter by J. M. Cook (*BSA.* 35 p. 173).

[16] Athens: Waldstein *Argive Heraeum* 2 pl. 67 (Hoppin); *BSA.* 35 pl. 52 with p. 191 (J. M. Cook). See also *AM.* 41 pp. 243–50 (Wrede).

[17] J. M. Cook in *BSA.* 35 p. 191.

[18] Kunze *Neue Meisterwerke griechischer Kunst aus Olympia* figs. 4–5.

[19] New York 11.210.1: *JHS.* 32 pls. 10–12 and pp. 372–373 and 377 (Richter), whence Pfuhl figs. 86–87; *ABS.* pl. 2, 1–2, with p. 9; A, Buschor *Vasen* p. 36 fig. 44. See also *AM.* 41 pp. 243–250 (Wrede) and *BSA.* 35 p. 192 (J. M. Cook).

[20] Berlin A 42: Karo *26 Hallisches Winckelmannsprogramm* pl. 1 and pp. 10–11; *CV.* 1 pls. 31–33. For the subject see *AM.* 62 p. 135 (Karouzou).

[21] Athens, Agora: *AJA.* 1936 p. 194 fig. 10.

[22] Athens, Acropolis 368: Graef pl. 13; combined by Gebauer with other fragments and tentatively ascribed to the Painter of the Ram Jug (*CV.* Berlin 1 p. 7 no. 14).

[23] Rome, Conservatori: Pfuhl figs. 64–65; Hoppin *Bf.* p. 7; Merlin pl. 11, 1; see *BSA.* 44 pp. 120–121 (Kirk).

[24] *JHS.* 53 p. 282; *BSA.* 43 pl. 38, 534 and pl. 39 (Martin Robertson).

[25] Palermo: *ML.* 32 pls. 79–80, pl. 81, 1 and p. 303.

[25] Athens 192: *AM.* 6 pl. 3 (= Furtwängler *KS.* pp. 84–86); whence Perrot 10, 323, *AM.* 18 pl. 10; the inscription also Kirchner *Imagines inscriptionum atticarum* pl. 1, 1.

[27] The Painter of the Ram Jug: *CV. Berlin 1* p. 7 (Gebauer); *BSA.* 35 pp. 189–190 and *JHS.* 59 pp. 151–152 (J. M. Cook). The Menelas vase attributed by J. M. Cook (*BSA.* 35 p. 189). Berlin A 41 (*CV.* 1 pl. 30 and pl. 34, 2) is a stand of the same shape as the Menelas, with another processional scene, but by a different painter; a fragment in Florence, with head and breast of a man to right, should belong to this.

[28] Berlin A 32: *CV.* 1 pls. 18–21, whence (detail) Buschor *Vasen* p. 39. Attributed to the Painter of the Ram Jug by Gebauer (*CV. Berlin 1* p. 7 no. 3).

[29] Next, one of the metopes at Foce del Sele (Zancani Montuoro and Zanotti-Bianco *Heraion alla Foce del Sele*).

[30] See *Jb.* 52 pp. 184–185 (Karouzou).

[31] Compare also the fragmentary figure, near ours in time, on a Cycladic "candlestick" from Delos (Dugas *Délos* 17 pl. 10, 4).

³² Aegina: *AM.* 22 pl. 8 and pp. 325–327 (Pallat); part, *BSA.* 35 pl. 53 with p. 189 (J. M. Cook).

³³ Berlin A 9: *CV.* 1 pl. 5, whence (part) *Dragma* p. 183 (Johansen), (part) *Bull. Vereen.* 14, i, p. 4 figs. 1–2, (part) Buschor *Vasen* p. 38. Tentatively attributed to the Painter of the Ram Jug by Gebauer (*CV.* 1 p. 7 no. 10).

³⁴ *Bull. Vereen.* 14, i, pp. 4–6.

³⁵ Apollodorus 3, 13, 7.

³⁶ Statius *Ach.* 2, 96.

³⁷ *CR.* 54 pp. 177–180.

³⁸ Pind. *Nem.* 3, 48–49.

³⁹ Nonnus *Di.* 34, 145–147.

⁴⁰ *Iphigénie* iv, 1, 12.

⁴¹ Athens: *JHS.* 22 pls. 2–4 (Cecil Smith: the red is the usual dark red); *BSA.* 35 pls. 56–58 with pp. 196–198 (J. M. Cook).

⁴² On early black-figure painters see, besides the works quoted in note 7 above, Payne *NC.* pp. 190–202 and 344–347; *Hesp.* 13 pp. 38–57; Kübler in *Anz.* 1943 pp. 417 ff.

CHAPTER II
EARLY BLACK-FIGURE AND THE C PAINTER

¹ Athens 353: *Eph.* 1897 pls. 5–6, whence Perrot 10 p. 81 and (redrawn and spoilt) 83, and Pfuhl fig. 88; Buschor *Vasen* p. 43. See Payne *NC.* p. 346; J. M. Cook in *BSA.* 35 p. 201.

² Amphora in Athens, Ceramicus Museum: part, *Anz.* 1935 p. 294; *Anz.* 1943 p. 437. Attributed by J. M. Cook (*BSA.* 35 p. 198).

³ The Nessos Painter: *Anz.* 1923–24 pp. 46–49 (Rumpf); *ABS.* pp. 9–11; *BSA.* 35 pp. 200–201 and 205 (J. M. Cook); *Hesp.* 7 pp. 367–371 (Vanderpool); *BCH.* 1938 pp. 443–444 (Karouzou); *Hesp.* 13 p. 39.

⁴ Athens 1002: *AD.* 1 pl. 57 and p. 46, whence Perrot 10, 71 and (redrawn and spoilt) 72–73, and Pfuhl fig. 85 and *ABS.* pl. 3, 1; part of Gorgon, *BCH.* 1938 pl. 46, a; upper part of Nessos, *AM.* 60–61 p. 272; phot. Alinari 24457, whence (the neck) Pfuhl fig. 89 and Merlin pl. 17.2; part, Buschor *Vasen* p. 44; *Hesp.* 13 p. 39 no. 1.

⁵ The chase is over the sea on a late bf. skyphos in a private collection in Hamburg (*Anz.* 1943 pp. 7–8, von Mercklin); and in Eur. *El.* 458.

⁶ On early representations of Perseus, and of the gorgoneion, see Payne *NC.* pp. 79–89 and 362; *AM.* 60–61 pp. 269–299 (Hampe); Besig *Gorgo und Gorgoneion*.

⁷ Athens: I, *BCH.* 1938 pl. 45, a. *Hesp.* 13 p. 39 no. 6. Attributed by Karouzou.

⁸ The incised sketch appears on another vase belonging to the same group as the Nessos vase,

namely, the skyphos-krater with Prometheus, from Vari, in Athens. I have not noticed it on vases earlier than these.

⁹ Leipsic. Probably from an amphora. *Anz.* 1923–24 p. 46. *Hesp.* 13 p. 39 no. 3. Attributed by Rumpf.

¹⁰ Berlin 1682: *AZ.* 1882 pls. 9–10, whence Perrot 10 pp. 75–79 and (part) *CV.* 1 p. 38; Neugebauer pl. 8, 2; part, *CV.* pls. 46–47. *Hesp.* 13 p. 39 no. 4. Attributed by Rumpf. On the shape, *Jh.* 29 p. 126 no. 9 (Kenner).

¹¹ The Protocorinthian aryballos in Oxford (146: *JHS.* 24 p. 295, whence Pfuhl fig. 168; *CV.* 2 III C pl. 1, 5, 36, and 51) is dated by Payne at the end of the first quarter of the seventh century. Attic: Acropolis 604 (Graef pl. 29); and vases by the C Painter. I do not go into the date of the earliest Attic coins with the head of Athena, helmeted; but it would be somewhat surprising if they were much earlier than the first armed Athena on Attic vases.

¹² Agora P 1247: A, *Hesp.* 2 p. 457; *Hesp.* 7 pp. 368–371. *Hesp.* 13 p. 39 no. 2.

¹³ Hamburg 1917.229: *Anz.* 1928 p. 297. *ABS.* p. 11 and *Hesp.* 13 p. 39 no. 5.

¹⁴ Sirens: see Buschor *Die Musen des Jenseits.*

¹⁵ Chimaera Painter: *Hesp.* 13 p. 40.

¹⁶ Aegina: *Hesp.* 13 p. 40 no. 1.

¹⁷ London A 1531: B, *BCH.* 1898 p. 285; A and side, Jacobsthal *O.* pl. 7.

¹⁸ Ceramicus 154: *Anz.* 1943 pp. 433–436. Attributed by Kübler.

¹⁹ Athens: part, *AJA.* 1937 pl. 8; part, *Anz.* 1940 p. 130; part, *BCH.* 1939 pls. 49–50. *Hesp.* 13 p. 40, left. It is not certain that the lid belongs to the bowl, or the stand to either. According to Kübler (*Anz.* 1943 pp. 435–436) the stand is alien. The stand is by the Chimaera Painter; the lid and bowl may also be his.

²⁰ Athens: *Soc. Friends Nat. Mus.* 1934–35 p. 12 fig. 9a; Buschor *Vasen* p. 45.

²¹ Kübler in *Anz.* 1943 p. 440.

²² Gorgon Painter: Payne *NC.* pp. 191–194 and 340; *AM.* 62 pp. 111–135 (Karouzou); *Hesp.* 13 pp. 40–42; *BSA.* 44 p. 169 (Hopper).

²³ Louvre E 874: Pottier pls. 60–62; *CV.* 2 d pls. 15–17, pl. 14, 3 and pl. 18, 1; Perrot 10 pl. 2 and pp. 117–118; part, Pfuhl fig. 92; part, Merlin pl. 34; phot. Alinari 23688; detail, *AM.* 62 pl. 54, 1; part, *Enc. phot.* 2 pp. 278–279; part, Buschor *Vasen* p. 99; part, Lane *GP.* pl. 34 and pl. 35, b. (*Hesp.* 13 pl. 1, 1 is not from this, but from the amphora Louvre E 817.) *Hesp.* 13 p. 40 no. 1.

²⁴ See Jacobsthal *ECA.* p. 77, and p. 39 of the present work; compare the "whirlwind" basketry

design of the Hopi Indians (M. R. Coolidge, *The Rain-makers*, p. 105, 8).

[25] Middle Protocorinthian—

Aryballos in Syracuse: Johansen *Les Vases sicyoniens* pl. 26, 5: warrior between sphinxes.

Late Protocorinthian—

Aryballos in Taranto, 3090 (Johansen *Les Vases sicyoniens* p. 101 no. 70; Payne *NC*. p. 269 no. 13): swan between sphinxes.

Alabastron in Syracuse: part, Payne *NC*. pl. 10, 2 (with p. 271 no. 30a): swan between sphinxes.

Conical oinochoë from Perachora: Payne *Perachora* 2 pl. 15, 270 (Dunbabin): bull between lion and panther.

Conical oinochoë from Perachora: *ibid*. pl. 15, 264: two sphinxes between two animals and two lions.

Aryballos in Taranto: *CV*. 2 III Cd pl. 1, 7–9: stag between lions. Compare also two aryballoi in Taranto (*CV*. 2 III Cd pl. 1, 1–3 and pl. 3; *ibid*. pl. 1, 4–6).

Earlier are: (1) two animals confronted; (2) the same with a plant between (Geometric); (3) two animals confronted with an animal between, which they attack (early Orientalizing): but the quintet is anticipated by a Late Geometric Attic cup in Athens, 14475 (Kunze *Kretische Bronzereliefs* pl. 53, e), where a wee man is in the maw of two confronted lions, between two bulls.

I owe some of the references in this note to the kindness of T. J. Dunbabin.

[26] Sophilos: Payne *NC*. pp. 62, 74, 105–106, 200, and 346; Karouzou in *AM*. 62 pp. 111–135; *Hesp*. 13 pp. 50–52.

[27] Acropolis 587: Graef pl. 26, whence (inverted) Hoppin *Bf*. p. 337; part, *AM*. 62 pl. 51; part, Buschor *Vasen* p. 102. *Hesp*. 13 p. 50 no. 14. The interpretation: Studniczka in *Eranos Vindobonensis* pp. 233–240.

[28] Athens, stand of a skyphoid krater: *BCH*. 1939 pl. 51, 1.

[29] See Payne *NC*. pp. 14–15.

[30] On these figures see Hampe in *AM*. 60–61 p. 275 (the horizontal line near the tip of the donkey's tail is a chance scratch).

[31] Athens 15499: *Mon. Piot* 33 pp. 44–47 and 49 and pl. 6 (Béquignon), whence (part) Johansen *Iliaden* fig. 9: part, *AM*. 62 pls. 52–53; part, Buschor *Vasen* p. 110. *Hesp*. 13 pp. 50–51 no. 16.

[32] The Games for Patroklos may be represented on the dinos Agora P 334 (*Hesp*. 4 pp. 431–439) and the pyxis fragment Acropolis 2073 (Graef pl. 92), where there is a single athlothetes—Achilles (the hand, however, on the left of the Agora fragment is a difficulty); perhaps also on a fragment of

a hydria, not far from Kleitias, in Samos; and not impossibly on a Protocorinthian aryballos in Syracuse (*ML*. 25 pl. 14, whence Johansen *Iliaden* fig. 10). The picture on the hydria Vienna, Oest. Mus., 220 (Masner p. 23, whence *Jb*. 41 p. 188), is interpreted by Studniczka as representing Diomed victorious in the Games for Patroklos (*Jb*. loc. cit.).

[33] Acropolis 590: Graef pl. 27, *Hesp*. 2 p. 340 (Broneer), *Hesp*. 9 p. 146 (Roebuck) (Games for Pelias). Acropolis 2209: Graef pl. 9, 3. Geneva MF 156, Tyrrhenian ovoid neck-amphora (Thiersch *Tyrrh*. pl. 2, 1–4). See *AJA*. 1950 p. 310.

[34] See *Hesp*. 13 p. 52; on red contours see also Rodenwaldt in *Jb*. 36 p. 1.

[35] Komast Group: Payne *NC*. pp. 194–201; Greifenhagen *Eine attische schwarzfigurige Vasengattung*; *JHS*. 49 pp. 258–260; *Metr. Mus. St.* 5 p. 93; *AJA*. 1941 p. 69 (Amyx); *Hesp*. 13 pp. 45–50.

[36] Athens 528: *Hesp*. 13 pl. 5, 2 (with p. 45 no. 14). New York 22.139.22: Greifenhagen *op. cit*. pl. 1; A, Payne *NC*. pl. 51, 6; B, Richter and Milne fig. 152; Lane *GP*. pl. 35, a: *Hesp*. 13 p. 46 no. 17.

[37] On these, Webster in *Manch. Mem*. 82 pp. 10–12.

[38] On the Komast cups see, besides the works named in n. 35, Villard in *REA*. 48 pp. 155–157; on the Corinthian cup, Hopper in *BSA*. 44 p. 225.

[39] Samos: part, *AM*. 54 pl. 4; another fragment, *AM*. 62 pl. 57, 1. *Hesp*. 13 p. 46 no. 18.

[40] Payne *NC*. p. 118. Compare also the C Painter's Corinthianizing symposia, *Metr. Mus. St.* 5 p. 101.

[41] Samos: here after Buschor *Meermänner* p. 17. Berlin 3987: for the subject see p. 24 of the present work.

[42] Siana cups: *JHS*. 49 p. 260; *JHS*. 51 p. 275; *Metr. Mus. St.* 5 p. 93; Villard in *REA*. 48 (1946) pp. 157–159.

[43] *JHS*. 59 pp. 103–123 (Webster); Dorothy Burr Thompson, *The Charmed Circle in Archaeology*, 1 pp. 158–164. Praise of roundness: Σφαῖρος κυκλοτερὴς μονίῃ περιηγέϊ γαίων (Empedokles frr. 27–28 Diels).

[44] C Painter: *Metr. Mus. St.* 5 pp. 93–115. The "cup-krater" Louvre CA 2988, attributed to the C Painter in *REA*. 48 p. 161, is not his: the style somewhat recalls the BMN Painter (see p. 73 of the present work).

[45] New York GR 521: *Metr. Mus. St.* 5 pp. 94–95 (with pp. 93 and 102 no. 4); A, Buschor *Vasen* p. 104.

[46] Heidelberg S 1: *Metr. Mus. St.* 5 pp. 96–97 (with pp. 93–94 and 102 no. 1).

47 Herakles himself, as victor in games, lifts a large tripod on an amphora by the Princeton Painter in Munich (1378: *CV.* 1 pl. 11, 4).

48 Berkeley 8.1: *CV.* Univ. Calif. 1 pl. 14: attributed by H. R. W. Smith.

49 Athens 532: *Metr. Mus. St.* 5 p. 103 (with pp. 94 and 104 no. 12).

50 Payne *NC.* pp. 105–106.

51 Athens 531: *Metr. Mus. St.* 5 p. 106 (with pp. 94–96 and 111 no. 65).

52 Würzburg 451: Langlotz pls. 117 and 126–127; I and A, *Metr. Mus. St.* 5 p. 107 (with pp. 96 and 113 no. 80); A, Buschor *Vasen* p. 105.

53 Merrythought cups: *AM.* 59 pp. 1–8 (Kraiker); *REA.* 48 pp. 161–162 (Villard); H. R. W. Smith, *The Hearst Hydria*, p. 252.

54 Louvre CA 616: the picture on the top, *Met. Mus. St.* 5 p. 109 (with pp. 96 and 114 no. 85).

55 According to Payne (*NC.* p. 142), a Corinthian bronze plaque in Delphi (*FD.* 5 pl. 21) has much the earliest representation of the subject.—A fragment in Athens, North Slope (*Hesp.* 9 p. 174, 55), is also by the C Painter. See also p. 25. The fragments by Kleitias (Graef pl. 24, a–c and e) may be somewhat later.

56 Compare Zeus's stick on a cup by the Heidelberg Painter in Heidelberg (*JHS.* 51 p. 276).

57 See *Jb.* 52 p. 172 (Karouzos).

58 Berlin 1895, bf. hydria (Gerhard *EKV.* pl. 14), by the Antimenes Painter.

59 Payne *NC.* pp. 134–135. The Berlin fr., our pl. 7, 2 with p. 21.

60 Lekythos in London, B 30 (Walters pl. 1, above), Deianeira Group, near the Gorgon Painter (*Hesp.* 13 p. 41 no. 3). On the Gorgon Painter's dinos in the Louvre (above, pp. 16–18) the flesh of Athena is black like the men's.

61 Naples: *RM.* 27 pls. 5–6; *ML.* 22 pl. 57, whence (part) *Metr. Mus. St.* 5 p. 108 (with pp. 96–98 and 113–114 no. 82).

62 Hecuba is present at the death of Priam in Eur. *Tro.* 481; cf. also Virg. *Aen.* 2, 515.

63 Acropolis 2112: Graef pl. 92. *Metr. Mus. St.* 5 p. 114 no. 83.

64 Berlin 1655: FR. pl. 121, whence Pfuhl fig. 179.

65 The Siana cup London B 379 (*JHS.* 5 pl. 42; *CV.* 2 pl. 8, 2), in the manner of the C Painter and very close to him, may be a little earlier (*Metr. Mus. St.* 5 pp. 99 and 110 no. 63). The lekythos Athens 413 is also early (*AM.* 56 Beil. 44, 3; Haspels *ABL.* pl. 1, 2).

66 The Acropolis fr., Graef pls. 83 and 87, 1780, whence Hoppin *Bf.* p. 312; the other, *JHS.* 55 p. 224. The two joined by Martin Robertson.

CHAPTER III
THE FRANÇOIS VASE

1 FR. pls. 1–3 and 11–13 and i p. 62b; phots. Brogi; phots. Alinari. The drawings in FR. have often been reproduced, for instance in Perrot 10 pp. 141–173.

2 Acropolis 594: see p. 27 and our pl. 12, 1–2. The cornea of Althaia's eye has suffered.

3 In Reichhold's drawing the right arm of Demeter is not in order, but turning to the older drawing by Michalek in *Wiener Vorlegeblätter* one sees that before the accident in 1900 a broad band of restoration ran diagonally through the three figures. Reichhold reproduced the old restoration; and after the accident, the whole middle part of the figures having disappeared, Milani had them re-restored after Reichhold's drawing.

4 See Greifenhagen *Eine attische schwarzfigurige Vasengattung* pp. 69–75, and, more generally, Paul Friedländer *Documents of Dying Paganism* pp. 22–26; also Lullies in *AM.* 65 p. 3 and Rodenwaldt *Korkyra* 2 p. 139. The earliest frontal face in Greek *drawing* seems to be on the Boeotian vase with the Potnia Thērōn, Athens 220 (*Eph.* 1892 pl. 10, 1, whence, part, Perrot 10 p. 42, fig. 30; Zervos *L'Art en Grèce* pl. 55; Hampe *FGS.* pl. 17, 2), early seventh century.

5 *Il.* 3, 125. Andromache's web had flowers only (θρόνα: *Il.* 22, 441).

6 Payne *NC.* p. 73.

7 See Richter *AAG.* pp. 56–58, and Hatch and Miss Alexander here.

8 See Karouzou in *Jb.* 52 pp. 176–182.

9 Milani saw that the remains were of Okeanos—and not of the same monster as the tail. See Buschor *Meermänner* pp. 24–28.

10 Eur. *Or.* 1377.

11 The earliest in sculpture is much later, the Athena of Endoios.

12 Egyptian, see Möbius in *AM.* 41 p. 136; Mesopotamian, *ibid.* p. 143.

13 Aen. Tact. 38. 6.

14 Wilamowitz-Möllendorff in *Nachrichten . . . Göttingen* 1895 pp. 217–245 = *Kleine Schriften* 5, 2 pp. 5–35.

15 Early representations of Dionysos: *AM.* 59 p. 23 (Kraiker).

16 Early satyrs: H. R. W. Smith *The Origin of Chalcidian Ware* pp. 122 and 134; *AM.* 59 p. 96 (Kunze); Brommer *Satyroi* pp. 25–26 and 52.

17 A Late Geometric gold diadem in Berlin is from Athens and may be Attic (*AZ.* 1884 pl. 10, 1, whence Poulsen *Orient* p. 110); the griffin on it is the earliest extant Greek griffin.

[18] On early representations of boar-hunts, P. de La Coste-Messelière *Au Musée de Delphes* pp. 130–152; D. von Bothmer in *Bull. MFA.* 46 pp. 42–48.

[19] Xen. *Cyn.* 10.

[20] Xen. *Cyn.* 20–22.

[21] This explanation was given by Heberdey in *AEM.* 13 pp. 78–82; it has recently been supported by Johansen, *Thesée et la danse à Délos*, and attacked by P. de La Coste-Messelière in *RA.* 28 (1947) pp. 145–156.

[22] Acropolis 596: Graef pl. 29.

[23] Acropolis 598: Graef pl. 24; hitherto thought part of an amazonomachy.

[24] Johansen *Iliaden* pp. 47–52 and 119–120.

[25] R. M. Cook in *CR.* 1937 p. 208. The bronze, *Jb.* 52 Olympia-Bericht pl. 28; *Bull. Vereen.* June 1939 p. 8. In *AJA.* 1941 p. 596 I tried to show that an Attic fragment in the University of Vienna, from the later part of the seventh century, might preserve part of a Thessalian centauromachy. Now that it is published (*CV.* 1 pl. 5, 651) I perceive that my notes misled me, that the inscribed name pertains to the centaur rather than to his opponent, and was doubtless Petraios, my alternative suggestion and also Miss Kenner's reading.

[26] On the Potnia Thērōn, Bloesch *AKS.* pp. 26–36 and 150–157.

[27] On each side of the neck of a long-necked amphora in Eleusis: she is winged, wears a polos, and holds swans.

[28] For early representations see Hampe *FGS.* pp. 72–73.

[29] *NC.* p. 79.

[30] *Trudy Gosudarstvennovo Muzeya Izobrazitelnich Iskusstv imeni A. C. Pushkina* (Moscow 1939) figs. 32–33; attributed to "the circle of Kleitias" by Blavatsky (*ibid.* pp. 86–91).

[31] New York 31.11.4. *Bull. Metr. Mus.* 26 pp. 290–291 (Richter); part, Richter and Milne fig. 189.

[32] *Il.* 3, 1–7.

[33] They are deformed on a gold head-band, doubtless Eastern Greek, in Rhodes (*Cl. Rh.* 8 pp. 112–113), found at Ialysos with Attic black-figured vases of the same period as the François vase or hardly later.

[34] Plin. *N.H.* 7, 2, 26.

[35] Aesop no. 285 Chambry; also Babrius no. 13.

[36] Furtwängler in *FR.* i p. 7.

[37] The following unsigned fragments are from the hand of Kleitias.

Skyphos or the like, Delphi, *BCH.* 1924 pl. 13, 1 and p. 321; *FD.* 2 fasc. 5 p. 125, 2. Attributed by Demangel.

Skyphos-like or kantharos-like vases: Acropolis 597 a–e, Graef pl. 24, whence Robert *Hermeneutik* p. 354, 1–4. A new fragment, identified by Miss Pease, *Hesp.* 4 p. 227, 14. Acropolis 597, f–h, Graef pl. 24, whence Robert *Hermeneutik* p. 354, 5–6. Acropolis 598, Graef pl. 24, whence Robert *Hermeneutik* p. 354, 8. See p. 34. Acropolis 599, Graef pl. 29.

Column-krater: Moscow, Pushkin Museum, as in note 30 to chap. iii above. See p. 36, and n. 30, pl. 12, 3.

Hydria: Acropolis 594. Graef pl. 24 and p. 66. See p. 27 and our pl. 12, 1–2.

Shape uncertain (hydria?): Acropolis 596. Graef pl. 29, whence Robert *Hermeneutik* p. 357. See p. 34 and our pl. 12, 4–5.

In *ABS.* 16 I surmised that the hydria-fragments Acropolis 601 (Graef pl. 29) might be by Kleitias, and noted that they were by the same hand as the fragments London B 601.13 (*JHS.* 49 pl. 16, 17 and 6: probably from a "nuptial lebes" like Acropolis 474, Graef pl. 171). Bothmer has shown me that the two fragments come from different sides of the vase. I now see that they are not by Kleitias but by another excellent artist of the same period who may be called "the Painter of Acropolis 601." On the cups by Kleitias see pp. 26 and 52, and *JHS.* 52 pp. 185–186.

CHAPTER IV
LYDOS AND OTHERS

[1] Acropolis 606: part, Graef pls. 30–32 and pp. 68–69, whence (part) *ABS.* pl. 4; two new fragments identified by Mrs. Karouzou, *BCH.* 1947–48 p. 424, a–b. The painter: *ABS.* pp. 13–14; Rumpf *Sak.* p. 19.

[2] On animal-whirligigs see Jacobsthal *ECA.* pp. 59 and 210, and Anna Roos in *Studia Vollgraff* pp. 134–136.

[3] Berlin inv. 4823: *ABS.* pl. 2, 3 and pl. 3, 2. Tübingen D 4: A, Watzinger pl. 5.

[4] See *AM.* 18 pp. 151 ff. (Brueckner and Pernice) and Wilamowitz-Möllendorff *Glaube der Hellenen* 1 p. 153.

[5] Odessa: von Stern *Theodosia* pl. 2, 1. Also by the Painter of Acropolis 606, fragments of a column-krater in Athens, Acr. 633 (Graef pl. 38; attributed by Rumpf), fragments (of a volute-krater?) in Athens, Acr. 625 (part, Graef pl. 38; a new fragment, added by Miss Pease, *Hesp.* 5 p. 262, 9 and p. 263); and an ovoid neck-amphora in Geneva (MF 153: A, phot. Giraudon 4945).

[6] Nearchos: *JHS.* 52 pp. 176 and 291; Richter in *AJA.* 1932 pp. 272–273; Pease in *Hesp.* 4 p. 229; Rumpf *Sak.* p. 19.

[7] Acropolis 611: Graef pl. 36, whence Hoppin *Bf*. p. 173 (except two fragments which belong to Acropolis 693), (part) Perrot 10 p. 201, (part) Pfuhl figs. 236–237, (part) Johansen *Iliaden* fig. 14; part, Lane *GP*. pl. 45, b. On the subject of A, see Wrede in *AM*. 41 p. 232 and Johansen *Iliaden* pp. 56–60; on harnessing-scenes in general, Wrede *op. cit.* pp. 335–354. Miss Pease saw that the fragment Acropolis AP 67 (*Hesp*. 4 p. 227, 15) was by Nearchos, and took it to be part of Acropolis 611, not, however, of A, but of "a similar scene on B"; but it does not seem certain that there was a chariot on B.

[8] On harnessing-scenes, Wrede in *AM*. 41 pp. 232–234 and 335–354; and see pp. 40, 70, 78–79, and 79–80 of the present work.

[9] Berlin inv. 3319: *Anz*. 1895 p. 34. In *JHS*. 49 p. 258 Payne and I took the Attic kantharos-fragment London B 601.14 (*ibid*. pl. 15, 17), in the manner of the KX Painter, to be from a harnessing-scene; it would have been the earliest in Attica; and so Johansen *Iliaden* p. 69. But in *CV*. Cam. 2 p. 43 I pointed out that the Cambridge fragment N. 131.G71 joined London B 601.14, so that the subject was not harnessing, but a frontal chariot (*Hesp*. 13 p. 46 no. 19). Nearchos' harnessing-scene remains the earliest extant Attic.

[10] Athens Acr. 612: Graef pl. 36, whence Hoppin *Bf*. p. 175.

[11] New York 26.49: *AJA*. 1932 pls. 10–11 and p. 273 (Richter).

[12] Lydos: *JHS*. 51 pp. 282–284 ("Painter of London B 148," seen by Miss Richter to be Lydos); Richter in *Metr. Mus. St*. 4 pp. 169–178; *BSA*. 32 p. 18; Rumpf *Sak*.; H. R. W. Smith, *The Hearst Hydria*, p. 267, n. 5; *Cypr*. pp. 6–7. See also the present work, p. 49.

[13] Louvre F 29: Hoppin *Bf*. p. 164; Rumpf *Sak*. pl. 17, f; phot. Giraudon 16996, right.

[14] Acropolis 607: Graef pls. 32–35 (not complete), whence (details) Pfuhl figs. 238–240; the head of Dionysos, not figured by Graef, *AM*. 59 p. 19 (Kraiker); Rumpf *Sak*. pls. 18–20.

[15] On the costume of Herakles, Paola Zancani Montuoro in *Rend. Acc. Linc.*, 8th ser., 2 (1947) pp. 207–221. Cf. Lenzen, *The Figure of Dionysos on the Siphnian Frieze* (*Univ. Calif. Publ. Class. Arch.*, iii, no. 1), pp. 9–14.

[16] Harvard: *CV*. Hoppin pl. 3; A, Rumpf *Sak*. pl. 12, c. Attributed by Rumpf.

[17] Vase in Athens, mentioned in *AM*. 62 p. 114 n. 3 (Karouzou).

[18] Acropolis 474 (Graef pl. 17; detail, *AM*. 62 p. 121): *Hesp*. 13 p. 40 no. 2. On the motive, which already occurs in an engraved stone of Geometric style, see Payne *NC*. p. 74; Hafner; Amyx in *AJA*. 1939 pp. 164–166.

[19] London 1948.10–15.1. Attributed by Dietrich von Bothmer and Martin Robertson.

[20] Similarly Herakles, on an amphora in the British Museum (B 166: Gerhard *AV*. pl. 128; *CV*. 3 pl. 30, 3), is so embarrassed when brought into the presence of Zeus that he turns round and makes off.

[21] Florence 70995: A, *JHS*. 1886 pl. 7, whence Pfuhl fig. 211; A, Thiersch *Tyrrh*. pl. 2, 7; Rumpf *Sak*. pls. 2–3. Attributed by Rumpf. Compare the ovoid neck-amphora in the Kent collection at Harrogate, attributed by Charlton (*AJA*. 1944 p. 255 figs. 4–5).

[22] New York 31.11.11: *Bull. Metr. Mus.* 1932 pp. 75 and 77; *AJA*. 1932 p. 96 and p. 97 fig. 5; *Metr. Mus. St*. 4 pl. 1 and pp. 171–173; Rumpf *Sak*. pls. 21–23; A, Buschor *Vasen* p. 114. Attributed by Miss Richter.

[23] London B 148: *JHS*. 19 pl. 6; *CV*. 3 pl. 25, 5; A, *Bull. Metr. Mus.* May 1947 p. 225. *JHS*. 51 p. 282 no. 1.

[24] See Payne *NC*. p. 133.

[25] Taranto: Rumpf *Sak*. pl. 25; *CV*. 1 pl. 1, 1–2. *JHS*. 51 p. 284.

[26] Theseus wears a somewhat similar garment on an amphora by a colleague of Lydos, the Painter of Louvre F 6 (see p. 49), in the Vatican (313: *Mus. Greg.* 2 pl. 47, 1; Albizzati pl. 32). See also Kunze *Kretische Bronzereliefs* p. 225.

[27] Cab. Méd. 206: de Ridder p. 116 and pl. 5; *CV*. 1 pl. 34, 1–2 and 8; A, *BSA*. 32 pl. 10; B, Rumpf *Sak*. pl. 26, b. See also *Cypr*. p. 7.

[28] Naples 2770: A, *JHS*. 51 pl. 13 (with p. 284); *CV*. pl. 6.

[29] Göttingen and Cab. Méd.: *Eph*. 1937 pp. 14 and 16.

[30] Chicago, Univ.: *AJA*. 1943 p. 390 fig. 4 (F. P. Johnson) and p. 442. See also p. 91 of the present work.

[31] Oxford, Mississippi, D. M. Robinson: *AJA*. 1930 p. 354; *CV*. Robinson 1 pl. 19, 1.

[32] Acropolis 1757: Graef pl. 86.

[33] Ceramicus: *AM*. 59 Beil. 1, 1–3 and pls. 1–3. Attributed by Kraiker.

[34] Vlasto: Rumpf *Sak*. pl. 14.

[35] Villa Giulia M 430: Mingazzini *Cast*. pl. 44, 1, pl. 46, 1–2, and pl. 45, 1; Rumpf *Sak*. pl. 13, a and pl. 15, a–c. Attributed by Rumpf.

[36] Munich 1681: Rumpf *Sak*. pl. 7, d. Attributed by Rumpf.

[37] Louvre E 804: phot. Giraudon 25741, whence Rumpf *Sak*. pl. 12, b. Attributed by Rumpf.

[38] Oxford 190: Percy Gardner *Catalogue of the*

Greek Vases in the Ashmolean Museum pl. 1 and p. 6 fig. 10; *CV.* 2 pl. 12, 1–4 and 8: restored. Rhodes: *Cl. Rh.* 8 p. 111, 1 and p. 126. Louvre F 6: Pottier pl. 63; *CV.* 6 pl. 59, 1–2: now cleaned. See also p. 43 of the present work.

CHAPTER V
THE HEIDELBERG PAINTER—LITTLE-MASTER CUPS—AMASIS

[1] *JHS.* 51 pp. 275–282: I spoke of a "Group"; I now see that the vases are all by one painter.

[2] Florence 3893: *JHS.* 51 p. 280 no. 13 and p. 285 figs. 30–31.

[3] Munich inv. 7739: *Anz.* 1938 p. 452 fig. 33 and p. 449; attributed by Sieveking.

[4] First in Corinthian; see Payne *NC.* p. 114.

[5] Also in an athletic scene very like this on a cup by the same painter in the Cabinet des Médailles (314: *CV.* 1 pl. 45, 1–5: *JHS.* 51 p. 280 no. 15).

[6] Würzburg 452: Micali *St.* pl. 87, 1; A, Baur *Centaurs* pl. 10, 242; Langlotz pl. 126, pl. 128, and pl. 117, whence (A) *Dragma* p. 185. *JHS.* 51 p. 280 no. 8 (where for "Greek" read "Herakles").

[7] Strictly, Thetis should not be present in this version of the legend; see Johansen in *Dragma* pp. 181–205.

[8] Pind. *Nem.* 3, 43 ξανθὸς δ' Ἀχιλεὺς τὰ μὲν μένων Φιλύρας ἐν δόμοις. Cf. *Philyreia tecta* in Ovid *Met.* 7, 352.

[9] Pind. *Pyth.* 4, 102–103.

[10] Palermo: the left half, *ML.* 32 pl. 91, 3, the two halves joined in *JHS.* 51 p. 52 no. 1; *JHS.* 51 p. 280 no. 17.

[11] Berlin inv. 4604: Körte *Gordion* pl. 7 and p. 41, whence Pfuhl figs. 213–214; Hoppin *Bf.* p. 149.

[12] Gordion cups: *JHS.* 49 pp. 265–267 and 52 pp. 185–186; see also Villard in *REA.* 48 (1946) p. 164.

[13] *Shield* 207–210 εφοινεον in 210 may be corrupt, but is an old reading, as it occurs in the plus-line *Il.* 18, 608c.

[14] *Sylloge nummorum* 2 R. 37, 1073–1074, and 3 pl. 15, 811–816.

[15] Taranto: *BSA.* 34 pl. 30, 1; Lane *GP.* pl. 30.

[16] Taranto: *BSA.* pl. 30, 2; Munich 385 (Sieveking and Hackl *Die königliche Vasensammlung zu München* pl. 13).

[17] Vernier *La Bijouterie et la joaillerie égyptiennes* pl. 26; Bossert *Geschichte des Kunstgewerbes* 4 p. 120; a small cut in Breasted *Ancient Times* p. 298.

[18] Krönig in *Mitteilungen des Deutschen Instituts für ägyptische Altertumskunde in Kairo* 5 pp. 144–166 (I owe my knowledge of this work to Dr. Bernard V. Bothmer and Dr. Dietrich von Bothmer).

See also the silver-and-gold bowl from the tomb of Psusenes at Tanis (Montet in *Mon. Piot* 43 pl. 4 with pp. 20–30), 21st dynasty.

[19] Hayford Peirce and Royall Tyler *L'Art byzantin* pl. 117 ("c. 400 A.D."; "there is no more disconcerting object in the world." I owe this reference to Dr. D. A. Amyx); Berenson *Aesthetics and History in the Visual Arts* p. 31 fig. 2. Said to be Byzantine; West European?

[20] Eucheiros: *JHS.* 52 pp. 169, 175, 178, 192, and 200.

[21] Little-Master cups: *JHS.* 52 pp. 167–204; Villard in *REA.* 48 pp. 162–169.

[22] Payne, *Protokorinthische Vasenmalerei*, p. 13.

[23] London B 424: *VA.* pp. 189 and 136; Hoppin *Bf.* p. 315; *CV.* 2 pl. 13, 2; *ABS.* pl. 1, 1–2; *JHS.* 52 pl. 5.

[24] *JHS.* 52 pp. 194–195; *PP.* p. 33.

[25] See also Villard in *REA.* 48 p. 165.

[26] Vatican 317: Albizzati pl. 34; *JHS.* 52 pl. 6, 1; Buschor *Vasen* p. 106. On the Phrynos Painter, *ABS.* pp. 6–8 and 16–17; *JHS.* 52 pp. 170 and 199; *Cypr.* p. 10.

[27] Tleson Painter: *JHS.* 52 pp. 195–196, 172–173, 176, 180–182, 184, 186, 191, 193; *RG.* pp. 55–56; *Cypr.* pp. 3–6.

[28] Castle Ashby: Hoppin *Bf.* p. 377; *ABS.* pl. 5, 1. The same subject on a lip-cup by another painter in Rhodes (12584: *Cl. Rh.* 3 p. 373 fig. 421 and fig. 420, 2).

[29] Hoppin *Bf.* p. 379; p. 372; p. 378; p. 367. Nicosia C 438: *Cypr.* pl. 1, 1–2 with pp. 3–4.

[30] Munich: Sieveking, *Bronzen, Terrakotten, Vasen der Sammlung Loeb* pl. 43, 1 and p. 55; *JHS.* 52 p. 9. See *Cypr.* p. 4.

[31] Not mentioned in my previous lists, a band-cup by the Tleson Painter in the Pushkin Museum at Moscow, attributed to him by Losseva (*Trudy Gosudarstvennovo Muzeya Izobrazitelnich Iskusstv imeni A. C. Pushkina*, Moscow 1939, figs. 30–31: A, stag between sphinxes; B, goat between swans), and another in the National Museum, Warsaw (ex Wilanow, Branicki: B, *CV.* Pologne 3 pl. 113, 5; A, boar between panthers; B, stag between swans).

[32] London B 421: Hoppin *Bf.* p. 387; *CV.* pl. 11, 2; *JHS.* 52 p. 177 fig. 9; Lane *GP.* pl. 39, a.

[33] Munich 2243: *WV.* 1889 pl. 2, whence Hoppin *Bf.* pp. 60–61; *FR.* pl. 153, 1 and p. 219; A, Schaal *Sf.* fig. 34; A, Buschor *Vasen* p. 126.

[34] By Dietrich von Bothmer: *tecte* in *Bull. Metr. Mus.* May 1947 p. 224.

[35] Vatican 325: *ML.* 28 p. 265; Albizzati pl. 36 and p. 115; phot. Alinari.

[36] New York 17.230.5: detail of B, *ABS.* pl. 1, 3;

details of B, *JHS.* 52 p. 204; *Jb.* 52 p. 205. The foot of the cup is modern.

[37] Boston 10.213.

[38] Louvre F 75: A, Pottier pl. 69; *JHS.* 51 pl. 12 (with p. 274); *CV.* 6 pl. 81, 3–10; *Enc. phot.* 2 p. 288; B, *Hesp.* 8 p. 253 fig. 10.

[39] Cracow inv. 30: *CV.* pl. 5, 1.

[40] Amasis Painter: *ABS.* pp. 17, 21–22, and 31–36; *BSR.* 11 pp. 3–4; Kraiker in *Jb.* 44 pp. 141–150; *JHS.* 51 pp. 256–275; *JHS.* 52 p. 202; Karouzou in *AM.* 56 pp. 98–111; *BSA.* 32 pp. 18–19; Kraiker in *AM.* 59 pp. 19–24; Vanderpool in *Hesp.* 8 pp. 247–255 and 265–266; Roebuck in *Hesp.* 9 p. 150; H. R. W. Smith in *AJA.* 1945 p. 265.

[41] Cab. Méd. 222: *WV.* 1889 pl. 3, 2, whence Perrot 10 pp. 179–183; *CV.* 1, pls. 36–37; phots. Giraudon, whence Hoppin *Bf.* p. 35, Merlin pl. 36, and (A) Pfuhl fig. 220; A, Buschor *Vasen* p. 117; A, Lane *GP.* pl. 42; side, Jacobsthal *O.* pl. 35, a; part of the shoulder, *Jb.* 53 p. 108.

[42] The two shoulder-scenes are misdivided in *CV.*

[43] Boston 01.8027: *Jh.* 10 pls. 1–4 and pp. 2 and 16 (Hauser), whence Pfuhl figs. 218–219, Hoppin *Bf.* pp. 30–31, and (redrawn and spoilt) Perrot 10 pp. 184–187; *AJA.* 1901 pls. 12–13; side, Jacobsthal *O.* pl. 24, d; shape, Caskey *G.* p. 44. See also Johansen *Iliaden* p. 157. Now augmented by fragments recognised in Philadelphia by Payne. The fragment with the feet of Thetis seems slightly out of place.

[44] See Johansen *Iliaden* pp. 65–70.

[45] *JHS.* 51 p. 261; *AJA.* 1945 p. 467, 1 (H. R. W. Smith).

[46] Similar guide-lines appear below the tongue-ornament on the shoulder in a class of black-figure oinochoai not connected with the Amasis Painter: London B 521, B 523, B 496; Havana, Cuba, collection of the Conde de Lagunillas (Athena mounting chariot, with Herakles, Apollo, and Hermes). Guidelines on inscribed stones: see Raubitschek *Dedications from the Athenian Acropolis* p. 439.

[47] Louvre F 30: *WV.* 1889 pl. 4, 3, whence Perrot 10 pp. 188–189; Hoppin *Bf.* p. 37; *AM.* 56, Beil. 51; *Enc. phot.* 2 p. 283.

[48] On a neck-amphora by the Antimenes Painter in Tarquinia (RC 1871), Herakles walks to right, towards Poseidon who stands to left; Herakles looks round at Hermes, who follows him.

[49] New York 06.1021.69: Sambon *Coll. Canessa* pl. 14 and p. 57; A, Richter and Milne fig. 3; A, *AM.* 56, Beil. 49; A, Buschor *Vasen* p. 108, fig. 127.

[50] Berlin inv. 3210: Adamek *Unsignierte Vasen des Amasis* pls. 1–2 and p. 7; *ABS.* pl. 9, 1 and pl.

10, 1; *Jb.* 44 p. 115: A, Neugebauer pl. 29. Attributed by Furtwängler.

[51] Würzburg 265: *JHS.* 19 pl. 5 and p. 136, whence Perrot 10 pp. 190–191; A, Pfuhl fig. 222; Langlotz pls. 73–74. Attributed by Dümmler.

[52] Samos: the larger fragment, *AM.* 56 pl. 3. Attributed by Karouzou.

[53] Vienna, Oest. Mus. 218: A, Masner pl. 2, right; part of B, FR. 1 p. 260; G. von Lücken *Greek Vase Paintings* pls. 62–63.

[54] The motive will be treated in my forthcoming continuation of Caskey *Attic Vase Paintings in the Museum of Fine Arts, Boston.*

[55] London B 524: *ABS.* pl. 11, 1. On the frontal chariots of the Amasis Painter see also Hafner pp. 22–23.

[56] Palermo. *ML.* 32 pl. 91, 1. *ABS.* p. 36 no. 40, and *JHS.* 51 p. 266.

[57] Bonn 504: *BSA.* 32 pl. 11, 1, with pp. 18–19; *Anz.* 1935 p. 422 fig. 10 (Greifenhagen).

[58] Louvre CA 2918: *CV.* 9 pl. 84, 1–5; A, *Hesp.* 8 p. 253 fig. 11. Attributed by Plaoutine. See also Villard in *REA.* 48 pp. 160–161.

[59] Louvre A 479: Pottier pls. 17–18, whence (A) Perrot 10 p. 230; *CV.* 9 pl. 92. *ABS.* p. 35 no. 36. See also Villard in *REA.* 48 p. 166; and *Cypr.* p. 19.

[60] No number.—Another work by the Amasis Painter in Boston is the fragment 86.616 (F 352.4: Fairbanks, *Catalogue of Greek and Etruscan Vases* pl. 38: boxers) from a vase of uncertain shape.

[61] On these three cups see *JHS.* 51 pp. 266–270. The fragments of the signed cup are now assembled in the Vatican (369a), those of the unsigned ex Vatican and Dorchester in Oxford (1939.118: *Ashm. Rep.* 1939 pl. 5, 1), those ex Florence and Villa Giulia in Florence (A, *Boll. d'Arte* 29 p. 259 fig. 2; the foot falsely restored). See also Bloesch *FAS.* pp. 42–43 and Villard in *REA.* 48 p. 179.

CHAPTER VI
EXEKIAS

[1] On Exekias: *ABS.* pp. 17–21 and 29–31; *BSA.* 32 pp. 1–3; Technau.

[2] Louvre F 53: *WV.* 1888 pl. 5, 1, whence Hoppin *Bf.* pl. 101 and Perrot 10 pl. 3 and pp. 193–195; *CV.* 3 pls. 19–20; A, Merlin pl. 37, 1; *Enc. phot.* 2 pp. 286–287.

[3] Group E: *BSA.* 32 pp. 3–8. See also Hafner pp. 28–29.

[4] London B 194: A, Walters pl. 4; A, *CV.* 3 pl. 37, 1; *BSA.* 32 p. 7 no. 35. Roš: Bloesch *AKS.* pls. 14–17.

[5] Bf. hydria in Florence, 70994.

[6] Plaoutine has shown that the lid was bought separately.

[7] Berlin 1720: *WV.* 1888 pl. 6, 3, whence Hoppin *Bf.* p. 93 and (B) Pfuhl fig. 228; A, Pfuhl fig. 227; side, Jacobsthal *O.* pl. 22, a; B, Neugebauer pl. 30; Technau pls. 1–2; B, Buschor *Vasen* p. 118 fig. 135; the signature, Kirchner *Imagines inscriptionum atticarum* pl. 4, 8.

[8] This adventure is common in Attic vase-painting from the second half of the sixth century onwards; one of the Corinthian pictures is much earlier: see Payne *NC.* p. 126.

[9] London B 210: *WV.* 1888 pl. 6, 2, whence Hoppin *Bf.* p. 95 and (part) Pfuhl fig. 232; side, Jacobsthal *O.* pl. 37, a; *CV.* 4 pl. 49, 2; Technau pl. 25; B, Lane *GP.* pl. 43.

[10] Vatican 344: FR. pls. 131–132 and 3 pp. 65 and 71–73, whence (B) Pfuhl fig. 230; A, Pfuhl fig. 229; phots. Alinari, whence (A) Merlin pl. 38 and (B) *ABS.* pl. 6; Albizzati pls. 40–42 and pp. 127–133; Technau pls. 20–21; A and part of B, Buschor *Vasen* pp. 120–121; Lane *GP.* pl. 44 and pl. 45, a.

[11] See Hauser in FR. 3 pp. 65–72, Chase in *Bull. MFA.* 44 pp. 45–50; and *Cypr.* pp. 32–33, where other references are given.

[12] Κύβος means "pip" as well as die: see Wuilleumier in *Istros* 1 pp. 14–18.

[13] Also on the amphora by Exekias in the Faina collection at Orvieto, 78 (Technau pl. 13, left; *ABS.* p. 29 no. 6), and on the column-krater fragment Acropolis 647 (Graef pl. 41), which may be by Exekias, as Hauser saw (FR. 3 p. 71).

[14] On thigh-guards, Wrede in *AM.* 41 p. 367; on the rerebrace, *EVP.* pp. 136–137 and 301.

[15] So already Panofka in *Annali* 1835 p. 230.

[16] *Il.* 11, 765.

[17] FR. pl. 132.

[18] Cups by Exekias: *JHS.* 52 pp. 178 (now *CV.* Louvre 8, pl. 77, 1–3), 180, 183, 185, and 200.

[19] Munich 2044: FR. pl. 42 and 1 p. 227, whence Hoppin *Bf.* p. 99 and (I) Pfuhl fig. 231; I, Merlin pl. 39, 1; A–B, Jacobsthal *O.* pl. 68a; Technau pls. 5–6; Bloesch *FAS.* pl. 1, 1, with pp. vi–x and 2; Buschor *Vasen* pp. 127–128; A, Lane *GP.* pl. 41. See also Villard in *REA.* 48 (1946) p. 174, and Neutsch *Henkel und Schalenbild* (in *Marburger Jahrbuch* 14, 1948) pp. 1–7.

[20] On cup A see Bloesch *FAS.* pp. 1–40, and Villard in *REA.* 48 (1946) pp. 173–180.

[21] Leipsic T 355 and T 391; ex Barone: Technau pl. 19, c–f. Attributed by Hauser (*Jb.* 11 p. 179).

[22] Lund, Univ.: attributed to Exekias by Gjerstad.

[23] Philadelphia MS 3442: *Mus. Journ.* 6, pp. 91–92; *AJA.* 1935 pl. 8; Technau pl. 23. Attributed by Furtwängler.

[24] On homonyms in the Iliad and the Odyssey, Bassett *The Poetry of Homer* p. 256 note 40.

[25] Bf. amphora Munich 1415: Gerhard *AV.* pl. 227; *CV.* 1 pl. 45, 2 and pl. 47, 3.

[26] A pair of greaves in Leningrad (*ABC.* pl. 28). Another, in which the gorgoneion is eked out to make a complete gorgon, in London (249: Walters *Select Bronzes* pl. 5; *AJA.* 1949 pl. 18, b). Leg of a bronze statue in the British Museum (*JHS.* 7 pl. 69). On rf. vases: skyphos by Makron in Boston, 13.186 (FR. pl. 85); cup in the late manner of Douris, London E 60 (*ARV.* p. 296 no. 23); calyx-krater by the Altamura Painter in the Louvre, G 342 (*VRV.* p. 412 no. 8).

[27] Hdt. 7, 69. On bf. vases: neck-amphora by Exekias in London, B 209 (*CV.* 4 pl. 49, 1; Technau pl. 26); neck-amphora in New York, GR 547 (*AJA.* 1935 pl. 7, b); hydria in Bristol; neck-amphora, near the Nikoxenos Painter, in Munich, 1507.

[28] Philadelphia MS 4873: B, *Mus. Journ.* 4 p. 158; part, *Univ. Mus. Bull.* 4 pp. 60, 66, and 68 (Dohan). *BSA.* 32 p. 2.

[29] Boulogne 558: Pottier *Musées de province* pl. 16, 3, whence (A) Pfuhl fig. 234 and (A, redrawn and spoilt) Perrot 10 p. 199; A, *ABS.* pl. 7; A, Technau pl. 34; part of A, Buschor *Vasen* p. 119.

[30] Boston 89.213 (R. 315): Jacobsthal *O.* pl. 39, c; A, Buschor *Vasen* p. 115; the shape, Caskey *G.* p. 38. See also Wrede in *AM.* 41 pp. 372–373.

[31] One of the pole-horses is seen from the front in the harnessing-scene on the bf. lekythos Syracuse 8776, by the Taleides Painter (Haspels *ABL.* pl. 14, 1).

[32] Athens, North Slope: *Hesp.* 6 pp. 468–486 (Broneer); part, *AJA.* 1938 pl. 16, b; detail of A, Buschor *Vasen* p. 122. Attributed by Broneer. Compare the hydria Florence 3790, from Orvieto (small phots. Alinari 17073, 4 and Brogi 10754), attributed to the Andokides Painter in *ARV.* p. 4 no. 24; "manner of the Andokides Painter," more cautiously, in *ABS.* p. 41 no. 9. If it is by the painter himself it must be an early work, close to his master Exekias.

[33] Berlin 1811–1826 and Athens 2414–2415: *AD.* 2 pls. 9–10 and pp. 5–6 (Hirschfeld), whence (part) Perrot 9 pl. 12 and pp. 251–255, (one) Pfuhl fig. 278, (part) Swindler figs. 236–238; Technau pls. 14–18 and pl. 19, a–b. Attributed by Rumpf.—A building of this sort is roughly rendered on bf. "kyathoi" (one-handled kantharoi) in the Cabinet des Médailles: 353, de Ridder p. 244, *CV.* 2 pl. 71, 7–9 and pl. 72, 1–4; 355, *CV.* 2 pl. 71, 2, 4, 6 and pl. 73, 1–3 (Perizoma Group, *RG.* p. 53).

[34] Nikosthenes: Hoppin *Bf.* pp. 177–293; *ABS.*

pp. 23–24; *BSR.* 11 p. 6; *JHS.* 52 p. 20; *BSA.* 32 p. 22; *JHS.* 55 p. 81; *RG.* p. 64; Bloesch *FAS.* pp. 9–12 and 23–27.

³⁵ London B 295: Hoppin *Bf.* p. 202; Jacobsthal *O.* pl. 14, b; *CV.* 4 pl. 72, 1; Norman Gardiner *Athl.* fig. 155.

³⁶ See Norman Gardiner *Athl.* p. 204.

³⁷ London B 403: A, *CV.* 2 pl. 12, 4; Lane *GP.* pl. 39, b and pl. 40, a. Berlin 1797.

³⁸ The Painter of Berlin 1686: *CV.* Oxford 2 p. 98; *BSA.* 32 pp. 10–11; *JHS.* 59 p. 305. Foot and mouth of the Washington amphora 136415 (*BSA.* 32 pl. 5, 1, with p. 11) are genuine; the foot is as described there, the mouth is that of "amphora type C."

³⁹ Berlin 1686: Gerhard *EKV.* pls. 2–3; *BSA.* 32 p. 10, middle, no. 1.

⁴⁰ Oxford 1918.64: *CV.* 2 pl. 4, 3 and pl. 5; *BSA.* 32 p. 10, middle, no. 2.

⁴¹ Faina 73: *AM.* 53 pl. 22 and pl. 23, 1.

⁴² Berlin 1697: A, Bieber *Th.* p. 66; A, Pickard-Cambridge *Dithyramb, Tragedy and Comedy* p. 246; A, Bieber *HT.* p. 68; *BSA.* 32 p. 10 no. 8.

⁴³ Vatican 350: A, phot. Alinari 35757, whence (part) Pfuhl fig. 290; A, *ABS.* pl. 8 (with p. 21); Albizzati pl. 44 and p. 137.

⁴⁴ The second warrior often present in this scene may be Odysseus rather than Agamemnon (*Od.* 8, 517).

⁴⁵ *Anz.* 1935 p. 490 figs. 64–65 (Greifenhagen).

⁴⁶ On other painters of this period see *BSA.* 32 pp. 9–22, and *JHS.* 59 p. 305.

CHAPTER VII
LATER BLACK-FIGURE

¹ *ARV.* pp. 1–7, 946 and 948; see also note 32 to chap. vi, above.

² A, *Cat. Christie July 15, 1948* p. 5: amphora type B; now in the Hearst collection at San Simeon.

³ Munich 2301: FR. pl. 4, whence Pfuhl figs. 315 and 265; A, Schaal *Rf.* fig. 11; B, *AM.* 62 pl. 26, 2. *ARV.* p. 2 no. 8. Attributed by Furtwängler.

⁴ *Cat. Sotheby Dec. 19 1927* pl. 5; B, *ABS.* pl. 10, 2. *ARV.* p. 3 no. 16. The painter's neck-amphora with the same subject, in Zurich, is now published by Bloesch (*AKS.* pls. 24–29 with pp. 54–57 and 166–167; detail of A, Lane *GP.* pl. 49, b).

⁵ Villa Giulia 24998: *ML.* 14 pp. 283–286; *CV.* 1 pl. 1, 1–2; phots. Alinari 41152 and another. *ARV.* p. 3 no. 14.

⁶ See Dugas in *REG.* 57 (1944) pp. 61–70.

⁷ Theocr. 24, 110.

⁸ Boston 99.538: C. H. Smith *Forman* no. 305 pls. 5–6, whence Pfuhl figs. 316 and 266 and (A)

VA. p. 4; shape, Caskey *G.* p. 60. *ARV.* p. 2 no. 10. Attributed by Cecil Smith.

⁹ Oxford 208: *CV.* 2 pl. 10, 3–4 and pl. 7, 1–5. *ARV.* p. 3 no. 19. See also Hafner, p. 25.

¹⁰ London B 211: *CV.* 4 pl. 49, 3. *ARV.* p. 3 no. 18.

¹¹ London B 302: *Jb.* 21 pl. 1; *CV.* 6 pl. 74, 3 and pl. 75, 3. *ARV.* p. 4 no. 26. Pernice's explanation (*Jb.* 21 pp. 42–45) does not seem right: on wine-skins as cushions see Caskey *G.* p. 29.

¹² Sappho fr. 135–136 Diehl, inc. 26 Lobel. In Lucian *Dial. deor.* 4, 5, Zeus tells Hermes to show Ganymede how to offer the wine-cup. On a bf. amphora in the Hearst collection at San Simeon, in the manner of the Andokides Painter (H. R. W. Smith in *AJA.* 1945 p. 471, b, with p. 473), Hermes, holding an oinochoë, stands in front of Dionysos, ready to serve him; a satyr plays the flute and two others dance. See also note 15.

¹³ Bf. amphora in Madrid (10916: *Jh.* 3 pp. 64–65; *CV.* 1 pl. 21, 3 and pl. 22); rf. cup by Oltos in Munich (2618: FR. pl. 83; *ARV.* p. 39 no. 59); rf. cup by the Hegesiboulos Painter in New York (07.286.47: FR. pl. 93, 2; Richter and Hall pl. 10; *ARV.* p. 77).

¹⁴ *Il.* 18, 408–427.

¹⁵ This should be the context of the satyr musicians, and the Hermes holding oinochoë and kantharos, on the Berlin Painter's masterpiece, Berlin 2160 (FR. pl. 159 and 3 p. 255; *Berl.* pls. 1–5. *ARV.* p. 131 no. 1). Compare also an rf. chous of about 430 B.C. in Athens, 16258, where Dionysos reclines, holding a kantharos, with Ariadne seated on his couch holding a dish of fruit, while Hephaistos is ushered in by a satyr; perhaps also a late bf. cup in Vienna (La Borde *Coll. des vases grecs* 1 pls. 71–72).

¹⁶ Psiax: see *ARV.* pp. 7–11 and 948, with the literature given there.

¹⁷ Cup in Odessa, attributed by Miss Peredolski: A, *AJA.* 1934 p. 551 no. 8 (Richter). *ARV.* p. 11 no. 31.

¹⁸ Castle Ashby: *Burl. 1888* pl. 18, whence Pfuhl figs. 267–268 and Hoppin *Bf.* p. 51; *Burl. 1903* pl. 92, G. 21. *ARV.* p. 10 no. 19. On the shape see *BSR.* 11 p. 10.

¹⁹ Madrid 11008: *Jh.* 3 pp. 70–71, whence Hoppin *Rf.* 1 p. 34; Pfuhl figs. 317 and 264; *CV.* 1 pl. 23, 1, pls. 24–25, and pl. 26, 1. *ARV.* p. 8 no. 2. Attributed by Buschor.

²⁰ Leningrad 381: Waldhauer *KO.* pl. 2. *ARV.* p. 10 no. 23 and p. 948.

²¹ Berlin 1897: FR. pl. 154, 2; Neugebauer pl. 35. *ARV.* p. 10 no. 20; Buschor *Vasen* p. 132. Attributed by Zahn.

²² See *AM.* 41 p. 338 (Wrede). Other good examples of this cross on hydriai by the Rycroft Painter in Hamburg (1917.476: *Anz.* 1928 p. 314), and Munich (1720, J. 138: Gerhard *AV.* pl. 211–12, 1–2; *AM.* 41 pl. 31, 2): on the artist, *JHS.* 54 p. 91, r.

²³ The Antimenes Painter: *JHS.* 47 pp. 63–91; *ABS.* p. 41; *AM.* 41 p. 351 (Wrede: "73" is added in error); *RG.* p. 46; Hafner pp. 25–28; Bloesch *AKS.* pp. 51–53 and 165–166.

²⁴ London B 304: *JHS.* 47 pl. 13 with p. 67 and p. 87 no. 46; *CV.* 6 pl. 76, 1 and pl. 77, 1.

²⁵ Vatican 426: Albizzati pl. 65 and p. 197. London B 336: *CV.* 6 pl. 90, 4 and pl. 93, 2. On fountain-scenes, Dunkley in *BSA.* 36 pp. 142–204.

²⁶ Leyden 14e 28: *JHS.* 47 pl. 11 (with pp. 63–65 and p. 88 no. 52); *ABS.* pl. 12, 2.

²⁷ London B 226: *JHS.* 47 p. 66 and pl. 12, 1 (with pp. 65–67, 70–72, and p. 82 no. 1); A, *ABS.* pl. 12, 1; *CV.* 4 pl. 55, 4.

²⁸ The Leagros Group: Buschor in FR. 3 p. 229; *ABS.* pp. 26–28 and 43–46; *CV.* San Francisco pp. 27–31 (H. R. W. Smith); *ARV.* pp. 929–930 and 940; *JHS.* 59 p. 305, foot.

²⁹ London B 327: *Archaeologia* 32 pl. 12; *ABS.* pl. 14, 2; *CV.* 6 pl. 86 and pl. 89, 1.

³⁰ *Od.* 8, 75.

³¹ Although in the *Achilles Thersitoktonos* of Chairemon (fr. 3) Achilles says ὡς οὐχ ὑπάρχων ἀλλὰ τιμωρούμενος, "not beginning the quarrel but defending my right."

³² See *AJA.* 1950 p. 313.

³³ London B 310: *CV.* 6 pl. 78, 3 and pl. 80, 2.

³⁴ Munich 2309: FR. pl. 33, whence Pfuhl figs. 368–369; Pfuhl *Mast.* figs. 41–42; *ARV.* p. 25 no. 3. The woman carried off must be Helen, but the inscriptions have got mixed: so Gerhard (*AV.* 3 p. 53) and Robert *Griechische Heldensage* p. 699.

³⁵ Munich 1719: the shoulder, and part of the body, Johansen *Iliaden* fig. 20.

³⁶ Leningrad 610, from Vulci. The background is of course black. Now published by Brommer in *Marburger Winckelmann-Programm* 1949 pl. 3. Attributed to Euphronios himself in *ARV.* p. 17 no. 8, but I should now class it as in his manner. See also Haspels *ABL.* p. 44.

³⁷ London B 313; *JHS.* 26 p. 17; *CV.* 6 pl. 79, 2 and pl. 80, 3.

³⁸ Ares was present at this scene in the group described by Pausanias (6, 19, 12).

³⁹ London B 314: *CV.* 6 pl. 79, 3 and pl. 81, 4. This is also the subject of the rf. column-krater by the Syracuse Painter in Capt. Spencer-Churchill's collection at Northwick Park (*ARV.* p. 352 no. 7).

⁴⁰ Munich 1708: *AZ.* 1878 pl. 10, whence (part)

JHS. 26 p. 21 = Norman Gardiner *GAS.* p. 441 = Norman Gardiner *Athl.* fig. 194. Attributed by Buschor.

⁴¹ Munich 1709: Klein *Die griechischen Vasen mit Lieblingsinschriften* p. 71; Schaal *Sf.* fig. 45. Attributed by Buschor.

⁴² London B 326: *AZ.* 1856 pl. 9, 1, 3; *CV.* 6 pl. 86, 2 and pl. 87, 3.

⁴³ Munich 1700: *Mon.* 1 pl. 34; detail, Schaal *Sf.* fig. 48. Attributed by Buschor.

⁴⁴ The throwing of the head and the throwing of the whole body are incompatible and must be alternative motives. It has been thought that the motive of Achilles holding Troilos by the leg, upside down, was borrowed from pictures of Neoptolemos and Astyanax: this may be so, but it occurs on the middle-Corinthian column-krater Louvre E 638 bis (*Mon. Piot* 16 pl. 14; Payne *NC.* no. 1196), which seems to be earlier than any extant picture of Neoptolemos and Astyanax (Achilles may have held the sword in his right hand, which is missing). In the third example of the motive, on a late bf. lekythos in Copenhagen (97: *CV.* 3 pl. 112, 3), Neoptolemos stands on the altar, has his shield on his left arm, and hurls the body at the two warriors (Hector and Aeneas?) who advance towards him.

⁴⁵ On the gesture see Greifenhagen in *Anz.* 1935 p. 488. Amphora of the Leagros Group, London B 196 (A, *JHS.* 26 pl. 5; *CV.* 3 pl. 38, 2).

⁴⁶ Würzburg 311: *RM.* 3 p. 108; Langlotz pl. 88, pl. 93, and pl. 97. Attributed by Buschor.

⁴⁷ Pindar *Paeans* 6, 112; translated freely. A woman raises her arms in somewhat earlier pictures of the subject on neck-amphorae in Berlin (3996: Furtwängler *Coll. Sabouroff* pl. 48, 3) and Würzburg (179: Langlotz pl. 57).

⁴⁸ Munich 1717: the shoulder-picture only, FR. 1 p. 159, whence Richter *Craft* p. 64 and *PP.* pl. 2, 1.

⁴⁹ So also in other pictures of the subject: neck-amphora in the Roman market (Gerhard *AV.* pl. 231, 1–2); neck-amphora in Berlin, 1861 (Gerhard *EKV.* pl. 25: Leagros Group). Compare also the relief with the Death of Aegisthus, Ny Carlsberg 30 (Furtwängler *AG.* 3 p. 266; *Billedtavler* pl. 3).

⁵⁰ See note 48, and *PP.* pl. 2, 1 with pp. 6–7. The old master of the establishment also figures in the foundry scenes on a lost bf. lekythos (*El. cer.* 1 pl. 51; much restored, but this particular certain).

⁵¹ Berlin 1902: Gerhard *TG.* pl. 16; *Jb.* 29 p. 225. Other pictures of the same subject on the "Tyrrhenian" neck-amphora London 97.7–27.2 (*JHS.* 18 pl. 15, whence Perrot 10 p. 11, Homann-Wedeking *Archaische Vasenornamentik* fig. 8), and

the Etrusco-Campanian bf. neck-amphora London B 70.

[52] Munich 1712: FR. 3 p. 228. Attributed by Buschor. See also Haspels *ABL*. p. 46.

[53] London B 323: *CV*. pl. 84, 3 and pl. 85, 4; detail, Lane *GP*. pl. 47.

[54] The Acheloös Painter: *ABS*. pp. 28 and 46–47; *JHS*. 54 p. 91. A new and characteristic work, the pelike New York 49.11.1, has been assigned to the Acheloös Painter by Dietrich von Bothmer and will be published by him in *Bull. Metr. Mus.* (A, Capture of Silenos; B, boxers.)

[55] Berlin 1851: Gerhard *EKV*. pl. 15–16, 1–2, whence (A) *ABS*. pl. 14, 1. Some repainting.

[56] Somewhat similar in motive the Herakles on a small rf. cup near the work of the Hermaios Painter, in Berlin (2271: *ARV*. p. 78); but there no terrain.

[57] New York 26.60.29: A, Richter and Milne fig. 4. Compare the amphora by the Acheloös Painter in Basle (A, *Historische Schätze Basels* fig. 2).

[58] London B 167: A, *Mon*. 4 pl. 11; *CV*. 3 pl. 34, 1.

CHAPTER VIII
PANATHENAIC AMPHORAE

[1] Recent matter on Panathenaic amphorae: Peters *Studien zu den panathenäischen Preisamphoren* (1942), and "Zwei panathenäische Preisamphoren des Aristophanes" in *Jb*. 57 (1942) pp. 143–157; Beazley "Panathenaica" in *AJA*. 1943 pp. 441–465 (with a list of earlier studies on p. 441). Something also in "Miniature Panathenaics" (*BSA*. 41 pp. 10–21).

[2] London B 130: Millingen *AUM*. 1 pls. 1–3; *Mon*. 11 pl. 48, i and k; A, Pfuhl fig. 299; *CV*. 1 f pl. 1, 1; A, Buschor *Vasen* p. 108 fig. 125. See *AJA*. 1943 p. 441, and Peters pp. 14–18.

[3] See Rumpf *Sak*. p. 21 note 51 and Peters p. 14.

[4] See *Hesp*. suppl. 2 p. 210 (Rodney S. Young). A curious representation of a Panathenaic-shaped amphora is on a seventh-century oinochoë in the Agora Museum at Athens (*Hesp*. 7 p. 417, R. S. Young); the vase is shown standing on a short ground-line (shelf?), between two broad vertical bands which recall the cock-columns (p. 91) of the prize Panathenaics.

[5] London B 134: *CV*. 1 e pl. 2, 2. London B 133: *CV*. 1 e pl. 2, 1. London B 606: *CV*. 1 f pl. 1, 2. London B 604: *CV*. 1 f pl. 2, 1. London B 611: *CV*. 1 f pl. 4, 1. We recur to all these later.

[6] Louvre F 77: *CV*. 9 pl. 82, 9.

[7] London B 131, *CV*. 1 e pl. 1, 2 and B 132, *CV*. 1 e pl. 1, 3.

[8] *AM*. 53, Beil. 10, 31; see also *AJA*. 1943 p. 441. Both halves are now in the Louvre.

[9] Langlotz *Zeitbestimmung* pl. 1, 1; Rumpf *Sak*. pl. 8, c and pl. 27, a. See also Peters pp. 18–19, and *AJA*. 1943 p. 441, H. R. W. Smith *The Hearst Hydria* pp. 246, 250, 251.

[10] The vase is incomplete to left of the letters, but there does not seem to be room for another word—στάδιον or δίαυλος, and ἀνδρῶν was perhaps alone both here and on the contemporary Panathenaic of which Acropolis 1043 is a fragment (Graef pl. 63).

[11] On this see a work of much interest, Gründel *Die Darstellung des Laufens in der griechischen Kunst* (1934). The warriors at the double on the Chigi vase raise the back leg from the ground (*AD* I pl. 44; Payne *Protokor.*, pls. 27–29), so do the runners in the race on a seventh-century bronze relief from Perachora (Payne *Perachora* I pl. 50, 7–8); those on a Corinthian amphora in the Villa Giulia lift the forward leg (Mingazzini *Cast*. pl. 33, 1), but the vase is not earlier than the earliest Attic examples, if so early.

[12] Agora P 2071: Vanderpool in *Hesp*. 15 pl. 14, 1 and pl. 13 with pp. 121–122.

[13] See Kunze *Kretische Bronzereliefs* p. 125 and Jacobsthal *ECA*. p. 73.

[14] Acropolis 917 (Graef pl. 60); 918, same painter as the last; 915; 913 (Graef pl. 58); 916 (Graef pl. 60); 925 (*ibid*.); 920 (Graef pl. 57; attributed to Nearchos by Rumpf *Sak*. p. 19 note, and Peters pp. 18–19); 1043 (Graef pl. 63).

[15] Florence, no number, from Orvieto. A tiny photograph of A is reproduced in Milani *Museo Topografico* p. 48, left.

[16] This is the only prize Panathenaic on which a votary is shown in the presence of Athena. There are other bf. pictures of Athena in fighting attitude attended by votaries, but they are not just like ours: amphora of Panathenaic shape in the Cabinet des Médailles, 243 (A, de Ridder p. 151; *CV*. 2 pl. 88: boys with branches); another in Bonn, 43 (*Anz*. 1935 p. 455 fig. 32 and p. 454: woman); lekythos by the Athena Painter in Buffalo (*AJA*. 1944 p. 123: trainers or judges).

[17] It has been held recently (Brunn-Bruckmann *Denkmäler griechischer und römischer Sculptur* text to pls. 786–790) that if Herodotos of Thebes drove his own chariot (Pind. *Isthm*. 1, 15) it was because he could not afford to hire a driver. This is to misconceive the nature of sportsmen.

[18] Berlin 1732: *WV*. 1889 pl. 1, 2; Pfuhl fig. 242; Hoppin *Bf*. p. 157; *Metr. Mus. St*. 4 pp. 176–177; Rumpf *Sak*. pls. 29–31.

[19] London B 134: A, Walters pl. 3; B, *JHS*. 27

pl. 18, whence Norman Gardiner *Athl.* fig. 139; *CV.* 1 e pl. 2, 2. *AJA.* 1943 p. 442 no. 1.

[20] Ion fr. 53 Nauck.

[21] On the Euphiletos Painter, *AJA.* 1943 pp. 442–443; Peters pp. 21–46; and *Cypr.* p. 33.

[22] Leyden xv.i.77: A, *Mon.* 10 pl. 48 n, whence Perrot 10 p. 293 and Pfuhl fig. 305; B, *AZ.* 1881 pl. 9, 1, whence Norman Gardiner *Athl.* fig. 148. *AJA.* 1943 p. 442 no. 2.

[23] New York 14.130.12: Bröndsted pl. 3; B, Alexander *Greek Athletics* p. 8, 2; A, Richter and Milne fig. 24; B, Norman Gardiner *Athl.* fig. 89; A, Lane *GP.* pl. 50. *AJA.* 1943 p. 443 no. 6.

[24] Copenhagen 99: *CV.* 3 pl. 104. *AJA.* 1943 p. 444, top, where fragments of two other Panathenaics by the same hand are mentioned; one of these, Acropolis 1054, is also attributed by Peters, pp. 59–60.

[25] Nauplia: B, *AJA.* 1938 p. 504 fig. 11. See *AJA.* 1943 p. 443, below. A blot has spoilt one of the fetlocks.

[26] Paus. 6, 2, 8.

[27] *Anth. Pal.* 6, 135; Paus. 6, 13, 10. See Friedländer and Hoffleit *Epigrammata* pp. 97 and 143.

[28] London 816, from Crannon in Thessaly, Millingen *AUM.* 2 pl. 16, 1. Acropolis, Walter *Beschreibung der Reliefs im Kleinen Akropolismuseum* p. 111 no. 244. See also Walter in *Epitymbion Tsounta* pp. 408–412. On an Italiote bellkrater in London (Zahn *Sammlung Schiller* pl. 31; *BMQ.* 4 pl. 17) a mounted youth crowns his horse; so also on the Tarantine coins quoted by Zahn. The horse on the early rf. cup by Oltos in Bonn has a wreath round its shoulders and may have won a race (*CV.* 1 pl. 1, 1: *ARV.* p. 36 no. 15). Compare the enigmatic horse on the cup by the Euergides Painter, Acropolis 166 (Langlotz pl. 6; *ARV.* p. 62 no. 60).

[29] London B 144: Gerhard *AV.* pl. 247; *CV.* 1 pl. 6, 2; B, Norman Gardiner *Athl.* fig. 207.

[30] The Swing Painter: *BSA.* 32 pp. 12–16; *RG.* pp. 41–42; Webster and Charlton in *Manch. Mem.* 83 pp. 191–201.

[31] Boulogne 441: *Mon.* 1 pl. 22, 5; B, *Musée* 2 p. 268 fig. 15 and p. 272 fig. 15a, whence Norman Gardiner *GAS.* p. 390; B, Norman Gardiner *Athl.* fig. 162. *AJA.* 1945 p. 444, where two other vases by the same artist are mentioned.

[32] New York 07.286.80: A, Richter and Milne, p. 5, 2; B, Alexander *Greek Athletics* p. 27, 2; B, *V. Pol.* pl. 2, 1; B, *ABS.* pl. 16, 1. *AJA.* 1943 p. 444, below, no. 3.

[33] Sparta: *BSA.* 13 pl. 5, whence (A) Norman Gardiner *GAS.* p. 456; B, *Burl. Mag.* 14 (1908) pl. at p. 65. *AJA.* 1943 p. 444, below, no. 1.

[34] Taranto: *Dedalo* 2 pp. 619–620; A, Quagliati *Mus. Tar.* pl. 54, 1. *AJA.* 1943 p. 444, below, no. 1.—Two uninscribed Panathenaics also belong to the Leagros Group. New York GR 565: B, McClees p. 106; A, Athena; B, chariot. Norwich 4: Gerhard *EKV.* pl. B, 5–6; A, Athena; B, acontist.

[35] Acropolis 931, Graef pl. 56: attributed by Peters, pp. 56–57.

[36] *ARV.* pp. 128–129; *AJA.* 1943 p. 445; Peters pp. 65–71. The Mikas Panathenaic is published in Peters, pl. 8. The Leyden Panathenaic xv.i.79 (B, and the shield on A, *Mon.* 1 pl. 22, 8, whence, B, Norman Gardiner *GAS.* p. 439), connected with the Kleophrades Painter in *ARV.* p. 952, middle, and attributed to his "manner" in *AJA.* 1943 p. 445, was seen by Peters (p. 66 no. 6) to be by the artist himself. The Norwich vase (*ARV.* p. 131 note 4) is from his hand too. See also *Eph.* 1948–49 p. 24 (Karouzou) with suppl. pl. 4.

[37] New York 07.286.79: detail of A, *VA.* p. 44. *ARV.* p. 129 no. 98. Two inscribed Panathenaics by the Kleophrades Painter are at Yale, 1909.12 and 1909.13, both with a chariot on the reverse.

[38] New York 16.71: A, Bröndsted pl. 2; *Handbook Cl. Coll.*, 2d ed., p. 93; B, McClees p. 98; detail of B, Alexander *Gr. Athletics* p. 25, 2, and Norman Gardiner *Athl.* fig. 196. *ARV.* p. 129 no. 99.

[39] Munich 1456: Blümel *Sport der Hellenen* pp. 96–97. *ARV.* p. 128 no. 97.

[40] Hartwig *Die griechischen Meisterschalen der Blüthezeit* pp. 416–417; *Kl.* pl. 17 and pl. 18, 1–3. *ARV.* p. 123 no. 31.

[41] *ARV.* p. 129 nos. 100–103.

[42] *ARV.* pp. 157–158 and 953–954; *AJA.* 1943 pp. 446–447. See also Peters pp. 60–65; but Peters, and others, do not keep the Eucharidean Panathenaics apart from the Leagran, which seems to me essential.

[43] London B 133: *CV.* 1 e pl. 2, 1; *ARV.* p. 157 no. 68. Toronto 350: Robinson and Harcum pl. 54. *ARV.* p. 157 no. 69.

[44] *ARV.* pp. 144 and 952; *AJA.* 1943 pp. 448–450; Peters pp. 71–75.

[45] Castle Ashby: Micali *St.* pl. 88, 3–4; A, *V. Pol.* pl. 1, 2; *BSR.* 11 pl. 10, 1–2 and p. 14. *ARV.* p. 144 no. 210; see also *AJA.* 1943 p. 449.

[46] Gründel (pp. 65–66) dates this vase, which he knew only from the old drawing in Micali, a hundred years too late, and says that the first attempts, on Panathenaics, to replace the "Halle" type of running by what he calls the "free run" were not made before 370.

[47] "Diagonal" running occurs, exceptionally, as early as the second quarter of the sixth century:

Tyrrhenian neck-amphora in Geneva, Thiersch *Tyrrh.* pl. 2, 1–4: see Gründel p. 73.

[48] Czartoryski 164: Gerhard *EKV.* pl. A, 3–4; *V. Pol.* pl. 1, 1 and pl. 2, 2; B, *ABS.* pl. 16, 2; B, Norman Gardiner *Athl.* fig. 206; *CV.* pl. 12, 1. *ARV.* p. 144 no. 209; *AJA.* 1943 p. 449.

[49] Vatican 375: *Mus. Greg.* 2 pl. 43, 1: B, phot. Alinari 35781; Albizzati pl. 51. *ARV.* p. 144 no. 211.

[50] Benghazi: *Notiziario archeologico* pp. 112–113. *ARV.* p. 144; *AJA.* 1943 p. 449.

[51] Bologna 12: Pellegrini *VF.* pp. 8–9; *CV.* 2 g pl. 2; *AJA.* 1943 p. 448, below, no. 2. Bologna 11: *JHS.* 32 pl. 4; B, Pellegrini *VF.* p. 7; B, Norman Gardiner *Athl.* fig. 91; *CV.* 2 g pl. 3; *AJA.* 1943 p. 448, below, no. 1. On both see *AJA.* 1943, 448–450, and Peters pp. 83–88.

[52] Oxford, Mississippi, Professor D. M. Robinson: B, *CV.* 1 pl. 31, 3 and pl. 32, a. *AJA.* 1943 p. 448 no. 5.

[53] The Robinson Group: see *AJA.* 1943 pp. 450–453. Vanderpool has added the Panathenaic Agora P 10007 (*Hesp.* 15 pl. 15 and pl. 16, 1 and 3).

[54] The Kuban Group: *AJA.* 1943 pp. 453–454; see also Peters pp. 97–99.

[55] London 1903.2–17.1: B, *JHS.* 27 pl. 10, whence Norman Gardiner *GAS.* p. 357 and Alexander *Greek Athletics* p. 19; *CV.* 1 f pl. 1, 1; B, Norman Gardiner *Athl.* fig. 12, left (fig. 12, right, is from another vase, London B 612, of the Kittos Group). *AJA.* 1943 p. 453 no. 1.

[56] Norman Gardiner *Athl.* p. 176.

[57] Leningrad inv. 17553: *Anz.* 1914 p. 287 figs. 108–109; *Izv. Mat. Kult.* 3 pl. 3; B, *Ant. class.* 5 pl. 37, 2. *AJA.* 1943 p. 453 no. 2.

[58] London B 606: *Mon.* 10 pl. 48c and pl. 48h, 13, whence Pfuhl fig. 306; *CV.* 1 f pl. 1, 2. *AJA.* 1943 p. 453 no. 3.

[59] London B 605: *Mon.* 10 pl. 48d and pl. 48h, 14; the shield-device, *Anz.* 1919 p. 86, a; *CV.* 1 f pl. 2, 3 and 6 and pl. 6. *AJA.* 1943 p. 453 no. 4.

[60] The Hildesheim Group: see *AJA.* 1943 pp. 454–455, and Peters in *Jb.* 57 pp. 143–157.

[61] Berlin inv. 3980: E. Schmidt pl. 2, 2 and pl. 4, 2; Peters pl. 12. On the date, Schefold *U.* pp. 108 and 111, Süsserott p. 72, Peters pp. 105–107.

[62] August Mommsen *Feste der Stadt Athen* p. 82; Norman Gardiner in *JHS.* 32 pp. 179–193; Peters pp. 7–9.

[63] *AJA.* 1943 pp. 456–457.

[64] Süsserott p. 72.

[65] See note 63 above.

[66] London B 604: *Mon.* 10 pl. 48b and pl. 48g, 12; B, *JHS.* 26 pl. 3, whence Norman Gardiner *GAS.* p. 442 and *Athl.* fig. 192; Hoppin *Bf.* p. 141;

CV. 1 f pl. 2, 1 and 4; detail of B, and one of the symbols, Süsserott pl. 3, 3 and pl. 12, 1. *AJA.* 1943 p. 455 no. 1. See also Peters p. 99.

[67] The Polyzelos Group: *AJA.* 1943 pp. 455–456. A of the Hearst Panathenaic, *Jb.* 57 p. 149.

[68] London B 603: *Mon.* 10 pl. 47 and pl. 48e, 1, whence (A) Pfuhl fig. 307; *CV.* 1 f pl. 2, 2 and 5; detail of B, *RM.* 47 pl. 21, 3; detail of B, and a symbol, Süsserott pl. 3, 4 and pl. 12, 2. *AJA.* 1943 p. 456 no. 4.

[69] See *AJA.* 1943 pp. 457–465.

[70] Harvard 1925.30.124: *AJA.* 1906 pl. 16 and pp. 386–392; *CV.* Hoppin *Rf.* pl. 6; A, Richter and Milne fig. 26; B, *RM.* 47 pl. 24, 1; B, Süsserott pl. 4, 4 and pl. 6, 1–2. *AJA.* 1943 p. 458 no. 2.

[71] Schmidt pl. 7, 1. See *AJA.* 1943 p. 457.

[72] D. S. Robertson in *CR.* 37 (1923) p. 6.

[73] *N.* 10, 61.

[74] London B 607: *Mon.* 10 pl. 47a and pl. 47e, 2, whence (A) Pfuhl fig. 308; B, Norman Gardiner *GAS.* p. 407; *CV.* 1 f pl. 3, 1; detail of B, Norman Gardiner *Athl.* fig. 175; B, *RM.* 47 pl. 24, 2 and pl. 23. *AJA.* 1943 p. 458 no. 4.

[75] On "bakchoi" see *Num. Chron.* 1941 pp. 1–7.

[76] This gives a *terminus post quem* for dating the Ficoroni cista: see *JHS.* 1949 p. 2.

[77] Berlin inv. 3981, see *AJA.* 1943 p. 460.

[78] London B 608: *Mon.* 10 pl. 47b and pl. 48e, whence (A) Pfuhl fig. 309; *CV.* 1 f pl. 3, 2. *AJA.* 1943 p. 461 no. 1.

[79] Munich inv. 7767. *AJA.* 1943 p. 461 no. 2.

[80] London B 610: *Mon.* 10 pl. 47d and pl. 48f, 5; B, *JHS.* 26 pl. 4, whence Norman Gardiner *GAS.* p. 443 and *Athl.* fig. 191; *CV.* 1 f pl. 4, 3; B, Süsserott pl. 6, 3 and pl. 7, 3–4. See *AJA.* 1943 p. 460.

[81] Above, same page; see *JHS.* 59 p. 38.

[82] London B 611: *Mon.* 10 pl. 47f and pl. 48f, 7; *CV.* 1 f pl. 4, 1. *AJA.* 1943 p. 458 no. 7 and p. 460.

[83] Leningrad: *CR.* 1876 pl. 1, 1–3, whence (B) Norman Gardiner *GAS.* p. 283; *Ant. class.* 5 pls. 39–40. *AJA.* 1943 p. 460 no. 16 and pp. 461–462.

[84] *AJA.* 1896 p. 332.

[85] On the Hellenistic Panathenaics, Dow in *Hesp.* 5 pp. 576–589, and N. M. Kondoleon in *Eph.* 1937 pp. 576–579. Mitsos and Karouzou, in *Eph.* 1948–49 pp. 5–32, publish a Hellenistic Panathenaic bearing the name of the agonosthetes for the year, a foreign monarch, benefactor of King Ariarathes of Cappadocia, who reigned from 163 to 130 B.C.

[86] Berlin inv. 4950: *Sammlung Vogell* pl. 4, 5 and p. 14 (whence pl. 48, 4). See *Anz.* 1909 p. 564 note 20, Schmidt pp. 84–85, Kondoleon in *Eph.* 1937 p. 579.

ADDENDA TO THE NOTES

I have not been able to use the new book by Kübler, *Altattische Malerei* [*A*.], which includes a good many of the vases described in our first two chapters, but in the addenda that follow I give references to his illustrations.

CHAPTER I

Note 10. The motive of the lion setting one paw on its cowering prey is Oriental; Jacobsthal refers me to a Mitannian cylinder in the British Museum (Frankfort *Cylinder Seals* pl. 31, a). See also Fraenkel *Aeschylus Agamemnon* p. 412, top.

Note 11. Part, Kübler *A*. p. 9, p. 39 above, p. 48 right.

Note 15. Part, Kübler *ibid*. p. 49, right.

Note 19. Part, *ibid*. p. 46, below, and p. 59.

Note 20. Part, *ibid*. p. 58.

Note 32. Part, *ibid*. p. 60, below; Kraiker *Aigina: die Vasen des 10. bis 7. Jahrhunderts v. Chr.* pl. 44 and pl. 45, above.

Note 33. Part, Kübler *A*. p. 60, above.

Note 34. Bear, lion, wolf are mentioned together by the comic poet Antiphanes (fr. 42 Kock).

Note 41. Part, Kübler *A*. p. 64.

CHAPTER II

Note 1. Kübler *A*. p. 71.

Note 2. *Ibid*. pp. 72–73.

Note 4. Part, *ibid*. p. 81.

Note 10. Part, *ibid*. p. 28.

Note 12. *Ibid*. p. 26, above, and p. 79, below.

Note 16. Part, Kübler *A*. p. 75, above; Kraiker *Aigina: die Vasen des 10. bis 7. Jahrhunderts* pl. 45, 2 and pls. 46–47; the Chimaera Painter is greater than the Nessos Painter.

Note 17. A, Kübler *A*. p. 23.

Note 18. *Ibid*. pp. 24 and 74: our illustration gives only part, much reduced.

Note 20. *Ibid*. p. 82, above; our illustration again gives part only, much reduced; other fragments of this vase are in the Louvre.

Note 28. Kübler *A*. p. 70, below.

CHAPTER IV

Note 2. See also *BSA*. 35 pp. 167 and 199 (J. M. Cook), *JHS*. 68 p. 12 (Barnett), *Mus. Helv.* 7 p. 99 (Yalouris), Kübler *A*. p. 55, above.

Note 20. In Colluthus 123 Paris flees from Hermes.

CHAPTER V

Note 26. The upper part (1) of our plate 22 should be tilted so that the hair of Achilles falls straight down.

CHAPTER VI

Note 12. Pherecrates fr. 124 ἢ τρὶς ἒξ ἢ τρεῖς κύβοι.

Note 26. See *RA*. 1939, i pp. 224–235 (Deonna).

CHAPTER VIII

Note 6. In London B 131 the animals are mules as I said in *ARV*. p. 131; in London B 132 one cannot be sure, owing to the restorations, whether they are mules or horses; it must be considered whether the Burgon animals are not also mules.

INDEXES

In these indexes, references to the *notes* are only given if the vase or other topic is not mentioned in the *text*. From a mention in the *text* the relevant matter in the *notes* is easily found.

GENERAL INDEX

INDEX OF COLLECTIONS

PLATES

PLATE I

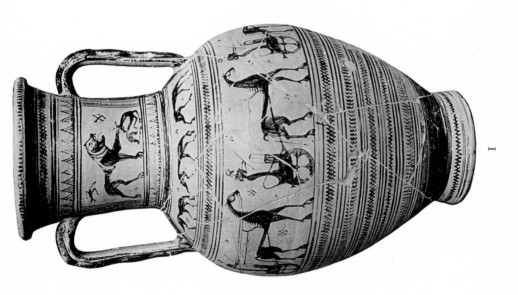

2

1

PLATE 2

PLATE 3

PLATE 4

PLATE 5

I

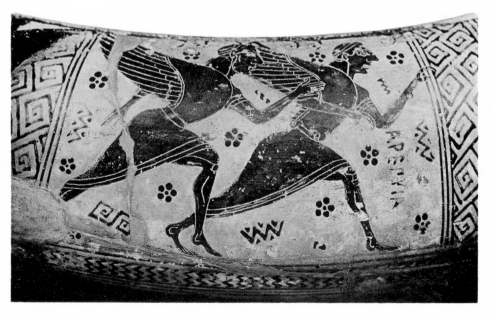

2

PLATE 6

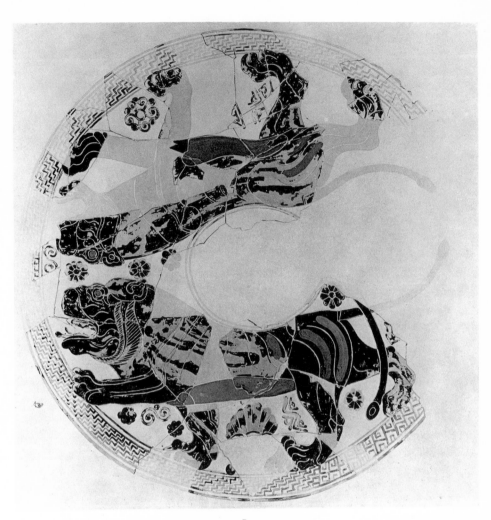

1

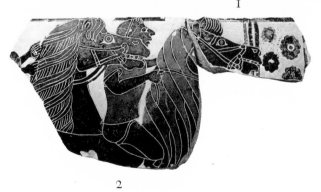

2

3

PLATE 7

1

2

3

4

PLATE 8

1

2

PLATE 9

PLATE 10

PLATE II

I

2

3

PLATE 12

PLATE 13

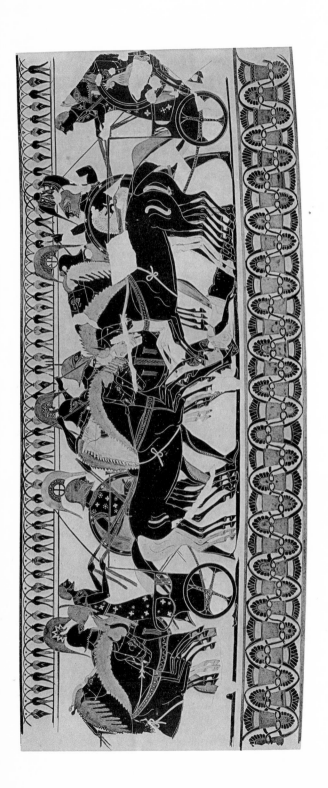

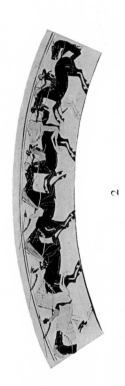

1

2

3

PLATE 14

I

PLATE 15

I

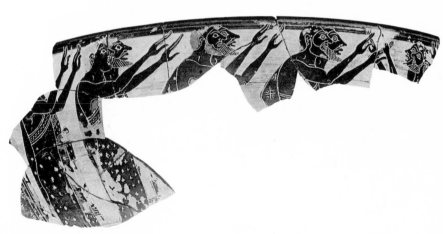

2

PLATE 16

PLATE 17

I

2

PLATE 18

PLATE 19

PLATE 20

1

2

3

PLATE 21

1

2

3

PLATE 22

1

PLATE 23

I

2

PLATE 24

PLATE 25

1

2

9

3

4

5

6

7

8

PLATE 26

2

3

4

I

PLATE 27

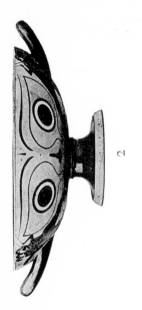

2

3

1

PLATE 28

PLATE 29

PLATE 30

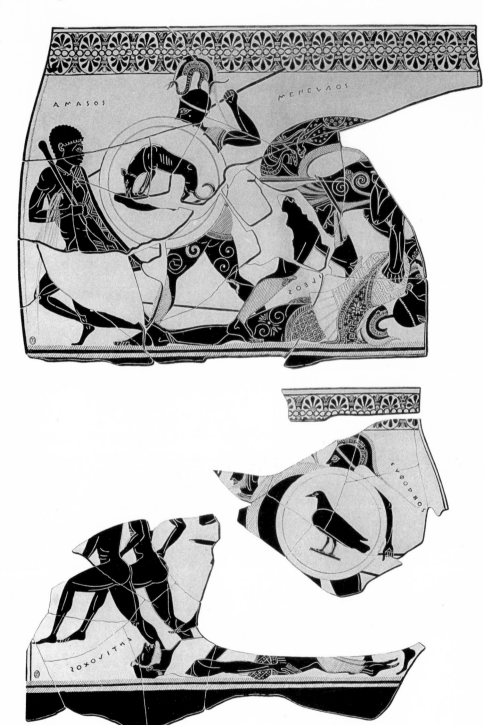

PLATE 31

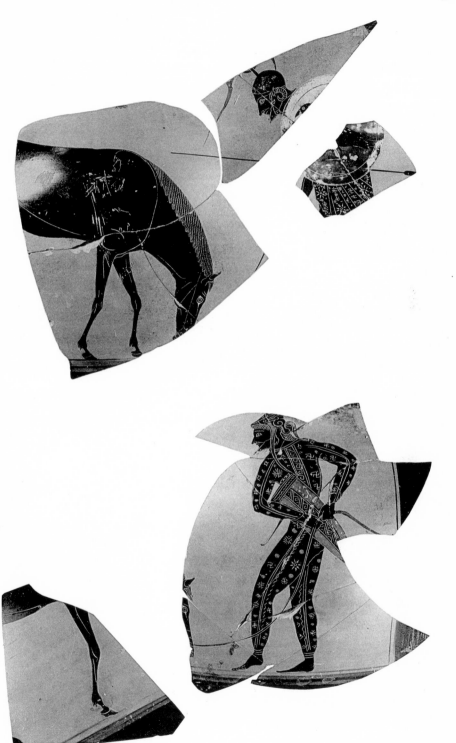

PLATE 32

1

2

PLATE 33

PLATE 34

PLATE 35

PLATE 36

I

2

PLATE 37

PLATE 38

I

2

3

PLATE 39

1   3

2

PLATE 40

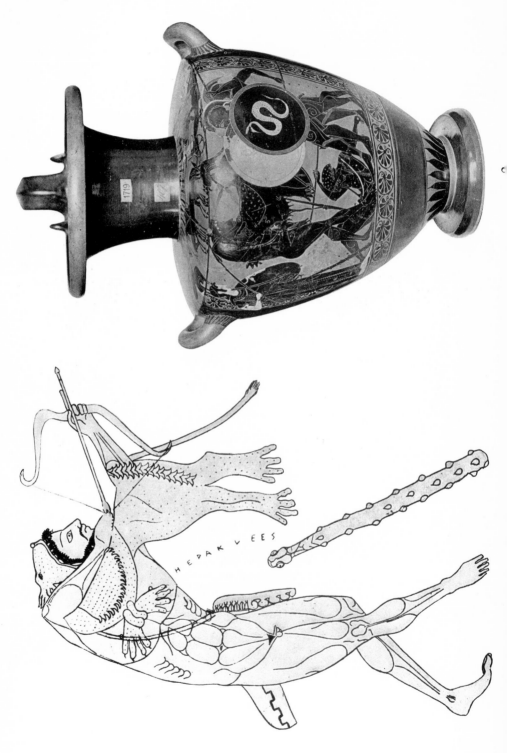

HEPAKLEES

PLATE 41

PLATE 42

PLATE 43

I

2

PLATE 44

1

2

PLATE 45

2

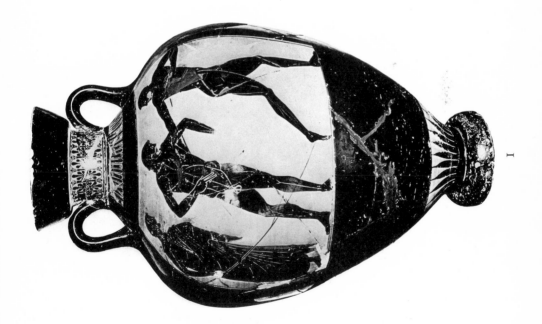

1

PLATE 46

1

2

3

4

PLATE 47

1

2

PLATE 48

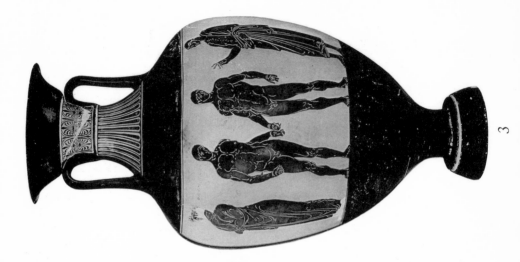

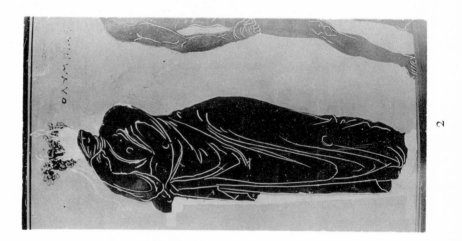

PLATE 49

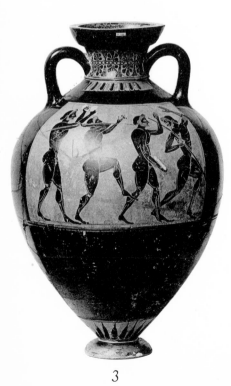

1

2

3

4